BALZAC AND THE MODEL OF PAINTING
ARTIST STORIES IN *LA COMÉDIE HUMAINE*

LEGENDA

LEGENDA, founded in 1995 by the European Humanities Research Centre of the University of Oxford, is now a joint imprint of the Modern Humanities Research Association and Maney Publishing. Titles range from medieval texts to contemporary cinema and form a widely comparative view of the modern humanities, including works on Arabic, Catalan, English, French, German, Greek, Italian, Portuguese, Russian, Spanish, and Yiddish literature. An Editorial Board of distinguished academic specialists works in collaboration with leading scholarly bodies such as the Society for French Studies and the British Comparative Literature Association.

MHRA

The Modern Humanities Research Association (MHRA) encourages and promotes advanced study and research in the field of the modern humanities, especially modern European languages and literature, including English, and also cinema. It also aims to break down the barriers between scholars working in different disciplines and to maintain the unity of humanistic scholarship in the face of increasing specialization. The Association fulfils this purpose primarily through the publication of journals, bibliographies, monographs and other aids to research.

MANEY
publishing

Maney Publishing is one of the few remaining independent British academic publishers. Founded in 1900 the company has offices both in the UK, in Leeds and London, and in North America, in Boston. Since 1945 Maney Publishing has worked closely with learned societies, their editors, authors, and members, in publishing academic books and journals to the highest traditional standards of materials and production.

RESEARCH MONOGRAPHS IN
FRENCH STUDIES

The *Research Monographs in French Studies* (RMFS) form a separate series within the Legenda programme and are published in association with the Society for French Studies. Individual members of the Society are entitled to purchase all RMFS titles at a discount.

The series seeks to publish the best new work in all areas of the literature, thought, theory, culture, film and language of the French-speaking world. Its distinctiveness lies in the relative brevity of its publications (50,000–60,000 words). As innovation is a priority of the series, volumes should predominantly consist of new material, although, subject to appropriate modification, previously published research may form up to one third of the whole. Proposals may include critical editions as well as critical studies. They should be sent with one or two sample chapters for consideration to Professor Ann Jefferson, New College, Oxford OX1 3BN.

❖

Editorial Committee
Professor Ann Jefferson, New College, Oxford (General Editor)
Professor Adrian Armstrong, University of Manchester
Dr Janice Carruthers, Queen's University Belfast
Professor Nicholas Harrison, King's College London
Professor Bill Marshall, University of Glasgow
Professor Michael Moriarty, Queen Mary University of London

Advisory Committee
Professor Wendy Ayres-Bennett, New Hall, Cambridge
Professor Celia Britton, University College London
Professor Sarah Kay, Princeton University
Professor Diana Knight, University of Nottingham
Professor Keith Reader, University of Glasgow

PUBLISHED IN THIS SERIES

www.rmfs.mhra.org.uk

Balzac and the Model of Painting

Artist Stories in 'La Comédie humaine'

❖

Diana Knight

l

LEGENDA

Research Monographs in French Studies 24
Modern Humanities Research Association and Maney Publishing
2007

Published in association with the Society for French Studies by the
Modern Humanities Research Association and Maney Publishing
1 Carlton House Terrace
London SW1Y 5DB
United Kingdom

LEGENDA is an imprint of the
Modern Humanities Research Association and Maney Publishing

Maney Publishing is the trading name of W. S. Maney & Son Ltd,
whose registered office is at Suite 1C, Joseph's Well, Hanover Walk, Leeds LS3 1AB

ISBN 978-1-905981-06-9

First published 2007

Printed in Great Britain

Cover: 875 Design

Copy-Editor: Richard Correll

CONTENTS

❖

FOR
MARIAN HOBSON

ACKNOWLEDGEMENTS

❖

This monograph derives from research funded by the exceptional generosity of The Leverhulme Trust, whose award of a Major Research Fellowship allowed me to reinvent myself as a Balzac specialist. Sections of Parts 1 and 3 have been presented to the French Departments of University College Cork, The University of Leeds and The University of Nottingham, as well as to the editors of *Paragraph*, in which an early version of chapter 1 was first published. I am grateful for the many useful questions put to me by these audiences, for the very constructive suggestions of the Legenda Editorial Committee and for those of its anonymous readers. Of the friends who have directly or indirectly supported my work on Balzac, both in Nottingham and in Paris, I am especially indebted to Owen Heathcote.

Honoré Daumier, *Pygmalion*

INTRODUCTION

❖

Balzac's artist stories, scattered across the internal subdivisions of *La Comédie humaine*, form a significant corpus that I have placed at the centre of this monograph. While there have been many scholarly investigations of Balzac's interest in the visual arts, of the frequent references in his writing to real painters and paintings, and of his own creative exploitation of painterly metaphors and visual effects, no critical study to date has engaged in detail with the content of this corpus of texts about fictional artists. The creation, replication, donation or circulation of fictional works of art plays a part in all of their plots. Moreover, the erotic investments of the artists in their art, and their real erotic relations with their human subject matter, place these stories on the familiar Balzacian terrain of the sexual politics of prostitution and marriage. In that the myth of Pygmalion conflates creative and erotic desire with mimetic representation, and bestows upon art the paradoxical power to transform the stony prostitute that is woman into a chaste flesh-and-blood spouse, it is no surprise that a number of these artist stories can be read as 'versions of Pygmalion'.[1] Balzac's passing allusions to Ovid's myth are ironically couched, but they are integral to his psychological and social analyses. Indeed, with the famous pre-nineteenth-century exceptions of Frenhofer and Sarrasine, Balzac's Pygmalions are vehicles of his realist representations of post-Revolutionary France.

Texts about paintings, painters and sculptors are obvious test cases for issues of representation. From Marx to Lukács to Barthes's enormously influential *S/Z*, and from the attacks of the 1950s *nouveaux romanciers* to those of feminist critics writing in the wake of Naomi Schor, Balzac has been a key figure for critical-theoretical debates around realism. In the first instance, 'the model of painting' of my title is an explicit allusion to *S/Z*, where Barthes elaborates, through his critical dissection of *Sarrasine*, the metaphorical *modèle de la peinture* that, in his persuasive analysis, underpins realist discourse.[2] In the first part of this study, 'From Sculpture to Painting', analyses of *Sarrasine* and *Le Chef-d'œuvre inconnu* are framed by consideration of the commonly proclaimed 'emptiness' of their subject matter. In particular, I attempt to draw out from *S/Z*, beneath Barthes's provocative 'castration' of *Sarrasine* as an emblematic realist text, an intriguing and fertile obsession with the inner content of Balzac's representational writing. In *S/Z*, the focus of this obsession is the sculptor, his statue and its model. Barthes's curiously empathetic engagement with Sarrasine's aesthetic betrays an ambivalent relation to realism which I pursue to open up a wider analysis of texts that are replete with social as well as psychic significance. In the second instance, then, 'the model of painting' is a play on words that serves to highlight my exploration, across Balzac's artist stories, of the relations between painters and sculptors, their models and their works of art. Artists and their models are variously gendered in these stories, but in every case the aesthetic relationship is overlaid not only with erotic desire, but with the sexual politics of a real social context. This is no less true of *Le Chef-d'œuvre inconnu* and *Sarrasine* than of the early feminocentric marriage stories (*La Bourse, La Vendetta* and *La Maison du chat-qui-pelote*) that are set in the Empire and early years of the Restoration, and that I discuss in 'From Painting to Marriage', my second and longest part. In Part 3, 'From Model to Artist', I place Joseph Bridau at the centre of an analysis of *La Rabouilleuse*, and by tracing his appearances in other texts in which he plays a minor or very minor role (*Illusions perdues, Un début dans la vie, Pierre Grassou* and *La Cousine Bette*), I map a more metaphorical relation of artist to model onto Balzac's profoundly cynical representation of homosocial power structures in a period that extends through the early nineteenth century to the July Monarchy.

The core of my monograph is an intense engagement with this small corpus of artist stories. The context I have sketched constitutes the horizon of my close readings, which draw broad issues into their orbit without claiming to do more than explore them through arguments that remain centred in Balzac's texts. To maintain this focus, I have restricted most of my critical debts, comparisons and disagreements to endnotes. There is, of course, an infinite critical literature not only on Balzac and some of his artist stories, but also on all of the wider areas that have directly or indirectly informed my research. Apart from scholarly and theoretical studies of, for example, Balzac and painting, the relations between other nineteenth-century French authors and the visual arts, or the Pygmalion motif as represented over the centuries in literature, painting, sculpture, theatre and opera, there is a considerable body of feminist cultural history concerned with family and conjugal institutions, as well as the regulation of sexuality, in nineteenth-century France. In recent years I have silently absorbed large quantities of all such studies, many of which include substantial and excellent discussions of Balzacian texts. However, from this insufficiently acknowledged critical hinterland, I should like to single out for brief introductory comment two studies, both published in 2001, that intersect in particularly significant ways with the subject matter of this monograph.

The first is Alexandra K. Wettlaufer's *Pen vs Paintbrush: Girodet, Balzac and the Myth of Pygmalion in Postrevolutionary France*. Wettlaufer's book contains a very useful historical overview of manifestations of Pygmalion in literature and the visual arts, as well as a wealth of fascinating material on Girodet, who is an intriguing parallel for Balzac, as well as a familiar point of reference in his fictional work. She then devotes three chapters to readings of *Sarrasine, Le Chef-d'œuvre inconnu* and *La Maison du chat-qui-pelote* as Pygmalion stories. I shall not here engage with Wettlaufer's argument that Balzac seeks to establish through these plots the generic superiority of literature over painting; what is most striking, however, is that she reads all three artist stories as expressions of Balzac's sexism.[3] While I leave my own counter-readings to defend themselves as best they can, I remain unconvinced by the well-established tradition of feminist criticism that denounces realism as literary mode for compounding Balzac's misogyny (the latter is sometimes assumed to exist rather than demonstrated from contextualized analyses of his texts). According to this argument, which derives from Naomi Schor's work on the historical gendering of aesthetic categories — and has been fuelled by a critical focus on the construction and deconstruction of gender identity — Balzac writes women out of subjecthood by his very choice of literary form.[4] As will be seen, nothing could be further from my own view that 'the model of painting', in both senses of the word, is both focus and vehicle of Balzac's lucid realist critique of the gender politics institutionalized by the 1804 Civil Code.

The second study that may appear relevant to my own is Marie Lathers's *Bodies of Art: French Literary Realism and the Artist's Model*. Lathers establishes an interesting nineteenth-century corpus of fictional works about sexual relations between artists and their models (with marriage or prostitution as the usual context), and analyses the artist's studio as a privileged literary space. In fact, despite taking *Le Chef-d'œuvre inconnu* as the *urtext* of this canon (she also discusses *La Peau de chagrin*, *La Maison du chat-qui-pelote*, *Illusions perdues* and *La Cousine Bette*), her declared focus is the professional model; for this reason, her book serves as a useful cultural history of the economics and gender politics of the studio. Although none of my own Balzacian 'models' are paid models in this sense — I would not include Gillette (*Le Chef-d'œuvre inconnu*) in this category — I shall borrow one of Lathers's starkest literary examples to frame the argument that will unfold in the chapters of this monograph.

Maupassant's short story *Le Modèle* (1883) depicts the misogynistic treatment of a professional model by two male artists, one of whom recounts the tale — '"il l'a épousée... comme on épouse, parbleu, par sottise!"'[5] — to a third male friend without a hint of regret for his complicity in an episode that took place in his own studio. The story opens with a painterly tableau of a beach scene at Étretat in which Jean Summer mournfully accompanies the invalid carriage that transports Joséphine, his crippled wife and ex-model, along the esplanade. The tableau opens onto a narrative flashback that recounts Joséphine's attempted suicide, when Summer, tiring of the model he had passionately loved and had persuaded to become his mistress, tries to buy her off with 20,000 francs raised in part by the sale of all his paintings. Leaving this sum on the mantelpiece with a farewell note, he takes refuge in the narrator's studio, only to be followed there by a hysterical Joséphine who throws the money at his feet: '"Je ne veux pas être traitée comme une fille. Vous m'avez implorée, vous m'avez prise. Je ne vous demandais rien. Gardez-moi!"' (p. 1107). By way of helping his friend out of his difficulty, the narrator invents the fiction that Summer still loves her but is being forced by his parents into a bourgeois marriage. When Joséphine threatens to kill herself by jumping through the window, Summer provokes her into action by opening the window with a sarcastic flourish: '"Voici la route. Après vous!"' (p. 1108). Whereas, in *La Maison du chat-qui-pelote*, Théodore de Sommervieux will smash to pieces the canvas and frame of his spurned wife's portrait, Jean Summer (whose name suggests a literary filiation) dispenses with the pictorial intermediary, enlisting the help of his *confrère* to provoke the self-destruction of the once desirable model. Joséphine's running jump over the balustrade is focalized by the artist-narrator, as is his subsequent framing of the empty space of the open window: 'Je n'oublierais jamais l'effet que me fit cette fenêtre ouverte, après l'avoir vu traverser par ce corps qui tombait; elle me parut grande comme le ciel et vide comme l'espace' (p. 1108). However, by the time the narrator tells his tale, he has dismissed Joséphine's leap through the window as the ultimate act of female manipulation: 'Son amant, fou de remords et peut-être aussi de reconnaissance, l'a reprise et épousée.' (p. 1109) If ever a scene in an artist story gave the lie to the empty contents of representational art, it is the empty frame of the studio window through which Maupassant's rejected mistress-model, watched by two cynical male painters, has just made the terrifying leap from unacknowledged prostitution into a begrudged and condescending marriage.

A general aim of this study is to reverse claims for the supposed theoretical emptiness at the core of *le modèle de la peinture* and to refill it, not least in Balzac's artist stories, with the social realities of nineteenth-century prostitution and marriage. In *Courbet's Realism*, Michael Fried suggests that his approach to nineteenth-century realism has been conditioned by his 'early and continuing involvement with abstract painting and sculpture'. This is not because a knowledge of abstraction has enabled him 'to see past the realistic appearance of Courbet's paintings to some (non-existent) abstract core, but rather because, being at home in abstraction, it's realist painting like Courbet's and Eakins's that has particularly seemed to [him] to require explanation'.[6] In my view, it is in a similar spirit that Barthes approaches Balzac in *S/Z*. It is because Barthes is at ease with those French theoretical positions of the 1950s and 1960s that proclaim the hollowness of the realist literary illusion that he has the confidence to approach Balzac's representational artist story for what it is, and to push his analyses of the 'readerly' codes that structure the text of *Sarrasine* to their limit. In my own case, fascination with the how and why of representation has always accompanied my sense that nineteenth-century realist fiction is critically challenging in its apparent simplicity. More recently, a parallel interest in celibacy and homosexuality in *La Comédie humaine* has alerted me to all that requires explanation in the supposedly straightforward realities of nineteenth-century marriage.[7] While the scope of that interest extends far beyond the small corpus of texts explored here, issues surrounding the representation of the sexual politics of marriage and prostitution are brought into especially sharp focus when they are mediated by an artist story. That Balzac was well aware of the constructed status both of literary representation and of marriage as a social institution is demonstrated, I hope, in the readings that constitute *The Model of Painting*.

Notes to the Introduction

1. The phrase is Jane M. Miller's. See her very useful 'Some Versions of Pygmalion', in *Ovid Renewed: Ovidian Influences on Literature and Art from the Middle Ages to the Twentieth Century*, ed. by Charles Martindale (Cambridge: Cambridge University Press, 1988), pp. 205–14.
2. See Roland Barthes, *S/Z* (Paris: Seuil, 1970), pp. 61–62. All further references to *S/Z* will be included in the text.
3. See, for example, the following claim: 'Despite Balzac's reputation as a harsh critic of the institution of marriage, his fiction proposes implicit support for the status quo, and his first major publication, *Physiologie du mariage* (1829) presents nothing less than a breviary of postrevolutionary strategies to "remettre les femmes à leur place."' (*Pen vs Paintbrush* (New York: Palgrave, 2001), p. 175).
4. See Naomi Schor, *George Sand and Idealism* (New York: Columbia University Press, 1993), p. 54. Dorothy Kelly argues of *Le Chef-d'œuvre inconnu*: 'The real woman must return to invisibility

in this text and cannot be "represented," is that which is missing in a representational text.' See *Fictional Genders: Role and Representation in Nineteenth-Century French Narrative* (Lincoln: University of Nebraska Press, 1989), p. 178.

5. Guy de Maupassant, *Contes et nouvelles*, ed. by Louis Forrestier, 2 vols (Paris: Gallimard (Bibliothèque de la Pléiade), 1974), I, 1103–09 (p. 1104). Further quotations from *Le Modèle* are included in the text. For Lathers's reading of the story, see *Bodies of Art* (Lincoln: University of Nebraska Press, 2001), pp. 197–200.

6. *Courbet's Realism* (Chicago: University of Chicago Press, 1990), pp. 51–52.

7. See Diana Knight, 'Skeletons in the Closet: Homosocial Secrets in Balzac's *La Comédie humaine*', *French Studies*, 57 (2003), 167–80 and 'Celibacy on Display in Two Texts by Balzac: *Le Cabinet des Antiques* and the Preface to *Pierrette*', *Dix-Neuf*, 2 (April 2004), 1–15.

PART I

❖

From Sculpture to Painting

Il faut donc passer *dans* le modèle, *sous* la statue, *derrière* la toile.
Roland Barthes, *S/Z*

CHAPTER 1

❖

S/Z, Sarrasine and *Le Chef-d'œuvre inconnu*

(i) 'Le fantasme du *dedans*'

In what have become the best known of Balzac's artist stories, *Sarrasine* and *Le Chef-d'œuvre inconnu*, the secrets of art embrace both sculpture and painting, as well as the relationship between them. Both narratives are structured around the delayed revelation of a sexual secret: in *Sarrasine* the discovery of Zambinella's sexual identity (a castrated young man kept by a jealous Roman cardinal); in *Le Chef-d'œuvre inconnu*, the uncovering of the ultimate male sexual fetish, a perfectly formed female foot, poking through the abstract chaos (an apparent jumble of lines and layers of paint) of Frenhofer's secret canvas. Yet both stories, so buried in critical discourse that it is hard to write about them at all, have become virtual emblems — within and beyond Balzac studies — of the notion that the secrets of art are ultimately empty, contentless secrets. It is especially difficult to dissociate *Sarrasine* from *S/Z*, Barthes's notorious commentary whereby a broadly psychoanalytic reading of the castration theme is extended to an influential argument about the undermining in this text of the stable values of representational art: Sarrasine thought he had found in Zambinella the founding masterpiece of female beauty; his statue of a castrato figures, therefore, not only the death of desire, but also the empty centre of his art. *Le Chef-d'œuvre inconnu*, for its part, has long fascinated real painters, most famously Cézanne and Picasso, and generations of commentators have been intrigued by the possibility of transforming Frenhofer's *Catherine Lescault* into a precursor of abstract, post-representational art. However, if Balzac's story and its reception have together forged 'a fable of modern art', the relation of Frenhofer's painting and its subject matter — the uncanny status of the buried, partial or absent woman — still fuels critical interpretation of the text as a whole.[1]

   Chantal Massol, the only Balzac specialist to have worked systematically on the functioning of secrets in *La Comédie humaine*, argues that the contents of Balzac's secrets — not least those of art — are subsumed into narrative effects. Typically, the much emphasized 'rien' of Frenhofer's canvas — ' "Rien sur ma toile" '; ' "Rien, rien!" '[2] — is taken as proof that 'l'effet-de-secret n'a nul besoin, pour être agissant, de l'existence d'un secret véritable'.[3] The misguided quest of Poussin — believing that Frenhofer's secret is a hidden 'something' he wants to discover what — is opposed by Massol to the supposedly superior understanding of Porbus, who has grasped that the secret of secrets is that they are merely 'empty envelopes'. This last notion derives from what Pierre Fédida describes as the best possible example of the 'le pouvoir d'illusion du secret', a case history of a young woman who pretends to write love letters, to the extent of posting empty envelopes.[4] Louis Marin's essay on the secrecy-effect forms part of a compulsory corpus for this sort of approach,[5] as does Todorov's 'Le Secret du récit', which presents James's *The Figure in the Carpet* as the ultimate example of the structural transmission of an empty secret.[6] For Massol, Balzac is playing this same game of empty secrets. His narratives pretend to contain secrets that are concealed but amenable to discovery, to be depositaries of external truths buried deep in the story, like envelopes that must be slit open to arrive at the meaning within. But such depth is 'aussi fausse que celle de la toile de Frenhofer', for just as the picture has no 'dessous' so the enigmatic text has no 'dedans'.[7] In *Le Chef-d'œuvre inconnu*, 'le leurre sur lequel tout repose est révélé: la nouvelle fait attendre le secret au lecteur pour lui avouer qu'il se réduit à "rien"' (p. 54). Secrets, however weighty and resonant, are equated with enigmas, with purely textual questions depending on the writer's manipulation of what Barthes calls the hermeneutic code: 'le secret ne saurait être qu'absence de contenu: il n'a d'autre existence que celle des actes métalinguistiques [...] qui le font surgir, qui signalant "il y a mystère" ou "énigme" dessinent les contours de cette absence' (p. 53).[8] Frenhofer's death derives, in this argument, from his lack of hermeneutic sophistication ('cherchant le secret à l'intérieur de l'œuvre, le peintre trouve la mort au terme de cette démarche' (p. 56)), while a similar death sentence is pronounced upon Sarrasine for trying to uncover, through his sketches, the reality of Zambinella: 'Mais on ne peut aller derrière le papier. "*Sous* la Zambinella, nous dit R. Barthes, il y a le 'rien' de la castration, dont mourra Sarrasine."' (p. 57)

As can be seen, it is in the name of Barthes that Massol reduces the resonant 'rien' to little more than 'le mot de l'énigme'. Arguably, she distorts Barthes's position by giving insufficient weight to the relation in *S/Z* between the hermeneutic and symbolic codes. The digression to which Massol alludes, *Derrière, plus loin* (pp. 128–29), is indeed a key passage for Barthes's delineation of the shared aesthetic of Frenhofer and Sarrasine. However, Sarrasine's 'fantasme du *dedans*' (p. 214) is approached via the symbolic code — 'SYM. La réplique des corps' (p. 127); 'SYM. Le déshabillage' (p. 128); 'SYM. Le scénario fantasmatique' (p. 129) — whose field Barthes designates as the human body. Sarrasine draws Zambinella from memory in every conceivable pose — 'sans voile, assise, debout, couchée, ou chaste ou amoureuse' — and yet wants to go still further: 'Mais sa pensée furieuse alla plus loin que le dessin.'[9] Barthes notes that this imaginary undressing, which will culminate in Sarrasine's passionate sculpting of Zambinella, exactly matches Freud's equation of the activities of both sculpture and psychoanalysis with excavation:

> l'une et l'autre sont *via di levare*, pratique d'un déblaiement. Reprenant un geste de son enfance (il déchiquetait le bois des bancs pour sculpter des ébauches grossières), le sculpteur arrache à la Zambinella ses voiles pour atteindre ce qu'il croit être la vérité de son corps. (p. 128)

The twin gestures of Sarrasine's feverish creativity are whittling and kneading: 'il s'agit d'enfoncer la main, de faire céder l'enveloppe, d'appréhender l'intérieur d'un volume, de saisir le *dessous*, le *vrai*' (p. 131); they are subsumed into 'le *forage*', a probing that is at once manual and visual: 'l'impulsion de percée, sorte d'énergie endoscopique qui, écartant les voiles, les vêtements, va chercher dans l'objet son essence intérieure. *Scruter* veut dire, à la lettre, *fouiller, sonder, visiter, explorer*' (p. 174). As ever, Barthes is developing the letter of Balzac's text, here Sarrasine's use of the verb 'scruter': ' "Crois-tu pouvoir tromper l'œil d'un artiste? N'ai-je pas, depuis dix jours, dévoré, scruté, admiré tes perfections?" ' (VI, 1069). With this example of what Barthes calls 'la preuve esthétique' (p. 172) — one of the categories of false syllogism that ground Sarrasine's mistaken belief that Zambinella is a woman — the sculptor, 'à travers des leurres répétés, se dirige fatalement vers l'état du castrat, le vide qui lui tient lieu du centre' (p. 128). Sarrasine's obsession with the underside of appearances leads him ineluctably to a subjective disaster ('la chute du plein rêvé dans le vide châtré' (p. 214)) that is magnified by Barthes's rhetoric.

If Sarrasine is gradually transformed into the tragic hero of *S/Z*, it is because his aesthetic is generalized, in the first instance by association with the parallel quest of Frenhofer:

> L'artiste sarrasinien veut déshabiller l'apparence, aller toujours *plus loin*, *derrière*, en vertu du principe idéaliste qui identifie le secret à la vérité: il faut donc passer *dans* le modèle, *sous* la statue, *derrière* la toile (c'est ce qu'un autre artiste balzacien, Frenhofer, demande à la toile idéale dont il rêve). (p. 128)

In this aspiration, Balzac's fictional artists are joined by the 'realist writer', of whom their own author is such a famous example, and by all those critics who choose to delve into a reality behind the words: 'même règle pour l'écrivain réaliste (et sa postérité critique): il faut aller *derrière* le papier' (p. 128). In the argument of *S/Z*, Sarrasine's failure is emblematic of the inherent impossibility of the realist enterprise: 'Ce mouvement, qui pousse Sarrasine, l'artiste réaliste et le critique à tourner le modèle, la statue, la toile ou le texte pour s'assurer de son dessous, de son intérieur, conduit à un échec — à l'Échec.' (p. 129) While painting, literature and criticism are all implicated, sculpture remains the privileged vehicle of Barthes's analysis. The mythical embodiment of this representational art form par excellence is of course Pygmalion's statue, whose place in Sarrasine's aesthetic Barthes convincingly glosses:

> La statue parfaite, selon Sarrasine, eût été une enveloppe sous laquelle se fût tenue une femme réelle (à supposer qu'elle-même fût un *chef d'œuvre*), dont l'essence de réalité aurait vérifié et garanti la peau de marbre qui lui aurait été appliquée (ce rapport, pris dans l'autre sens, donne le mythe de Pygmalion: une femme réelle naît de la statue). (p. 213)

In the two sections that follow, I shall pursue my own analyses of *Sarrasine* and *Le Chef-d'œuvre inconnu* as Pygmalion narratives. This will lead me, in the fourth and fifth sections of this first chapter, to engage in greater detail with Barthes's mythical castration reading of *Sarrasine*, and to consider further his own neurotic probing under the surface of realist representation.

(ii) '*Sous* la statue'

Balzac's masterly narrator makes explicit if ironic use of the Pygmalion myth when he describes the antisocial and largely asexual Sarrasine who was Bouchardon's pupil in Paris: 'Il n'eut pas d'autre maîtresse que la Sculpture et Clothilde, l'une des célébrités de l'Opéra. Encore cette intrigue ne dura-t-elle pas.' (VI, 1059) It is Clothilde herself who returns the sculptor to his 'amour des Arts', to the amusement of her friend Sophie Arnould, who 's'étonna [...] que sa camarade eût pu l'emporter sur des statues' (VI, 1059). Less than a page later we re-encounter Sarrasine in the Roman opera house, squashed up in the stalls but well positioned close to the stage. The curtain rises and Jommelli's music prepares the way for Sarrasine's reaction to Zambinella's entrance.[10] Sarrasine's carefully charted build-up of physical pleasure is very specifically grounded in the aesthetic admiration of a sculptor, for whom 'la beauté idéale' (VI, 1060) had hitherto been dispersed in mere fragments of 'perfection', the crucial concept for Sarrasine (as, also, for Frenhofer in *Le Chef-d'œuvre inconnu*). Previously obliged to assemble his perfect (whole) woman from the bits and pieces of scattered and partial models (a finely curved leg here, a well-shaped breast there, and so on for shoulders, neck, hands and knees), Sarrasine has sought in vain in Paris for the consummate creations of ancient Greece.[11] Here at last, gathered into the single living model of Zambinella, are those 'exquises proportions de la nature féminine si ardemment désirées, desquelles un sculpteur est, tout à la fois, le juge le plus sévère et le plus passionné' (VI, 1060). And if, according to the narrator, a painter would likewise marvel at such perfection, it is the sculptor in Sarrasine who fills it out, who gives it volume, through his recognition of 'toutes les merveilles des Vénus révérées et rendues par le ciseau des Grecs' (VI, 1060). Only an ancient Greek sculptor could have attached the arms so beautifully to the bust, could have shaped the curves, lines and contours of the neck and face, of the eyebrows, eyelashes and voluptuous eyelids: 'C'était plus qu'une femme, c'était un chef-d'œuvre! [...] Sarrasine dévorait des yeux la statue de Pygmalion, pour lui descendue de son piédestal.' (VI, 1061) It is at this moment in the text that Balzac makes Zambinella sing; appropriately, this ultimate proof that the statue has come to life transforms Sarrasine's first cries of pleasure into an hallucinatory sexual possession during which he can 'sentir le vent de cette voix, [...] voir les méplats de ce visage, [...] y compter les veines bleues qui en nuançaient la peau satinée' (VI, 1061).

Balzac allows Sarrasine to recreate and act out this mythical scenario on a daily basis. After his first frenzy of drawing and mental undressing he spends every morning for a week working on his statue: 'occupé le matin à pétrir la glaise à l'aide de laquelle il réussissait à copier la Zambinella, malgré les voiles, les jupes, les corsets et les nœuds de rubans qui la lui dérobaient' (VI, 1062). Then, every evening, in a theatre box close to the stage and especially hired for the purpose, he derives a controlled and solitary pleasure from the sight and sound of his metamorphosed statue: 'Le soir, installé de bonne heure dans sa loge, seul, couché sur un sofa, il se faisait, semblable à un Turc enivré d'opium, un bonheur aussi fécond, aussi prodigue qu'il le souhaitait.' (VI, 1062–63) The next morning — and every morning — he will return to the creation and recreation of his statue. If this is an entirely successful two-stage scenario it is because it is organized by Sarrasine alone, protected as he is by self-imposed isolation; it will be destroyed when the world of real, other people intervenes in the form of the hoax set up by Zambinella's friends, and specifically in the impossible role allotted by them to Zambinella himself. Appropriately, Sarrasine brings his own tragedy to its climax when his abduction of Zambinella from the French ambassador's concert — he had lined up horses and carriage for an elopement — is diverted into an enforced confrontation between Zambinella the model and Zambinella the statue in the sculptor's own studio. This is no longer the setting of a creative phantasy but an 'atelier sombre et nu', where the life drains out from a terrified Zambinella: 'Le chanteur, à moitié mort, demeura sur une chaise, sans oser regarder une statue de femme, dans laquelle il reconnut ses traits.' (VI, 1073) As Sarrasine works through the layers of his denial a gesture of disgust causes him to turn from Zambinella to the statue: '"Et c'est une illusion!"'; he then addresses his despair directly to Zambinella, forcing the singer to look at the statue, as if he himself were to blame for the fact that, for Sarrasine, this 'femme imaginaire' will have stamped every 'femme réelle' — 'toutes les autres femmes' — 'd'un cachet d'imperfection' (VI, 1074). The metamorphosis of Pygmalion's statue, revealed as a male artist's phantasy, has gone into reverse, redividing the living masterpiece into statue and model. It is logical, therefore, that Sarrasine, in his violent but lucid rage, should attempt two separate acts of destruction: the sword for Zambinella, but first, and more urgently, the sculptor's mallet for the statue, 'ce monument de sa folie' (VI, 1074). Indeed, from Sarrasine's point of view, it is now a monument rather than a statue, a mere illusion with the life gone out of it.

To suggest that the myth of Pygmalion has gone into reverse is to follow to its logical conclusion Sarrasine's 'passion d'artiste'.[12] However, it is also to remain within the parameters of the inner narrative, as well as those of Sarrasine's blinkered value system. In fact, by the time of the narrator's evening at the Lanty ball, Sarrasine's lifeless 'statue de femme' has undergone a whole sequence of metamorphoses; along the way it has been transformed into the beautiful painting of Adonis that hangs in a blue, satin-lined, semi-circular boudoir, softly illuminated by an alabaster lamp. Put the other way round, the secret of this painting, so carefully established as a mystery worthy of Mme de Rochefide's and the reader's curiosity, turns out to be the story of a statue. Painting subsumes sculpture, while the myth of a creation brought alive by desire outlives the erroneous readings that are mischievously encouraged, in *Sarrasine*, by narrator and author alike.

Indeed, it is a brilliant irony of Balzac's narrative that the 'original' of the picture, once a desirable Italian boy but now a skeletal centenarian decked out in gaudy finery, should interrupt Mme de Rochefide's rapt contemplation of the painted image of his former self. Even as the narrator bemoans his first experience of jealousy of a work of art — 'Oublié pour un portrait!' (VI, 1055) — the soft footsteps and rustling dress of Marianina herald the painful passage of Zambinella through the 'petit cabinet' that houses the portrait in question. Marianina is leading Zambinella to a door hidden in the wall covering, and the roulade that completes her '"*Addio, addio!*"' will cause the old man to pause, carried back to his past, on the threshold of this 'réduit secret' (VI, 1055). Thus the 'spectre habillé' (VI, 1055), ghost indeed of his former self, is framed against the same blue-satin wall covering as the magnificently framed painting of Zambinella as Adonis. The boudoir is the antechamber of the 'sanctuaire inconnu' (VI, 1048) in which Zambinella remains hidden for months on end. Effectively, then, and as if by magic, Zambinella escapes from and returns to his portrait.[13]

The Adonis painting is the structural hinge of the text as a whole, in that Mme de Rochefide's imperious curiosity as to the identity of its model — '"Mais qui est-ce? [...] Je veux le savoir"' (VI, 1054) — motivates the story of a sculptor that will explain, eventually, the origin of the painting itself. At the same time, the description of the painting, and of Mme de Rochefide inspecting it from close to, is the climax of a pictorial metaphor that has been built up in layers throughout the opening sequence of *Sarrasine*. In the first paragraph of the text, the narrator develops a sparkling antithesis between the two tableaux, the external and internal, that are framed by the window recess in which he sits hidden by the curtains.[14] In the garden of the Lanty *hôtel*, 'les arbres, imparfaitement couverts de neige, [...] ressemblaient vaguement à des spectres mal enveloppés de leurs linceuls, image gigantesque de la fameuse *danse des morts*' (VI, 1043). It is a sober and silent picture of death, of a bleak, chilly nature in mourning. Its counterpart for this witty narrator is 'la danse des vivants!' (VI, 1043), the joyfully mingling sounds and sights — 'les décentes bacchanales de la vie' (VI, 1044) — of the Lanty ball. The antithesis is maintained by the narrator's action of turning from one scene ('je pouvais contempler') to the other ('je pouvais admirer') (VI, 1043) and, as he points out, his body both marks the dividing line ('moi, sur la frontière de ces deux tableaux si disparates') and participates physically in his mental phantasy: 'je faisais une macédoine morale, moitié plaisante, moitié funèbre. Du pied gauche je marquais la mesure, et je croyais avoir l'autre dans un cercueil.' (VI, 1044)

A lengthy digression on the unresolved mystery of the Lanty fortune, and the identity of their mysterious elderly relative, is motivated by gossip overheard from the narrator's hiding place. Some ten pages later, the narrator picks up his meditation where he had left off, and has just drawn it to a close with a summary of the two sides of the human coin when he is disturbed by a stifled laugh. Not only has Zambinella sprung up from the depths — 'Il semblait être sorti de dessous terre, poussé par quelque mécanisme de théâtre' (VI, 1050) — he has emerged right next to Mme de Rochefide. The narrator's contrasting tableaux, nourished by his imagination as much as by his eyes, have merged into the single hybrid image that takes on human shape through this literal juxtaposition of Zambinella and Mme de Rochefide:

> Je restai stupéfait devant l'image qui s'offrit à mes regards. Par un des plus rares caprices de la nature, la pensée en demi-deuil qui se roulait dans ma cervelle en était sortie, elle se trouvait devant moi, personnifiée, vivante, elle avait jailli comme Minerve de la tête de Jupiter, grande et forte, elle avait tout à la fois cent ans et vingt-deux ans, elle était vivante et morte. (VI, 1050)

Both halves of the narrator's pictorial 'pensée' have come to life — 'personnifiée, vivante' — including the half that was death-like: 'Ils étaient là, devant moi, tous deux, ensemble, unis et si serrés, que l'étranger froissait et la robe de gaze, et les guirlandes de fleurs, et les cheveux légèrement crêpés, et la ceinture flottante.' (VI, 1050) This composite figure is a chiasmus, with youth and life at its centre: 'elle avait tout à la fois cent ans et vingt-deux ans, elle était vivante et morte'. With her delicate forms and fresh colouring, Mme de Rochefide was already the object of a strikingly endoscopic male gaze: 'une de ces figures [...] si frêles, si transparentes, qu'un regard d'homme semble devoir les pénétrer, comme les rayons du soleil traversent une glace pure' (VI, 1050). Now, by seeming to touch all at once the outer trappings of Mme de Rochefide, it is as if Zambinella were the first external layer to be peeled off, before that male gaze could pass through her gauze dress and translucent body.

The detailed description of Zambinella that follows is the first of 'Les Deux Portraits' by which Balzac originally entitled the first part of the text. It is initially focalized through the eyes of Mme de Rochefide, to whom Zambinella is still metaphorically glued, having fetched a folding stool to sit next to her when she herself, for protection, has sat down next to the narrator. Despite the dull, glaucous eyes that turn to meet her gaze, she is sufficiently emboldened to engage in active examination of this bizarre old man. The conflation of her viewpoint with that of an impersonal 'on' ('on s'apercevait facilement'; 'quand une fatale attention vous dévoilait'), as well as that of a hypothetical specialist of the human anatomy ('un anatomiste eût reconnu') (VI, 1051), establishes a sculptural perspective on the emaciated forms and angular planes of 'ce corps étrange' (VI, 1051). The outdated, tasteless luxury of the clothes — a dazzling white shirt and waistcoat embroidered with gold, a diamond of incalculable worth in the middle of a rust-coloured ruff — throws Zambinella's face into relief ('faisaient encore mieux ressortir la figure de cet être bizarre'), again in the sculptural sense of the term:

> Le cadre étaient digne du portrait. Ce visage noir était anguleux et creusé dans tous les sens. Le menton était creux; les tempes étaient creuses; les yeux étaient perdus en de jaunâtres orbites. Les os maxillaires, rendus saillants par une maigreur indescriptible, dessinaient des cavités au milieu de chaque joue.
> (VI, 1052)

The framed, sculpted face is literally painted in red and white: 'Les sourcils de son masque recevaient de la lumière un lustre qui révélait une peinture très bien exécutée', and the pretension and 'coquetterie féminine' attributed to him are brought out not only by his luxuriant blond wig, his earrings, and the sparkling rings on his skeletal fingers, but above all by the comparison of his watch chain with 'les chatons d'une rivière au cou d'une femme' (VI, 1052). After a last description of the skull-like head of this 'espèce d'idole japonaise', Zambinella as a whole is described as a statue — 'silencieuse, immobile autant qu'une statue' (VI, 1052) — the movement of whose eyes must be produced by some trick mechanism. It is at this point that the narrator produces a second version of his composite figure, one that integrates Mme de Rochefide in terms that are so specifically sculptural as to suggest that he is now describing a hybrid statue. The link between the two figures is the women's neck (supporting a simile in Zambinella's case), but Mme de Rochefide's neck, like the rest of her body, is beautiful and unadorned:

> Voir, auprès de ces débris humains, une jeune femme dont le cou, les bras et le corsage étaient nus et blancs; dont les formes pleines et verdoyantes de beauté, dont les cheveux bien plantés sur un front d'albâtre inspirait l'amour, dont les yeux ne recevait pas, mais répandaient la lumière, qui était suave, fraîche, et dont les boucles vaporeuses, dont l'haleine embaumée semblaient trop lourdes, trop dures, trop puissantes pour cette ombre, pour cette homme en poussière; ah! c'était bien la mort et la vie, ma pensée, une arabesque imaginaire, une chimère hideuse à moitié, divinement femelle par le corsage. (VI, 1053)

Balzac's sculpted chimera superimposes outside and inside, so that the spectral centenarian is the slough to be cast off, like that of the snake who forms the third part of the chimera, to reveal the beautiful, living creature inside. Indeed, Zambinella's wafer-thin, yellow skin has been glued to his bones by his many years, and the sunken contours his skin traces make him seem like the mould of a statue seen from the inside or turned inside out.

Appropriately, it is Mme de Rochefide who initiates the transfer of the group to the boudoir, and sets in train its metamorphosis: '"C'est une horrible vision"', she declares, logically unaware of the fuller picture that includes herself, '"Si je le regarde encore, je croirai que la mort elle-même est venue me chercher. Mais vit-il?"' (VI, 1053). Unsure, she touches him to find out, and initiates by this transgressive gesture the nightmare sequence whereby, terrified by the rattle he emits and by the ferocious glances of his family, she escapes with the narrator to her ironically chosen retreat at the end of the *enfilade* of reception rooms. As in every bad dream, the 'spectre habillé qui [leur] avait fait fuir du salon de musique' (VI, 1055) will inevitably catch up with her. However, before this has happened, a new coupling takes place, in the blue lunar boudoir, between Mme de Rochefide and the beautiful Adonis: '"Ah! le beau tableau!" ajouta-t-elle en se levant, et allant se mettre en face d'une toile magnifiquent encadrée.' (VI, 1054) This time, Mme de Rochefide is subject, and Zambinella object, of the strange attraction that links them. This is no longer the 'craintive curiosité qui pousse les femmes à se procurer des émotions dangereuses' (VI, 1051), but an admiration that is both aesthetic and erotic. Touched by Mme de Rochefide's bold hand, the metaphorical statue has indeed cast off the corpse-like slough ('le cadavre ambulant') that will shuffle back to its lair in the lunar boudoir. Retreating, as it were, behind the painting that mythologizes his youthful desirability, the elderly model will pay no more attention to Mme de Rochefide than to his portrait, at which she is gazing. Yet her rapt contemplation has restored Zambinella to his rightful sex and has completed the transformation of a lifeless 'statue de femme' into a painting of a beautiful young man.

(iii) '*Dans* le tableau'

By way of transition to *Le Chef-d'œuvre inconnu*, I shall briefly examine a real-life performance of the Pygmalion myth. Set some time before 1830, the episode is recounted in the 1860s in the *Mémoires* of Louis Canler, who rose through the ranks of the police in the Restoration and July Monarchy to become head of the *Brigade de la Sûreté*. If only for their immersion in *la vie privée*, these memoirs are on Balzacian territory, and this most likeable and literary of policemen is an accomplished raconteur. In a chapter that bears the intriguing title 'Les Poses mythologiques', Canler relates an anecdote from a period when he was based in the Marché du Temple in Paris and found himself in need of information from the boyfriend of a local brothel owner, Mlle S★★★. Always keen to keep in with the local police, the latter invites Canler, whilst waiting for her boyfriend's return, to witness a spectacle that may be new to him. Agreeing not to make a sound he follows her into a pitch-black cabinet; already, he confesses, 'cette espèce de mystère et les ténèbres qui m'entouraient avaient excité ma curiosité'.[15] Mlle S★★★ pulls back a curtain to uncover a carefully crafted chink in the woodwork; left alone, he spies on the scene on the other side of the wall:

> sur un piédestal rond, recouvert d'un tapis vert, était placée une statue de femme de grandeur naturelle, le poli du corps était blanc rosé; un vieillard, un septuagénaire, affublé d'une écharpe verte, un maillet et un ciseau de sculpteur à la main, était en extase au pied de la statue. (p. 86)

After gazing at the statue for a few moments, the old man touches the pedestal which proceeds to revolve slowly, and it is not only the brothel customer, but Canler himself who is able to admire, at his leisure, 'les formes gracieuses et bien proportionnées de cette statue' (p. 86).[16] The old man then immobilizes the pedestal, kisses the statue the length of its body — 'des pieds à la tête' — before dropping to his knees to act out, with incomprehensible words and dramatic gestures, Pygmalion's invocation to Venus. The answer to his prayers is achieved by his action of placing his hand on the statue's hip, for the statue 's'anima insensiblement en ouvrant les yeux. Ses bras et ses jambes s'agitèrent comme si un ressort les avait fait mouvoir; alors le vieillard se débarrassa de son écharpe, du maillet et du ciseau, et, à ma grande surprise, il disparut comme une ombre.' (p. 86) It is left to Mlle S★★★'s boyfriend to reveal that the old man is the comte de B★★★, and that he pays a hundred francs 'chaque fois qu'il venait jouer le rôle de Pygmalion avec sa statue' (p. 86).

   Canler is so intrigued that he is invited to spy on a second, more elaborate mythological performance. Returning to the brothel a week later, he is confronted by an empty room in which three statues of different shapes and sizes, but again with 'les formes aussi gracieuses que bien proportionnées' (p. 87), face each other in a circle. Only at the end will it be explained to him that he has witnessed the Judgement of Paris, and that the three statues represent Juno, Minerva and Venus, the latter in fact Pygmalion's Galatea, recycled for the occasion. Canler describes the entry of a decrepit old man who, as the judge of this beauty contest, proceeds to scrutinize all sides of all three statues from all angles:

> Il fit plusieurs fois le tour des statues en les touchant avec une sorte de frénésie, puis il fit tourner le piédestal par le moyen que j'ai déjà indiqué, et après vingt minutes de rotation, un bruit semblable à celui que produit le ressort d'une pendule qu'on remonte grinça jusqu'à moi. Alors les statues firent volte face en tournant sur elle-mêmes; cette nouvelle position électrisa le vieillard à un tel point que, les yeux enflammés, il se jeta à genoux, dans un état de surexcitation difficile à décrire. (p. 87)

When he has recovered, Paris places sixty francs at the feet of Juno and Minerva, a hundred francs at those of the winner, Venus, and a further hundred francs on the mantlepiece for Mlle S★★★. He then melts away, as had Pygmalion the previous week. Canler, who had set the scene of the three competing statues with an intriguing choice of words — 'J'étais à les considérer depuis quelques secondes, comme ferait un peintre réaliste' (p. 87) — self-consciously analyses the formal mechanisms of these staged performances, with their costumes, props and mechanical devices. Moreover, he builds into his narrative his own role as voyeur of a 'folie érotique' that is mediated, for the brothel customer, by participation in a phantasmatic scenario, for himself, by the carefully placed spyhole that creates a peep-show acted out as if for his benefit. As he retrospectively notes: 'Le spectacle que je venais de voir avait d'autant plus d'imprévu pour moi, qu'à cette époque les tableaux vivants n'étaient pas encore connus à Paris' (p. 87).

It is tempting to draw a comparison between Canler's Pygmalion and Paris and Balzac's Sarrasine and Frenhofer, especially the latter who, as Barthes puts it in *S/Z*, 'voudrait que l'on pût circuler *dans* le tableau, comme dans un air volumineux, contourner la chair des corps peints, de façon à les authentifier' (p. 214). At the centre of the first part of *Le Chef-d'œuvre inconnu* is a painting lesson, set in the studio of Porbus, and taking as its subject the latter's painting, a *Marie égyptienne*. This fictional painting — Porbus was a real painter — a commission for the Queen, portrays the moment in the saint's life when, wishing to give up her life as a prostitute and to withdraw to a life of prayer in the desert, she must prostitute herself one last time to pay the ferrymen to take her across the Nile. The painting has already become known as a masterpiece, and Frenhofer is presumably visiting Porbus in order to see it. Yet he is critical, and his lengthy lecture on how and why it lacks life is witnessed by Poussin who, young and unknown, has slipped in unnoticed for a veritable initiation into the world of art and artists. Poussin's ambitious desire for this world, which includes moments of modest *pudeur*, is eroticized by Balzac's metaphors, so that his first encounter with master painters and a masterpiece, his first entry into a proper studio with the material trappings of art — from canvases, easels, paints and sketches to pieces of armour, carefully arranged drapes, *écorchés* and bits of statues of Greek goddesses — might be thought to resemble a first visit to a brothel. In Frenhofer's analysis, Porbus's painting of the Egyptian saint lacks space and depth: '"on s'aperçoit qu'elle est collée au fond de la toile et qu'on ne pourrait pas faire le tour de son corps; c'est une silhouette qui n'a qu'une seule face, c'est une apparence découpée qui ne saurait se retourner, ni changer de position."' (x, 416) She therefore lacks life in terms that are sculptural and allude, obviously, to Pygmalion:

> 'je ne saurais croire que ce beau corps soit animé par le tiède souffle de la vie. Il me semble que si je portais la main sur cette gorge d'une si ferme rondeur, je la trouverais froide comme du marbre! [...] le sang ne court pas sous cette peau d'ivoire [...]: ici c'est une femme, là une statue, plus loin un cadavre. Ta création est incomplète.' (x, 417)

An indignant outburst from Poussin leads to an invitation to show off his future skills in front of the two older painters — '"A l'œuvre!" lui dit Porbus en lui présentant un crayon et une feuille de papier' (x, 420) — and it is the obvious brilliance of the copy that Poussin dashes off (and signs) that spurs Frenhofer to propose a rival performance, a practical demonstration in which he will add the crucial finishing touches to Porbus's painting and bring its saintly prostitute to life.[17]

The scene, which contains elements of the erotic Pygmalion phantasy played out in a Parisian brothel, is a short one relative to the long aesthetic lesson that precedes it. Frenhofer sends for palette and brushes, then rolls up his sleeves and mixes his colours in a ritualized pantomime of preparation that is marked by visible sexual excitement. This is charted in the twitching of the tip of his beard and the rapid movement of his brush as it jabs feverishly into the various mounds of paint, or occasionally runs the length of his palette like the hand of an organist showing off at his keyboard. Frenhofer as a physically aroused Pygmalion is himself framed by Poussin and Porbus who watch him, absorbed and motionless, one on each side of the canvas, as he slaps on warmth ('"paf, paf, paf!"') to those parts of the painted body ('"Pon! Pon! Pon!"') where he had earlier pointed out 'un défaut de vie' (x, 422).[18] Indeed the narrative focus is largely on Frenhofer's physical performance as, with a running commentary addressed exclusively to Poussin, he interferes — 'ici deux coups de pinceau, là un seul' (x, 421) — with every part of the painting:

> Il travaillait avec une ardeur si passionnée que la sueur se perlait sur son front dépouillé, il allait si rapidement par de petits mouvements si impatients, si saccadés, que pour le jeune Poussin il semblait qu'il y eût dans le corps de ce bizarre personnage un démon qui agissait par ses mains. (x, 421–22)

When he stops both Porbus and Poussin are 'muets d'admiration' (x, 422), but it is Frenhofer who pays for the pleasure he has given himself, offering two gold coins for Poussin's sketch, inviting both men to lunch at his house, and sending for two casks of Porbus's favourite wine: '"Une pour m'acquitter du plaisir que j'ai eu ce matin en voyant ta jolie pécheresse, et l'autre comme un présent d'amitié."' (x, 423–24) By the end of this archetypal episode of male bonding, set in Porbus's studio, and in which the *Marie égyptienne* has passed through the hands of all three men as it were — Porbus has painted her, Poussin has copied her, Frenhofer has touched up her portrait and set her blood circulating — Poussin is fully integrated into this confraternity of painters with its cross-generational hierarchies of masters and pupils. The three of them leave together, they saunter along 'en devisant sur les arts', and Poussin, 'le peintre en espérance', soon finds himself 'devant un bon feu, près d'une table chargée de mets appétissants, et par un bonheur inouï, dans la compagnie de deux grands artistes pleins de bonhomie' (x, 422–23).

The fourth (and founding) figure in the homosocial genealogy of Balzac's story is another real painter. As Porbus explains to Poussin:

> 'Le vieux Frenhofer est le seul élève que Mabuse ait voulu faire. Devenu son ami, son sauveur, son père, Frenhofer a sacrifié la plus grande partie de ses trésors à satisfaire les passions de Mabuse; en échange Mabuse lui a légué le secret du relief, le pouvoir de donner aux figures cette vie extraordinaire, cette fleur de nature, notre désespoir éternel.' (x, 426–27)

This is a retrospective explanation of Frenhofer's earlier lament — '"Ô Mabuse! ô mon maître! [...] tu es un voleur, tu as emporté la vie avec toi!"' (x, 420) — while Mabuse's painting *Adam* conveys to Poussin a hint at least of what this '"secret du relief"' might be: 'Cette figure offrait, en effet, une telle puissance de réalité, que Nicolas Poussin commença dès ce moment à comprendre le véritable sens des confuses paroles dites par le vieillard.' (x, 423) A second engagement with the Pygmalion myth is therefore set in motion — a Sarrasinian tragedy, however, rather than a *tableau vivant* à la Canler — when Porbus tries to exploit Frenhofer's good mood to gain access to the unknown masterpiece that the old man refers to as his 'mistress', and that is assumed by Porbus and Poussin to embody this secret: '"Montrer mon œuvre, s'écria le vieillard tout ému. Non, non, je dois la perfectionner encore."' (x, 424) Sarrasine's week of solitary pleasure, in which the *va-et-vient* between statue and living masterpiece was renewed on a daily basis, has expanded to the ten years during which Frenhofer, in the fortified isolation of his studio, has vacillated between euphoric certainty and depressed doubt:

> 'Hier, vers le soir, dit-il, j'ai cru avoir fini. Ses yeux me semblaient humides, sa chair était agitée. Les tresses de ses cheveux remuaient. Elle respirait! Quoique j'aie trouvé le moyen de réaliser sur une toile plate le relief et la rondeur de la nature, ce matin, au jour, j'ai reconnu mon erreur.' (x, 424)

> 'De près, ce travail semble cotonneux et paraît manquer de précision, mais à deux pas, tout se raffermit, s'arrête et se détache; le corps tourne, les formes deviennent saillantes, l'on sent circuler l'air tout autour. Cependant je ne suis pas encore content, j'ai des doutes.' (x, 425)

Ovid's Pygmalion is similarly indecisive. Knowing full well that his statue is simply a statue, still he 'would not yet admit that ivory was all it was'. And then, standing before the metamorphosed maiden of his prayers, he questions the evidence of his eyes and hands, 'afraid of being mistaken, his joy tempered with doubt'.[19] Frenhofer's hesitation may seem strategic, in that it refuels and endlessly prolongs the phantasy: '"Nous ignorons le temps qu'employa le seigneur Pygmalion pour faire la seule statue qui ait marché!"' (x, 425). Nevertheless, it is rationalized aesthetically, and in terms that repeat Sarrasine's ideal of a unity and wholeness to replace the previously scattered parts: '"il m'a manqué jusqu'à présent de rencontrer une femme irréprochable, un corps dont les contours soient d'une beauté parfaite, et dont la carnation... Mais où est-elle vivante, [...] cette introuvable Vénus des anciens, si souvent cherchée, et dont nous rencontrons à peine quelques beautés éparses?"' (x, 426). Perfection is the seme insistently attributed to Gillette, a living woman and Poussin's mistress. And since Poussin has been overtaken by 'une inexplicable curiosité d'artiste' (x, 425) that conflates 'l'art avec ses secrets' (x, 426) not only with Frenhofer, but with Frenhofer's secret painting, he conceives the idea of offering Gillette as a model — '"Il ne pourra voir que la femme en toi. Tu es si parfaite!"' (x, 429) — using Porbus as intermediary to propose the loan in exchange for a look at Frenhofer's picture: '"Le jeune Poussin est aimé par une femme dont l'incomparable beauté se trouve sans imperfection aucune"' (x, 431); '"avant que vous trouviez, même en Asie, une femme aussi belle, aussi parfaite, vous mourrez peut-être sans avoir achevé votre tableau"' (x, 432). And when the exchange is effected and Frenhofer emerges beaming from his studio, it is to announce that his work is indeed 'parfaite', and to suppose that Porbus and Poussin cannot see the picture precisely on account of the perfection of the image:

'"Ah! Ah! [...] vous ne vous attendiez pas à tant de perfection! Vous êtes devant une femme et vous cherchez un tableau.[...] Où est l'art? perdu, disparu!"' (x, 435) Frenhofer, 'dont les yeux pétillaient, et qui haletait comme un jeune homme ivre d'amour', has convinced himself at last: '"Ne semble-t-il pas que vous puissiez passer la main sur ce dos? [...] Mais elle a respiré, je crois! [...] Les chairs palpitent. Elle va se lever, attendez."' (x, 435)

Le Chef-d'œuvre inconnu is thus a more literal version of the Pygmalion myth than either the inner or outer narrative of *Sarrasine*. For all the passion with which Frenhofer describes the living qualities of the painted woman with whom he has shared ten years of his existence ('"ce n'est pas une toile, c'est une femme!"' (x, 431)), this relationship never ceases to be mediated by the fact that she is a picture, and that he has brought her alive with paint: '"Ne m'a-t-elle pas souri à chaque coup de pinceau que je lui ai donné? Elle a une âme, l'âme dont je l'ai douée."' (x, 431)[20] On the whole, Frenhofer seems to use the term mistress as a metaphor to characterize an eroticized investment in what he never ceases to regard as a painting:

> 'Ma peinture n'est pas une peinture, c'est un sentiment, une passion! Née dans mon atelier, elle doit y rester vierge, et n'en peut sortir que vêtue. La poésie et les femmes ne se livrent nues qu'à leurs amants! [...] l'œuvre que je tiens là-haut sous mes verrous est une exception dans notre art; ce n'est pas une toile, c'est une femme! Une femme avec laquelle je pleure, je ris, je cause, je pense. [...] Cette femme n'est pas une créature, c'est une création.' (x, 431)

Logically, it is the painter's gaze that he fears in Poussin: '"lui faire supporter le regard d'un homme, d'un jeune homme, d'un peintre? Je tuerais le lendemain celui qui l'aurait souillée d'un regard!"' (x, 432) And when Frenhofer first sees Gillette and begs after all to borrow her, it is his painter's instinct that brings a lively glint to his eye, and his painter's eye that mentally undresses her, as Poussin himself realizes, 'au désespoir d'avoir sorti ce beau trésor de son grenier' (x, 433). Once Frenhofer pronounces his work perfect, it is very specifically no painting, rather than no woman, that could ever match it: '"Jamais peintre, pinceaux, couleurs, toile et lumière ne feront une rivale à *Catherine Lescault*!"' (x, 435) And it is certainly a painting that Frenhofer is describing in the wonderful moment when Porbus and Poussin peer at the canvas from all angles in an attempt to decipher an image, while Frenhofer assumes they see only a real woman and are searching for the material existence of a picture on an easel: '"Oui, oui, c'est bien une toile [...]. Tenez, voilà le châssis, le chevalet, enfin voici mes couleurs, mes pinceaux."' (x, 436)

The text of Ovid's *Metamorphoses* makes it clear that Pygmalion has played at dressing and undressing his statue: 'He dressed the limbs of his statue in woman's robes [...]. All this finery became the image well, but it was no less lovely unadorned.' (p. 232) No wonder, then, that Frenhofer defers to sculpture when it comes to creating the human form, for only a sculptor could literally dress and undress his work of art:

> 'je n'ai pas marqué sèchement les bords extérieurs de ma figure et fait ressortir jusqu'au moindre détail anatomique, car le corps humain ne finit pas par des lignes. En cela, les sculpteurs peuvent plus approcher de la vérité que nous

autres. La nature comporte une suite de rondeurs qui s'enveloppent les unes
dans les autres.' (x, 424)

Still, he does his best to subsume this sculptor's privilege into his own creative
method. Like Sarrasine stripping the layers from his imaginary Zambinella,
Frenhofer has '"analysé et soulevé couche par couche les tableaux de Titien"' (x,
424); at the sight of Gillette, 'par une habitude de peintre, [le vieillard] déshabilla
pour ainsi dire cette jeune fille en devinant les formes les plus secrètes' (x, 433). In
the seclusion of his studio he can juxtapose *Catherine Lescault* with Gillette, and can
initiate and study Gillette's literal undressing: '"Ah! elle se déshabille. Il lui dit de
se mettre au jour! Il la compare!"' (x, 434) When he is satisfied at last ('"Entrez,
entrez [...]. Mon œuvre est parfaite"' (x, 434)), the depth of Frenhofer's picture
— '"Il y a tant de profondeur sur cette toile"' (x, 435) — is attested, even for
Porbus and Poussin, by 'les diverses couches de couleur que le vieux peintre avait
successivement superposées en croyant perfectionner cette peinture' (x, 436). What
for Poussin are 'des couleurs confusément amassées et contenues par une multitude
de lignes bizarres qui forment une muraille de peinture' (x, 436), for Frenhofer are
the layers by means of which he has lovingly dressed and undressed his sculpted
Catherine Lescault: '"mon cher Porbus, regarde attentivement mon travail, et tu
comprendras mieux ce que je te disais sur la manière de traiter le modelé et les
contours"' (x, 436–37). Indeed, it is a three-dimensional bare foot — 'mais un pied
délicieux, un pied vivant!' — that Porbus eventually sees poking through the layers
of paint:

> Ils aperçurent dans un coin de la toile le bout d'un pied nu qui sortait de ce chaos
> de couleurs, de tons, de nuances indécises, espèce de brouillard sans forme; mais
> un pied délicieux, un pied vivant! Ils restèrent pétrifiés d'admiration devant ce
> fragment échappé à une incroyable, à une lente et progressive destruction. Ce
> pied apparaissait là comme le torse de quelque Vénus en marbre de Paros qui
> surgirait parmi les décombres d'une ville incendiée. (x, 436)

Sculptural in its own right, the foot calls up the torso of a statue of Venus rising
from the debris of a burned-out city. As such, it is a perfect figuration of the 'secret
du relief' (x, 426) that was passed down to Frenhofer by his master Mabuse, and
the key to the painting is a *relief* in both French senses of the word: at once a *foot in
relief* and a *leftover foot*. The foot is sculptural and *vivant*: it is the leftover fragment of
a representational woman buried under the layers of paint.

(iv) '*Dans* le modèle'

As so often, the fetishist's indecision comes to turn on a foot. '"Il y a une femme là-
dessous"' (x, 436), exclaims Porbus, as if that were the end of the matter. '"Tôt ou
tard, il s'apercevra qu'il n'y a rien sur sa toile"' (x, 437), cries Poussin, in an apparently
dismissive final comment. What is the relation between these two statements and
the painting that has provoked them? In the context of an aesthetic of wholeness
and perfection that so clearly, in these artist stories, and from the perspective of
their knowledge-driven artists, involves an imaginary female anatomy, it would
be perverse not to read the foot as a Freudian compensatory fetish.[21] It would

be perverse, too, not to integrate the reactions of Porbus and Poussin, as well as Frenhofer's quest for the perfection of Venus, into this reading. If Gillette has been given a role in a male phantasy that involves a relation between the fragmentary left-over foot and the imaginary whole woman to whom it fetishistically relates, it is appropriate that Frenhofer's *entremetteurs* should provide an ironic frame for the missing scene. Eavesdropping in the absence of a voyeur's keyhole, Porbus provides the commentary that allows us to understand that Frenhofer is testing the 'truth' of *Catherine Lescault* against an undressed Gillette. Poussin, meanwhile, clings to the door of the forbidden studio, phallic dagger at the ready. Porbus and Poussin are a double act, contributing in turn and as appropriate to this triangular fetishistic performance. First they procure Gillette to play the crucial role of 'perfect woman'; then, by acting out their own uncertainty as to what they see on the canvas — first 'nothing', then the foot of a buried woman, then 'nothing' once more — they re-ignite Frenhofer's doubt after his moment of triumph and certainty. Such disappointment is structural, part and parcel of the fetishistic scenario, whereby Frenhofer moves from tears of despair ('"Rien, rien!"'), to denial ('"Moi, je la vois!"'), to a defiant reconcealment of his masterpiece ('recouvrait sa Catherine d'une serge verte') (x, 438).[22]

When Zambinella is brought face to face with his statue in Sarrasine's studio, he recognizes himself in what he sees there. There is no need for Balzac to spell out that this could not be the case when Gillette is confined with *Catherine Lescault* in Frenhofer's studio. Fetishistic phantasies presuppose that Ideal Woman is 'really' castrated and it is logical that Gillette — the only real woman in the tale, herself '"merveilleusement belle"' and, finally, 'oubliée dans un coin' (x, 438) — should be lucid from the outset about her treatment by these three male artists: 'Elle croyait aimer déjà moins le peintre en le soupçonnant moins estimable' (x, 430); '"Pour lui, répondit Gillette en regardant attentivement le Poussin et Porbus, ne suis-je donc pas plus qu'une femme?"' (x, 434) In this story of four people and a painting, clearly Gillette is the victim of the secrets of art that gather around the figure of Frenhofer. From the point of view of the sexual politics of the story, Balzac uses Gillette to introduce a critical perspective on the three male disciples of Pygmalion. By representing the fetishistic scenario at one remove, he exposes the narcissistic sexuality whereby an illusory view of 'perfect woman' feeds off a phantasy of woman's castration.

In *Le Chef-d'œuvre inconnu*, the phantasy is shown to have little connection with real women. In *Sarrasine*, it is more mischievously shown to have no connection with them at all in that the delusion is supported, for a long time successfully, by a cross-dressed young man. It is true, of course, that the young man in question is a castrato. Jean Reboul, an analyst who notes in passing that Freud was an obsessive reader of Balzac, is amazed to find the Freudian castration phantasy described so literally in a text dating from 1830. 'Sarrasine, ou la castration personnifiée', the 1967 essay whose influence on S/Z Barthes openly acknowledges (p. 23), is a writing out of that amazement.[23] Reboul's basic point is summed up in the neat formulation that castration personified (Zambinella) negates castration denied (the statue of perfect woman). The confrontation of masterpiece and model in Sarrasine's studio destroys the phantasy, whereas it had been confirmed for Frenhofer when he compared his portrait — *Catherine Lescault* with her compensatory fetish-foot — with the supposedly 'perfect' (whole) model that was Gillette. Zambinella, for his part, is the living negation of a phantasy designed to shore up Sarrasine's virility. While the scene with the snake — Zambinella's terror and Sarrasine's corresponding courage — is classic fodder for this narcissistic delusion (female inferiority as confirmation of male superiority), the discovery that Zambinella is literally castrated causes the structure to implode. The statue can no longer support the phantasy of an imaginary whole woman (her 'lack' compensated by a fetish), all women are stamped once more with a 'cachet d'imperfection' (VI, 1074), and Sarrasine is obliged to acknowledge the insecurity of his own condition in the mirror of Zambinella's real body.

To this extent, with his brilliant glosses on Sarrasine's spurious logic, Barthes follows the letter of Reboul's reading, while expanding it to a fuller engagement with the sculptor's psychology, ideology and aesthetics. However, Barthes parts company with Reboul — and with the latter's orthodox Freudian interpretation — in his evaluation of the ending of *Sarrasine*. For Reboul, Sarrasine's *angoisse* is ironized by the concluding exchange between the narrator and Mme de Lanty: 'fadaises mondaines [...], rite de sortie [...]. Ces deux-là pourront encore jouer à l'amour.' (p. 96) Reboul restricts the internalization of castration to Sarrasine, and considers Mme de Rochefide's subsequent love affairs to be perfectly programmed by Balzac's worldly conclusion. Barthes, however, wants this tailpiece to be 'castrated' too, implying that a reader without knowledge of other texts of *La Comédie humaine* would believe in a Mme de Rochefide permanently excluded from desire. To deny the irony of the ending, and to stay within the register of a tragically pandemic castration, he is obliged to attribute Mme de Rochefide's 'fadaises mondaines' to a defensive denial of the whole register of the symbolic. Her world-weary conclusions — '"Oui, les âmes pures ont une patrie dans le ciel! Personne ne m'aura connue!"' (VI, 1076) — are trumped four times in quick succession by versions of Barthes's rebuttal: 'SYM. Alibi de la castration'. Indeed, they are recuperated as castration come what may: 'SYM. Alibi suprême de la castration (le Ciel justifiera les castrats que nous sommes devenus).' (p. 220)

In short, once Barthes gets beyond Reboul's reading of the inner story, he launches into his own attempt to castrate the realist text, so that the galloping disease of castration, having swept through the statue and its copies *en route* to the painted Adonis, contaminates the narratee and rebounds onto the narrator, the better to reveal the empty interior of a whole system of representation. Barthes's main target is Balzac's narrator, who supposedly upholds the stable system of representation, only to see it fall away from him as an effect of the story he tells. Not only is he lined up by Barthes as the last victim of the castration pandemic — 'l'amoureux, pris à son propre piège, est rébuté: on ne raconte pas impunément une histoire de castration' (pp. 218–19) — he is admonished, from the outset, for his 'asymbolism': 'le narrateur feint de refuser le symbolique [...]; il sera d'ailleurs puni de son incrédulité' (p. 33). His rational descriptions of the elderly castrato, though recognized by Barthes as narrative exploitation of the hermeneutic code, are ultimately considered a form of *dénégation*. When the narrator follows his first reference to 'un personnage étrange' with a perfunctory 'C'était un homme' (VI, 1047), Barthes retorts: 'Le vieillard, en fait, n'est pas un homme' (p. 48).[24] The follow-up claim, 'l'étranger était tout simplement un *vieillard*' (VI, 1047), is deemed tautologous: 'il se fait défenseur de la lettre, [...] (*le vieillard était un vieillard*)' (p. 50), and when Mme de Rochefide is chided for her fear of Zambinella — ' "vous imitez les sots. Vous prenez un petit vieillard pour un spectre" ' (VI, 1054) — Barthes leaps in to denounce such bad faith: 'l'imaginaire du narrateur, c'est-à-dire le système symbolique à travers lequel il se méconnaît, a précisément ce caractère d'être asymbolique: il est, dit-il, celui qui ne croit pas aux fables (aux symboles)' (p. 73). Finally when, in the face of Mme de Rochefide's distressed reaction to the denouement (' "Laissez-moi seule" ' (VI, 1075)), the narrator attempts to pass off his story as evidence of the progress of Italian civilization — ' "On n'y fait plus de ces malheureuses créatures" ' (VI, 1075) — this 'realist' rejoinder is dismissed by Barthes with aggressive sarcasm:

> le narrateur tente d'opposer à la terreur d'une castration toute-puissante [...] le barrage de la raison historique, du fait positif: congédions le symbole, dit-il, revenons sur terre, dans le 'réel', dans l'histoire: il n'y a plus de castrats: *la maladie est vaincue*, elle a disparu d'Europe, comme la peste, la lèpre; proposition minuscule, rempart douteux, argument dérisoire contre la force torrentueuse du symbolique qui vient d'emporter toute la petite population de *Sarrasine*. (p. 219)

Curiously, Barthes is a lot less hostile to the character who, as the asymbolic narrator par excellence, might have been thought the real villain of the piece. The revelation to Sarrasine of the 'affreuse vérité' (VI, 1072) is delegated by Balzac to the elderly prince Chigi, first protector of the singer and, according to Barthes, 'castrateur littéral' (p. 192) insofar as he has organized and paid for the operation: ' "C'est moi, monsieur, qui ai doté Zambinella de sa voix. J'ai tout payé à ce drôle-là, même son maître à chanter." ' One of the ironies of Sarrasine's 'coincidental' address of his question to Chigi — ' "C'est sans doute par égard pour les cardinaux, les évêques et les abbés qui sont ici [...] qu'*elle* est habillée en homme?" ' (VI, 1072) — is Balzac's brilliantly staged confrontation of the two Pygmalions of his story. One is an artist who has sculpted a phantasmatic statue in line with his desire; the other, similarly motivated by desire, has formed him for his future by commissioning an intervention in his anatomy: ' "s'il fait fortune, il me le devra tout entière" ' (VI, 1072). The one is caught up in a symbolic structure; the other is both narrator and protagonist of a scenario that is as socially and historically specific as could be. Indeed, even in Barthes's account, for the space of Chigi's 'realist' narrative the symbolic code is briefly overshadowed: 'ce qui est opposé brutalement aux constructions retorses du symbole (qui ont occupé toute la nouvelle), ce qui est appelé en droit à en triompher, c'est la vérité sociale, le code des institutions — le principe de réalité' (pp. 190–91).

It is true that Barthes, with a disingenuous formulation, will make a half-hearted attempt to recuperate the social reality of this prostitution for the symbolic structure of the text: 'SYM. Avant la castration.' (p. 191) But the effect is simply to play up the realist register that makes of castration 'une opération chirurgicale parfaitement réelle (datée: pourvue d'un *avant* et d'un *après*)' (p. 192), and to stress that Chigi is the instigator of a single contingent event. The secret origin of the vast fortune of the Lanty family — 'thème initial d'une chaîne d'énigmes et "sujet" de cette "scène de la vie parisienne"' — turns out to be passably sordid: 'une opération de castration, payée par un prince romain (intéressé ou débauché) à un jeune garçon napolitain qui l'a ensuite "plaqué"' (p. 193). Sarrasine may be heading for metaphorical castration and death ('*ayant été touché par la castration, je dois mourir*' (p. 193)), but what leads him there is the trivial gossip of the asymbolic Chigi: 'médiateur falot, sans envergure symbolique, abîmé dans la contingence, gardien plein d'assurance de la Loi endoxale' (p. 192). The fatal absence, for this realist reading, is the fact of castration as a literal lacuna in the mishmash of stereotypes that constitute Sarrasine's social knowledge: '"ne savez-vous pas par quelles créatures les rôles de femmes sont remplis dans les États du pape?"' (VI, 1072) Appropriately, the lacuna is identified and then filled by what Barthes calls 'la voix d'un vieux courtisan "réaliste" (n'a-t-il pas voulu faire un bon placement sur la voix de son *ragazzo*?), porte-parole de ce savoir vital qui fonde la "réalité"' (p. 190).

The 'affreuse vérité' emerges, then, not indirectly and unreliably from the lips of a narrator in denial, but from a brief dialogue, recounted in direct speech, between the two Pygmalions. Having for once allowed himself to pursue the realist underside of castration, Barthes does so with his usual subtlety. In particular, he notes that Sarrasine guides himself to the facts of the matter by his full description of Zambinella's male dress: '"C'est sans doute par égard pour les cardinaux, les évêques et les abbés quit sont ici [...], qu'*elle* est habillée en homme, qu'elle a une bourse derrière la tête, les cheveux crêpés et une épée au côté?"' (VI, 1072). For Barthes, the crucial detail is Zambinella's '"cheveux crêpés"':

> ce détail est 'réaliste', non en ce qu'elle est précis, mais parce qu'il libère l'image d'un ragazzo napolitain et que cette image, conforme au code historique des castrats, contribue à la révélation du garçon, au déchiffrement de l'énigme, plus sûrement que l'épée ou le vêtement. (p. 189)

Led to the 'code historique des castrats' by the image of the crinkly haired *ragazzo*, Barthes happily supplies details and facts of his own concerning the history of castrati. Where earlier he had quoted Stendhal on the mass hysteria induced by the erotic voices of 'les castrats-vedettes', now he lends *vraisemblance* to Zambinella's fictional career (the fabulous wealth indirectly predicted by Chigi) by giving biographical details for two real castrati, Caffarelli and Farinelli ('*il ragazzo*').[25] Finally, with a barrage of those *effets de réel* that he famously defines as the stock-in-trade of the realist novelist — dates, places and proper names — Barthes will confirm the claim for which, in the immediately preceding lines, he had sarcastically mocked the asymbolic narrator:

> REF. Histoire des castrats. Le code historique auquel se réfère le narrateur nous apprend que les deux derniers castrats connus furent Crescentini, qui reçut l'Ordre de la Couronne de Fer après que Napoléon l'eut entendu à Vienne en 1805, qu'il fit venir à Paris et qui mourut en 1846, et Velluti, qui chanta en dernier lieu à Londres en 1826 et mourut il y a un peu plus de cent ans (en 1861). (pp. 219–20)

When Barthes himself, in his earlier analysis of Sarrasine's kiss, noted the presence in Zambinella of the *garçon* — 'Sarrasine embrasse passionnément un castrat (ou un garçon travesti)' (p. 171) — he brushed the latter aside with a gloss that turned the kiss into the familiar vehicle of castration: 'la castration se reverse sur le corps même de Sarrasine, et nous autres, lecteurs seconds, nous en recevons l'ébranlement' (p. 171). However, in Barthes's reading of the recognition scene, it is the turn of the *garçon tout court* to sideline symbolic castration and to nuance the image of the newly discovered castrato. According to Barthes, the image of the *ragazzo* 'donne à lire à Sarrasine dans son amante un garçon (seule note de pédarastie dans toute la nouvelle)' (p. 192). Above all, in Chigi's 'petit discours' (p. 191), it is the phrase '"ce drôle-là"' that fleshes out the image activated by the '"cheveux crêpés"' of Sarrasine's question:

> Suscitant le garçon à la place de la femme ou du castrat, *ce drôle-là* rétablit (ne serait-ce que fugitivement) un axe, si l'on peut dire, normal des sexes (altéré tout au long de la nouvelle par la situation incertaine du castrat, tantôt essence de féminité, tantôt dénégation de toute sexualité). (p. 191)

Barthes describes here an impossible conjunction of 'la Femme superlative' (Sarrasine's aesthetic ideal) and '[le] garnement' (the crinkly haired Neapolitan *ragazzo*). From Sarrasine's point of view, nothing could be further from 'la Sur-Femme, terme et fondement de l'Art' than 'un drôle sale et déguenillé qui court les rues de Naples miséreux' (p. 191). It is for this reason that Sarrasine's system of psychic and aesthetic beliefs implodes, that he accuses Zambinella of genderless monstrosity ('"Tu n'es rien. Homme ou femme, je te tuerais! [...] Monstre!"' (VI, 1074)), and that he assumes the metaphorical castration that is spelled out in Balzac's text as a permanent loss of desire: '"Tu m'as ravalé jusqu'a toi. *Aimer, être aimé!* sont désormais des mots vides de sens pour moi, comme pour toi."' (VI, 1074) As Barthes reasonably proposes, the truth that penetrates Sarrasine's understanding is somewhere between '*j'ai aimé un castrat*' and '*en Zambinella, c'est le castrat* que j'ai aimé' (p. 193). However, from the point of view of Chigi and Cicognara, such formulations would be wide of the mark. Not only is Zambinella loved by a jealous cardinal, it is the *garçon* behind the castrato whom both protectors have desired. By acquiring the statue of Zambinella and commissioning a marble copy, Cicognara takes over from Chigi the mantle of Pygmalion; indeed, Cicognara is a key mediator of the chain of artistic copies that comes to rest in the painting of Adonis-Endymion:

> Le cardinal Cicognara se rendit maître de la statue de Zambinella et la fit exécuter en marbre; elle est aujourd'hui dans le musée Albani. C'est là qu'en 1791 la famille Lanty la retrouva, et pria Vien de la copier. Le portrait qui vous a montré Zambinella à vingt ans, un instant après l'avoir vu centenaire, a servi plus tard pour l'*Endymion* de Girodet, vous avez pu en reconnaître le type dans l'Adonis. (VI, 1075)

(v) '*Derrière* la toile'

Much earlier in this chapter, we left Mme de Rochefide gazing with delight — '"Un être si parfait existe-t-il?"' (VI, 1054) — at the beautiful painted Adonis she had failed to connect with the centenarian Zambinella. It is the moment of

Balzac's narrative chosen by Barthes for an important digression, *Au-delà et en deçà*. The context of the latter is Barthes's insistent claim that beauty is a catachresis; it can be figured only metaphorically, typically by comparison with works of art that constitute an infinitely receding code. Sarrasine, however, unfortunately believed he had discovered in Zambinella its founding *chef-d'œuvre*:

> Le corps zambinellien est un corps réel; mais ce corps réel n'est total (glorieux, miraculeux) que pour autant qu'il descend d'un corps déjà écrit par la statuaire (la Grèce Antique, Pygmalion); [...] dans le corps zambinellien comme chef-d'œuvre, coïncident théologiquement le référent (ce corps réel qu'il faudra copier, exprimer, signifier) et la Référence (le commencement qui met fin à l'infini de l'écriture et conséquemment la fonde). (pp. 121–22)

It is because Zambinella is 'really' a castrato that Barthes considers his point proven: there is no origin for the chain of copies, its end-point is simply *rien*. Whereas, in his reading of the recognition scene, Barthes analyses the short-circuiting in the sculptor's model of the superlative *Sur-Femme* and a desirable *ragazzo*, here, discussing the picture of Adonis, he deems the *au-delà* of the code of Art interchangeable with its monstrous *en deçà*:

> Ainsi Zambinella est la Sur-Femme, la Femme essentielle, parfaite (en bonne théologie, la perfection est l'essence, et la Zambinella est un 'chef-d'œuvre'), mais en même temps, du même mouvement, elle est le sous-homme, le castrat, le manque, le *moins* définitif; en elle, absolument désirable, en lui, absolument exécrable, les deux transgressions se confondent. (p. 78)

So confident is Barthes of this argument that Mme de Rochefide's rapt comment, ' "il est trop beau pour un homme" ', is marshalled as evidence for his stark paradigm: 'il y a, implicites, un *au-delà* de la Femme (la perfection) et un *en deçà* de l'homme (la castrature). Dire que l'Adonis n'est pas un homme, c'est à la fois renvoyer à une vérité (c'est un castrat) et à un leurre (c'est une Femme).' (p. 79)

The possibility that Mme de Rochefide might desire a representation of the real-life Zambinella — the beautiful young man who appealed also to men — is simply bypassed in Barthes's account, which limits her desire for the Adonis as man to desire for his mythological referent.[26] However, Mme de Rochefide wants to know the identity of the model, and is no more likely to see Perfect Woman in the painting than does Gillette in *Catherine Lescault*, or Cardinal Cicognara in the statue of Zambinella. In fact, nobody in Balzac's story shares the sculptor's delusion; every other mediator of the artistic chain perceives its referent to be a beautiful young man. When, in 1791, the Lanty family commissions the transformation of its famous relative from a statue into a painting, Vien copies the statue as an Adonis, not as a woman, and Girodet's well-known painting of Endymion, conflated by Balzac with Vien's Adonis, is the last of the beautiful young men in the chain of representations.[27] In short, when Balzac had the intriguing idea of inventing a past for Girodet's *Le Sommeil d'Endymion*, a painting with which he seems to have been obsessed,[28] he invented the prostituted body of a beautiful Neapolitan *garçon* as the buried origin of an ostentatious aristocratic fortune. Barthes's digression *La lampe d'albâtre* (pp. 76–77) reveals that he is as alert as Balzac to the homoerotic qualities of Girodet's painting. Yet Barthes is determined to frame the general argument of *S/Z* under the sign of a symbolic *castration*, rather than a literal *castrature*. Despite having unearthed the desirable *ragazzo* in his reading of the recognition scene, he refuses to give the fictional painting of Balzac's story a stable realist foundation. Thus he severs the link between the beauty of the painted Adonis and the beauty, so clearly spelled out in Balzac's story, of its 'real' model.[29] He can do so only by restricting his reading of the painting to the aesthetic perspective of Sarrasine. The 'trois coups de stylet' (VI, 1074) that kill the sculptor are delivered in the name of Cardinal Cicognara. Barthes responds by castrating the painting of Adonis in the name of Sarrasine.

Barthes's empathy with Sarrasine contaminates his own analysis, to the extent of blinding him, ironically in the context, to the evidence before his eyes. On at least four occasions in *S/Z*, he refers to Sarrasine's destruction of the statue of Zambinella: 'brisant pour finir la statue creuse' (p. 119); 'après avoir détruit dans la statue illusoire le témoin de son échec' (p. 129); 'et la statue détruite' (p. 174); 'mais encore l'art se brise (la statue est détruite)' (p. 206). Yet Barthes knows full well, and mentions elsewhere, that the mallet is thrown with such force that it misses.[30] This repeated *lapsus* is explained, perhaps, by his claim that every statue, not just Sarrasine's, is already — by definition — castrated ('le creux intérieur de toute statue (qui attire sans doute bien des amateurs de statuaire) et donne tout son contexte symbolique à l'iconoclastie)', p. 204). Barthes's generalization gives him away: the unconscious of this phantasmatic iconoclast tells him the statue is not merely empty, but broken apart.[31]

The phantasy is a literary-critical one, of course, and the object of Barthes's neurotic anxiety is the realist text: 'L'œuvre "réaliste" doit être garantie par la vérité intégrale du modèle, qui doit être connu de l'artiste copieur jusqu'en ses dessous' (p. 204). Barthes's analysis of pandemic castration (the emptiness that links model, statue and copies) should be read in the context of *Pleine littérature*, the section that immediately follows *La pandémie* within the carefully planned structure of *S/Z*. Although Barthes generates a sequence of ironic metaphors to capture the infinite fullness of representational literature,[32] he ends with an elegiac lament, rather than a theoretical *cri de guerre*: 'Cette Pleine Littérature, lisible, ne peut plus s'écrire: la plénitude symbolique (culminant dans l'art romantique) est le dernier avatar de notre culture.' (p. 206) Barthes's reading of *Sarrasine* depends on the fact that, 'selon la métaphysique sarrasinienne, le sens, l'art et le sexe ne forme qu'une même chaîne substitutive: celle du *plein*' (p. 206). It is because Balzac's story presents itself as an emblem of plenitude — 'produit d'un art (celui de la narration), mobilisation d'une polysémie (celle du texte classique) et thématique du sexe' (p. 206) — that Barthes seems to have found in *Sarrasine* his own 'perfect' text. Fullness and emptiness are part of a single problematic of representation; the relation between them, captured in Barthes's reading of *Sarrasine* in the relation between sculpture and painting, is therefore the object of his critical anxiety:

> En passant du volume à la planéité, la copie perd, ou du moins atténue la problématique brûlante que la nouvelle n'a cessé de mettre en scène. Contournable, pénétrable, en un mot *profonde*, la statue appelle la visite, l'exploration, la pénétration: elle implique idéalement la plénitude et la vérité de l'*intérieur* (c'est pourquoi il est tragique que cet intérieur soit ici vide, châtré).
> (p. 213)

Sarrasine can be read as the emblematic castrated text, but the castrated text, like castrated Woman, is simply a phantasy. In *S/Z*, searching for the ideal *texte scriptible*, Barthes had found himself, like Frenhofer and Sarrasine, obliged to make do with scattered parts: 'Des textes scriptibles, il n'y a peut-être rien à dire. D'abord où les trouver? Certainement pas du côté de la lecture (ou du moins fort peu: par hasard, fugitivement et obliquement dans quelques œuvres-limites).' (p. 11) Like Zambinella's statue for Sarrasine, Balzac's story is 'un objet dont le dessous, le creux vont continuer à susciter son inquiétude, sa curiosité et son agression' (p. 119). *S/Z* stages the 'fantasme du *dedans*' of a fetishistic lover of *Pleine littérature*, obstinately whittling away the layers of the realist text, the better to convince himself of its fullness.[33]

Barthes's symbolic field is saturated by the body, but the body, as is apparent in *Sarrasine*, is crossed by many other codes. In Barthes's reading, the two narrative levels are linked above all by castration: the denouement of the inner story (the revelation of Zambinella's sexual status) leads to a loss of desire in the narratee and the breakdown of her sexual contract with the narrator. Although Barthes famously views this contract as a form of prostitution — 'une nuit d'amour contre une belle histoire' (p. 95) — his argument does not build in the obvious fact that prostitution is mirrored in the underlying 'realist' plot of the framed narrative, in what constitutes, as he elsewhere acknowledges, 'la vérité sociale, le code des institutions — le principe de réalité' (p. 191). The relation between the psychic and the social is brilliantly captured in Canler's 'Poses mythologiques', where his aged Pygmalion and Paris are framed historically, with comments on the power, corruptibility and complicity of the Head of the Vice Squad (p. 85), and a comparative disquisition on sexual depravity in the hypocritical Restoration period (p. 88). Canler's contextualization reveals the *envers* of the phantasy that places Venus on a pedestal, for it is in the nature of his job to deal with '[les] amateurs de juvénilité', as well as those who, like Mlle S★★★, 'avait le privilège de recevoir ces malheureuses jeunes filles prédestinées au service de Vénus' (p. 86). Similarly, for Balzac, there is no tension between the phantasmatic scenarios that his artists act out through their models, and the real social and historical contexts in which they do so. Indeed, with varying emphases, the two interact, and Balzac uses his artist plots, with versions of the Pygmalion myth that are at once ironic and serious, as a lever to open up the sexual politics of early nineteenth-century France.

Notes to Chapter 1

1. See Dore Ashton, *A Fable of Modern Art* (London: Thames & Hudson, 1960). Hubert Damisch describes a story 'qui semble n'avoir plus désormais d'autre *sujet* que la peinture, et la peinture dans ce qu'elle a de plus matériel' (*Fenêtre jaune cadmium, ou les dessous de la peinture* (Paris: Seuil, 1984), pp. 44–45). The more generally mythical status of Balzac's text is fostered by two influential readings, Michel Serres, *Genèses* (Paris: Grasset, 1982), and Georges Didi-Huberman, *La Peinture incarnée* (Paris: Minuit, 1985). Like Damisch, both write from close acquaintance with *S/Z*.

2. *Le Chef-d'œuvre inconnu*, ed. by René Guise, in Honoré de Balzac, *La Comédie humaine*, ed. by Pierre-Georges Castex and others, 12 vols (Paris: Gallimard (Bibiothèque de la Pléiade), 1976–81), X, 391–438 (p. 437, p. 438). All subsequent page references for the Pléiade edition of *La Comédie humaine* are included in the text.

3. Massol-Bédoin, 'Le Mot de l'énigme', in *Balzac: Une poétique du roman*, ed. by Stéphane Vachon (Paris: Presses universitaires de Vincennes, 1996), pp. 181–93 (p. 186).

4. Fédida, 'L'Exhibition et le secret de l'enveloppe vide', *Nouvelle revue de la psychanalyse*, 14 (1976), 275–80 (p. 280).

5. 'Le secret [...] n'est pas une chose ou un être mis à part, mais l'effet — négatif — d'un jeu de relations et d'interactions'; 'la logique du secret est celle de ses effets'. See Marin, 'Logiques du secret' (1984), in *Lectures traversières* (Paris: Albin Michel, 1992), pp. 247–57 (p. 251, p. 257).

6. Tzvetan Todorov, 'Le Secret du récit' (1969), in *La Poétique de la prose* (Paris: Seuil, 1971), pp. 151–85.

7. Massol-Bédoin, 'L'Artiste ou l'imposture: Le Secret du *Chef-d'œuvre inconnu* de Balzac', *Romantisme*, (1986), 44–57 (p. 54). Further page references are included in the text.

8. For Barthes's definition of the hermeneutic code see *S/Z*, p. 26.

9. *Sarrasine*, ed. by Pierre Citron, in *La Comédie humaine*, VI, 1033–76 (p. 1062).

10. Zambinella's stage performance is at the heart of Timothy Scheie's very original analysis of *S/Z* in *Performance Degree Zero: Roland Barthes and Theatre* (Toronto: University of Toronto Press, 2006), pp. 104–16.

11. In a well-known article, Jean Seznec convincingly establishes that Balzac is alluding here to the preamble to the 1767 Salon in which Diderot debates the Platonic *beau idéal* with an imaginary sculptor. See 'Diderot et Sarrasine', in *Diderot Studies IV* (Geneva: Droz, 1963), pp. 237–38.

12. *Sarrasine* was first published in two instalments in the *Revue de Paris* (November 1830), where it was divided into two chapters: 'Les Deux Portraits' and 'Une passion d'artiste'.

13. This is a common device of Pygmalion stories. An amusing example is Théophile Gautier's *Omphale* (1834): 'La tapisserie s'agita violemment. Omphale se détacha du mur et sauta légèrement sur le parquet; elle vint à mon lit en ayant soin de se tourner du côté de l'endroit. [...] "Adieu! dit-elle, à demain." Et elle retourna à sa muraille à reculons, de peur sans doute de me laissser voir son envers.' See Gautier, *Contes fantastiques* (Paris: Corti, 1986), pp. 63–76 (p. 70, p. 72).

14. See *S/Z*, pp. 33–35 and pp. 71–72 for Barthes's compelling analysis of the rhetorical structuring of this antithesis.

15. Louis Canler, *Mémoires de Canler: Ancien Chef du Service de Sûreté 1795–1865*, ed. by Jacques Brenner (Paris: Mercure de France, 1986), p. 86. Further page references are included in the text.

16. Wettlaufer, discussing Sommariva's collection of erotic statues, describes the manner in which Canova's well-known *Magdalene* was displayed in a brothel-like shrine 'with a mirror behind her to expose all sides' (p. 104).

17. Stephen Bann relates the rivalry of Balzac's three seventeenth-century painters to that played out in versions of the famous myth of Zeuxis' grapes: 'Rather than advertising the master artist's feats of mimetic realism, this material demonstrates that the master artist is caught up in a system of social exchange and that his illusionistic skills can only be estimated at their true worth as a function of this exchange.' See *The True Vine: On Visual Representation and the Western Tradition* (Cambridge: Cambridge University Press, 1989), p. 36.

18. Wettlaufer (pp. 107–09, p. 226) convincingly proposes a painting by François-Louis Dejuinne as an intertext for this scene. It portrays Girodet who, at work on *Pygmalion et Galatée*, is watched by two male figures, one of whom is Sommariva, who has commissioned it.

19. Ovid, *Metamorphoses*, Book X, trans. by Mary M. Innes (Harmondsworth: Penguin, 1955), pp. 231–32 (p. 231). Further page references are included in the text.

20. The mistaken belief that Catherine Lescault is or was a real model for Frenhofer's painting is occasionally encountered in the massive critical literature. Claude Bremond and Thomas Pavel, for example, think to defend Gillette's beauty by claiming: 'un idéal vaut l'autre et rien ne permet de penser que Gillette le cède en rien à l'ancien modèle de Frenhofer, Catherine Lescault'. See *De Barthes à Balzac: Fictions d'un critique, critiques d'une fiction* (Paris: Albin Michel, 1998), p. 222.

21. For an exemplary exposition of *Le Chef-d'œuvre inconnu* in these terms see P.-L. Assoun, 'La Femme et l'œuvre: Le Fétichisme dans *Le Chef-d'œuvre inconnu*', in *Analyses et Réflexions sur Balzac: 'Le Chef-d'œuvre inconnu', 'Gambara', 'Massimila Doni'*, collectif (Paris: Ellipses, 1993), pp. 102–08. See too Didi-Huberman, pp. 93–114, and Dorothy Kelly, who interweaves realism, castration and fetishism in the concluding chapter of *Fictional Genders*, pp. 169–79.

22. The history of the text reveals Balzac's own hesitations over whether and where to bring Frenhofer's vacillation to an end: an early version left him smiling at his imaginary women, oblivious of his friends' discovery of the 'nothing' on the canvas, while the tailpiece expulsion of his friends from the studio, and the burning of his paintings, was added only in 1837. See William Paulson, 'Pour une analyse de la variation textuelle: *Le Chef-d'œuvre* trop connu', *Nineteenth-Century French Studies*, 19 (1991), 404–16, and Pierre Laubriet, *Un catéchisme esthétique: 'Le Chef-d'œuvre inconnu' de Balzac* (Paris: Didier, 1961).

23. *Cahiers pour l'Analyse* (March–April 1967), 91–96 (further references in the text).

24. Barthes maintains fairly consistently that the gender of the singer is undecidable, to the extent of lamenting that French has no gender-neutral article ('SYM. Le neutre', p. 215). However, once we know that Zambinella is simply a castrated male, the hesitation between genders might be thought part of the rhetorical skill of a narrator manipulating the expectations of his narratee.

25. See *S/Z*, p. 116, pp. 192–93.

26. As will be seen in Chapter 3, in *La Vendetta* it is a female artist who makes a copy of Girodet's *Endymion* and who, when the picture comes alive as it were, falls in love with the image she then recopies from reality.

27. Until the Furne edition of *La Comédie humaine*, it was Girodet himself, not Vien, who was asked to copy the statue, and who later used it for his *Endymion*. Barthes is wrong that the date 1791 is 'un pur effet de réel' (p. 213); clearly it was chosen by Balzac to be consistent with the period Girodet spent in Rome (1790 to 1795). *Le Sommeil d'Endymion* was painted there in 1791.

28. Is this well-known fascination a fatal gap in Barthes's knowledge of Balzac? Girodet's homosexuality, openly discussed in the 'Notice biographique' published by Coupin in 1829, must certainly have been known to Balzac. See Anne-Louis Girodet de Roucy-Trioson, *Œuvres posthumes*, ed. by P. A. Coupin, 2 vols (Paris: Renouard, 1829), especially p. xlviii. On Balzac's interest in Girodet see Thomas Crow, 'B/G', in *Vision and Textuality*, ed. by Stephen Melville and Bill Readings (London: Macmillan, 1994), pp. 296–314. For Anne-Marie Baron's powerful interpretation of the significance to Balzac of *Le Sommeil d'Endymion* (a combination of psychoanalytic and textual readings), see 'Endymion, ou l'enfance idéale', in *Balzac, ou les hiéroglyphes de l'imaginaire* (Paris: Honoré Champion, 2002), pp. 49–62.

29. In Balzac's text, male beauty is also conveyed by the description of Filippo, who has clearly inherited Zambinella's sexuality as well as his beauty (while Marianina has inherited his voice). The homoerotic appeal of Filippo is suggested by one of Balzac's familiar sculpterly comparisons with Antinous (VI, 1046).

30. Since Barthes produces a line-by-line commentary on Balzac's text, the truth of the matter is inevitably built into his analysis: '★ ACT. "Statue": 6 : la statue épargnée. ★★ SYM. Réplique des corps: la chaîne, *in extremis*, est préservée.' (p. 209)

31. In fact, iconoclasm is built into the critical methodology of *S/Z*: 'On étoilera donc le texte, écartant, à la façon d'un menu séisme, les blocs de signification dont la lecture ne saisit que la surface lisse' (p. 20); 'le texte tuteur sera sans cesse brisé' (p. 21).

32. 'Littérature qui est pleine: comme une armoire où les sens sont rangés, empilés, économisés (dans ce texte, jamais rien de perdu: le sens récupère tout); comme une femelle pleine de signifiés dont la critique ne se fera pas faute de l'accoucher; comme la mer, pleine de profondeurs qui lui donnent son apparence d'infini, son grand drapé méditatif.' (p. 206)

33. Barthes's *Vita nova* (1979) contains a fascinating and specifically Frenhoferesque phantasy when he plays with the notion of creating a leftover fragment that would guarantee the lost integrity of the full text: 'Faire comme si je devais écrire ma grande œuvre (Somme) [...] et qu'il n'en restât que des ruines ou linéaments, ou parties erratiques (comme le pied peint par Porbus [*sic*]).' See Barthes, *Œuvres complètes*, ed. by Éric Marty, 5 vols (Paris: Seuil, 2002), V, 1007–17 (p. 1016).

PART II

❖

From Painting to Marriage

Nous aimons d'abord *un tableau* [...]: ce qui n'avait été encore jamais vu est
découvert dans son entier, et dès lors dévoré des yeux: l'immédiat vaut
pour le plein [...]: le tableau *consacre* l'objet que je vais aimer.

ROLAND BARTHES, *Fragments d'un discours amoureux*

CHAPTER 2

❖

La Bourse

(i) 'A la faveur du clair-obscur'

La Bourse opens with an evocation of that 'heure délicieuse' between day's end and nightfall when bizarre light effects incite expansive souls to reverie. It is a magical, silent moment that is especially prized by artists; unable to work once the daylight has faded, they can allow themselves to stand back and assess their labours, 'en s'enivrant du sujet dont le sens intime éclate alors aux yeux intérieurs du génie'.[1] In this quasi-supernatural atmosphere, artistic illusion reigns supreme:

> À la faveur du clair-obscur, les ruses matérielles employées par l'art pour faire croire à des réalités disparaissent entièrement. S'il s'agit d'un tableau: les personnages qu'il représente semblent et parler et marcher: l'ombre devient ombre, le jour est jour, la chair est vivante, les yeux remuent, le sang coule dans les veines, et les étoffes chatouillent.' (I, 413–14)

This Frenhoferesque fantasy of a painting so lifelike that it comes to life prefaces the love story of 'un jeune peintre, homme de talent, et qui dans l'art ne voyait que l'art même' (I, 414). At the bewitching twilight hour, Hippolyte Schinner has been transported out of the everyday world by avid contemplation of the vast painting he is close to finishing; engulfed in 'une de ces méditations qui ravissent l'âme et la grandissent, la caressent et la consolent' (I, 414), he loses all sense of reality. Unfortunately, since he is perched at the time on the trestle ladder from which he had been working on his canvas, when night falls so too does the artist, knocking himself out on a stool. But he has not, for all that, been brought down to earth, for it is 'une douce voix' that will entice him out of the 'espèce d'engourdissement dans lequel il était plongé' (I, 414). Through the veil that envelops his senses he deciphers the whispering of two women and the presence of 'deux jeunes, deux timides mains entre lesquelles reposait sa tête' (I, 414). Returning to full consciousness, in the light thrown by 'une de ces vieilles lampes dites *à double courant d'air*', he sees 'la plus délicieuse tête de jeune fille qu'il eût jamais vue, une de ces têtes qui souvent passent pour un caprice du pinceau, mais qui tout à coup réalisa pour lui les théories de ce beau idéal que se crée chaque artiste et d'où procède son talent' (I, 414).

Obviously, Balzac has invented this 'accident' to bring his two lovers together. At the same time, by rendering the artist briefly unconscious, he is able to motivate the direct transition from Schinner's contemplation of his painting to his first vision of the 'délicieuse tête de jeune fille'. In this way, the 'création accomplie' that is Adélaïde, born like Catherine Lescault in the artist's studio, appears to have stepped out of Schinner's own canvas. However, even as she does so, the living girl steps back into the model of painting. Her pure lines and virginal features are sketched with reference to a typical Balzacian code of works of art: 'Le visage de l'inconnue appartenait, pour ainsi dire, au type fin et délicat de l'école de Prudhon, et possédait aussi cette poésie que Girodet donnait à ses figures fantastiques.' (I, 414–15) As Schinner expresses his artist's admiration 'par un regard de surprise' (I, 415), he becomes aware of a handkerchief pressed to his forehead and, eventually, of an old woman 'qui ressemblait aux marquises de l'ancien régime' (I, 415). The girl's brisk summary of events has the exaggeratedly factual tone of a police witness statement: '"Monsieur [...], ma mère et moi, nous avons entendu le bruit de votre corps sur le plancher, nous avons cru distinguer un gémissement. [...] En trouvant la clef sur la porte, nous nous sommes heureusement permis d'entrer"' (I, 415). As such, it may appear to fuel an 'asymbolic' debunking of the twilight fantasies to which artists are prone, and to stop in its tracks the first hint of another castration narrative: '"Vous êtes blessé au front, là, sentez-vous?"' (I, 415). Indeed the mother, who is holding the lamp over the pair and directing operations, adds a comically ambiguous reassurance: '"Oh! cela ne sera rien [...]. Votre tête a, par bonheur, porté sur ce mannequin."' (I, 415) Is Schinner's manikin, mediator of this first *tête-à-tête* of the lovers, a parodic version of the artist's living model?

Certainly most critics seem unwilling to take the subject matter of *La Bourse* at all seriously. Balzac's sister Laure Surville was one of the first to find the plot *invraisemblable*: 'Comment? L'amoureux croit que son amante lui vole ses petits écus? Et puis, quand il voit qu'il n'est pas volé, il en conclut que c'est une belle âme et l'épouse!' For Anne-Marie Baron, who quotes this reaction in her introduction to the text, the episode of the purse 'transforme le drame en comédie', and she notes with surprise the inclusion in the *Scènes de la vie privée* of such a happy ending: 'après l'interrogation la plus cruelle, l'amour le plus tendre'.[2] For Jean-Louis Tritter, editor of the Pléiade edition, the story is devoid of psychological reach: 'On accablerait certes Balzac en évoquant, à propos d'une petite scène sans prétention comme *La Bourse*, la jalousie d'un Mosca ou d'un Swann: on le sent, cependant, capable de composer des scènes psychologiques d'une plus grande ampleur.' (I, 412) However, by common accord, what *La Bourse* lacks in ambition, it compensates for by its charming simplicity, and above all by the painterly qualities famously celebrated by Félix Davin: '*La Bourse* est une de ces compositions attendrissantes auxquelles excelle M. de Balzac, une page tout allemande qui tient à Paris par la description de l'appartement habité par une vieille femme ruinée, un de ses plus jolis tableaux de chevalet.'[3]

In his important study of the status of painting in Balzac's creative writing, Olivier Bonard quotes and extends Davin's claim for *La Bourse*, describing the 'joli tableau de chevalet' as a 'délicate scène de genre':

> Nous y retrouvons au centre du récit un personnage de peintre, c'est-à-dire une conscience et un regard de peintre, autour desquels tout s'ordonne et se colore: les décors et les visages, les sentiments et le développement même de l'intrigue. Une fois de plus, l'œuvre croît et mûrit à partir d'une sorte de noyau pictural.[4]

However, Bonard does not reduce *La Bourse* to its pictorial qualities. Rather, he identifies Balzac's conflation of the aesthetic and the erotic — 'le tableau qui se superpose [...] à une figure humaine et déclenche ce brusque réveil des sens' — as one of the 'lois profondes de sa psychologie amoureuse' and one of the 'constantes psychologiques de *la Comédie humaine*' (p. 33). It is a psychological law extended to the generality of amorous passion by Barthes in *Fragments d'un discours amoureux*. Through the rhetorically inflated discourse of his constructed, first-person lover, Barthes suggests, in the figure 'Ravissement', that a total, instantaneous and life-determining psychic investment is triggered by the perception of the love object as a metaphorically framed picture. His paradigmatic example is Werther's famous first sighting of Lotte, framed in the doorway of her house as she cuts *tartines* for her brothers and sisters:

> Nous aimons d'abord *un tableau*. Car il faut au coup de foudre le signe même de sa soudaineté [...]: et, de tous les arrangements d'objets, c'est le tableau qui semble le mieux se voir pour la première fois [...]: l'immédiat vaut pour le plein: je suis initié: le tableau consacre l'objet que je vais aimer.[5]

Barthes injects narrative as well as psychic content into this model of painting: 'il y a un leurre du temps amoureux (ce leurre s'appelle: roman d'amour)'. Although the *coup de foudre* is an 'épisode réputé initial', its contingent immediacy is constructed retroactively: 'lorsque je "revois" la scène du rapt, je crée retrospectivement un hasard: [...] je ne cesse de m'étonner d'avoir eu cette chance: rencontrer ce qui va à mon désir; ou d'avoir pris ce risque énorme: m'asservir d'un coup à une image inconnue' (pp. 228–29).

Barthes stresses here the huge risk for the subject who chooses his or her love object after this model. Bonard, too, raises the issue of risk, but only to state that it hardly applies to a *scène de la vie privée* like *La Bourse*. Indeed he makes a firm distinction between two categories of Balzacian artist: on the one hand, Sarrasine and Frenhofer, whose object choice will embroil them in a dramatic struggle with 'les secrets et les angoisses de la création artistique' (p. 71); on the other, Sommervieux (*La Maison du chat-qui-pelote*), Ginevra (*La Vendetta*) and Schinner, for whom the founding coincidence of an aesthetic and erotic ideal is a prelude — devoid of aesthetic consequence — to 'l'histoire d'un couple et d'un mariage':

> La fascination esthétique qui provoque ici l'éveil de l'amour, le trouble et l'émerveillement de Sommervieux, de Ginevra et de Schinner, [...] sont une invitation au bonheur et même un gage du bonheur. Car après tout, Balzac aurait pu exploiter à des fins dramatiques la part de risque et de menace que comportait cet éveil de l'amour dans un regard de peintre. Il n'en est rien. (pp. 71–72)

For Bonard, the fact that the love choices of Sommervieux and Ginevra lead to disaster has nothing to do with the aporias of art: though Balzac uses their painter's vision to motivate densely pictorial episodes, such scenes have no direct causal link with the conjugal dramas that ensue. As for *La Bourse*, it would seem that an absence of risk is built into the very fibre of this 'histoire heureuse' (p. 72): '*la Bourse* n'est pas un livre tragique mais l'histoire d'un couple promis au bonheur' (p. 32). In fact, Bonard successfully conveys the psychic enormity of Schinner's 'immense moment de crise, fait de perplexité, d'espoir et de doute, un moment d'affolement et de désespoir' (p. 34). However, he appears to have no interest in interpreting what he describes so well and reduces this 'intense mais bref moment de crise' to 'le petit drame qui va se jouer' (p. 61). The disappearance of the purse is simply the peripeteia of this drama, while its denouement is 'un dénouement de comédie': 'Adélaïde aura fait sans le savoir un bon calcul, [...] elle gagne tout simplement un mari!' (p. 34). In this way, even Bonard is able to conclude that the plot, 'qui est en effet une intrigue de comédie, [...] se réduit à fort peu de chose' (p. 35). Within the limits of the *Scènes de la vie privée*, the artist who falls in love with a picture is, according to Bonard, making a safe investment.[6]

Bonard does link the opening of *La Bourse* — the paintings whose subject matter comes alive for their artists in the twilight — with Frenhofer's belief that he has created a *Catherine Lescault* with whom he can laugh, cry and share his thoughts. Curiously, he does not see that this linking might undermine his own distinction between two sorts of artist in Balzac. Distancing himself from the sarcasm of André Wurmser, who denounces the aesthetic naivety — assumed to be Balzac's — of proposing a *trompe-l'œil* illusion as the high point of art, he notes that such claims 'n'ont en somme de sens profond que psychologique et romanesque' (p. 32).[7] What matters to Frenhofer is 'le rêve même de Pygmalion: être à la fois le créateur et l'amant, créer par l'art et posséder par la chair'. When the reader recalls the 'image incompréhensible et absurde du chef-d'œuvre inconnu', and reflects on 'la catastrophe' of the mad painter: 'c'est bien l'image de ce rêve anormal, de cette passion démesurée et, pourrait-on dire, incestueuse qui l'emporte dans notre esprit sur le souvenir de ses erreurs esthétiques' (p. 84). This is the only reference in Bonard's book to the Pygmalion myth, and he does not pursue the parallel with *La Bourse*. He does, however, sketch the 'vide affectif' that contextualizes Frenhofer's decision to seek erotic fulfilment in 'les seules créations de son génie': 'on ne lui connaît qu'un décor, son atelier, et quelques habitudes, ses pipes et ses amis peintres; mais on ne le sent pas engagé dans une affection, une tendresse humaines' (p. 83).

Frenhofer is the closest of Balzac's artists to the Pygmalion prototype, in that his work of art and his mistress-wife are literally one and the same *Catherine Lescault*. Yet Balzac's more metaphorical Pygmalions, with varying motivations, have sublimated at least part of their affective and sexual needs in art. This is why Balzac's artists, in taking a leap of faith into psychic-aesthetic investment in an image in the way Barthes and Bonard describe, seem to me to assume a level of subjective risk beyond that of a non-artist who might fall in love through the same process. Whereas Bonard refers to 'tous les personnages, peintres ou non, auxquels le romancier a prêté ce premier regard de l'amour' (p. 33), Barthes lends to all such lovers the metaphorical status of an artist: 'L'image — comme l'exemple pour l'obsessionnel — est *la chose même*. L'amoureux est donc artiste, et son monde est bien un monde à l'envers, puisque toute image y est son propre fin (rien au-delà de l'image).' (p. 159) In the case of a literal artist, the psychic structure (the constitutive role of an image) is, at the very least, overdetermined. But, more importantly, Balzac's artists fall in love with what is always, at some level of their psyche (as well as at some level of the narrative), their own work of art. It is in this sense that an artist positioned as the subject of this structure will necessarily play out a version of Pygmalion. Pygmalion has fashioned the ivory statue in the image of his desire — Venus will understand what he means when he asks for a wife '"like the ivory maid"' (p. 232) — and the narcissism and incest built into the myth are carried over, to some extent, to the narcissistic love choices of Balzacian artists such as Ginevra and Schinner. But, above all, Pygmalion has created his own love object to counter the risk inherent in loving a real woman, as Ovid very clearly spells out by linking Pygmalion's option for celibacy to his fear of woman as prostitute. In *Metamorphoses*, the Pygmalion narrative is immediately preceded by the story of the 'loathsome Propoetides' who were turned to stone for having 'dared to deny the divinity of Venus':

> [they] were the first women to lose their good names by prostituting themselves in public. Then, as all sense of shame left them, the blood hardened in their cheeks, and it required only a slight alteration to transform them into stony flints.
>   When Pygmalion saw these women, living such wicked lives, he was revolted by the many faults which nature has implanted in the female sex, and long lived a bachelor existence, without any wife to share his home. But meanwhile, with marvellous artistry, he skilfully carved a snowy ivory statue. He made it lovelier than any woman born, and fell in love with his own creation. (p. 232)

That Frenhofer shares this motivation for restricting his eroticism to his own creation is spelled out in his replies to Porbus: '"Elle est à moi, à moi seul."' (x, 431); '"Quelle maîtresse [...]. Elle le trahira tôt ou tard. La mienne me sera toujours fidèle!"' (x, 432). Like Pygmalion, who has no need to expend doubts concerning the exclusive possession of his modest maiden, Frenhofer need waver only as to whether he has brought *Catherine Lescault* to life.[8] *La Bourse* inverts the structure. There is no doubting the physical reality of the Adelaïde who, 'à la faveur du clair-obscur', steps out of the artist's canvas. However, for Schinner, who ventures for the first time to love a living being — because that being first imposed herself as a picture — Mme de Rouville's 'vieille lampe *à double courant d'air*' will cast the shadow of the mythical Propoetides.

(ii) 'Le tableau de mon fantasme'

As Barthes suggests, the *coup de foudre* takes form and is consolidated in the memory: 'Dans la rencontre, je m'émerveille de ce que j'ai trouvé quelqu'un qui, par touches successives et à chaque fois réussies, sans défaillance, achève le tableau de mon fantasme' (p. 234). It would be hard to capture more precisely, and with more appropriate metaphors, the way Schinner, in the three days spent at home recovering from his accident, fills out the inaugural scene of his passion:

> son imagination inoccupée lui rappela vivement, et comme par fragments, les détails de la scène qui suivit son évanouissement. Le profil de la jeune fille tranchait fortement sur les ténèbres de sa vision intérieure: il revoyait le visage flétri de la mère ou sentait encore les mains d'Adélaïde, il retrouvait un geste qui l'avait peu frappé d'abord mais dont les grâces exquises furent mises en relief par le souvenir. (I, 419)

In the first instance, Adélaïde is reconstructed aesthetically, in a reframing that picks up the pictorial language that had already, in the artist's studio, transformed a mere 'caprice du pinceau' into a 'création accomplie'. However, it is not the case, as Bonard claims, that Schinner loves Adélaïde only because he conflates her with a pictorial memory and aesthetic ideal ('La jeune fille n'a vraiment d'attrait aux yeux de Schinner qu'en vertu de cette confusion' (p. 33)). The text states clearly that, during his *réclusion*, his imagination has worked not just on her visual image but on the information gleaned from the *portière*: 'Cette fille, qui ne portait pas le nom de sa mère, avait éveillé mille sympathies chez le jeune peintre; il voulait voir entre elle et lui quelques similitudes de position, et la dotait des malheurs de sa propre origine.' (I, 419) The reader is told this as Schinner crosses the fourth-floor landing for the first time since his accident, his heart pounding at the sight of the brown door of the 'modeste appartement habité par Mlle Leseigneur' (I, 419). The outer door — with which Schinner's almost violent affective investment in the apartment will remain associated — had been left open on the first evening (whether by daughter or mother is the subject of a minor altercation between the two), and for all Adélaïde's deft opening and shutting of doors when the painter pays his first visit, it is spelled out that the material signs of extreme poverty, because recognized from his childhood, are a second cause of his active empathy: 'Hippolyte, qui jadis avait vu chez sa mère les mêmes signes d'indigence, les remarqua avec la singulière vivacité d'impression qui caractérise les premières acquisitions de notre mémoire, et entra mieux que tout autre ne l'aurait fait dans les détails de cette existence.' (I, 422)

If, for Schinner, the door opens onto 'le tableau de [son] fantasme', the underpainting of the picture, filled in by the narrator between the *rencontre* in the studio and the *portière*'s gossip, is an account of the painter's background as an illegitimate *enfant comblé*: 'Il était l'idole d'une mère pauvre qui l'avait élevé au prix des plus dures privations. Mlle Schinner [...] n'avait jamais été mariée. Son âme tendre fut jadis cruellement froissée par un homme riche qui ne se piquait pas d'une grande délicatesse en amour.' (I, 417) On finding herself betrayed at the height of her youth and beauty, 'Elle refusa les aumônes de celui qui l'avait trompée, renonça au monde, et se fit une gloire de sa faute'. By the age of twenty-five, Schinner understands better than ever 'sa situation dans le monde' (I, 417). He lives for his mother as she has for him, imitates her reclusive lifestyle and chooses his friends with care, as if to protect her reputation until such time as he can rehabilitate her socially: 'espérant à force de gloire et de fortune la voir un jour heureuse, riche, considérée, entourée d'hommes célèbres' (I, 417). These details, sketched to explain the impression made on the painter by the opening episode — 'tout ce que cette scène pouvait avoir de piquant et d'inattendu' (I, 416) — establish Schinner as good fodder for a neurosis that will play itself out across the space of his passion for Adélaïde. By projecting layers of his own life into the picture, he adds to and intensifies his initial investment in Adélaïde as image. However, even as he does so, the artist — who incarnates the 'faute' of the mother with whom he identifies so closely — creates the conditions for the delusion that will invade him in its turn.[9]

Barthes's 'Rencontre' is the figure that refers to the 'temps heureux qui a immédiatement suivi le premier ravissement, avant que naissent les difficultés du rapport amoureux' (p. 233). It takes shape as 'une découverte progressive (et comme une vérification) des affinités, complicités et intimités que je vais pouvoir entretenir éternellement (à ce que je pense) avec un autre, en passe de devenir, dès lors, "mon autre"' (p. 234). For Schinner, this Golden Age is the first week of his passion:

> Huits jours se passèrent ainsi, pendant lesquels les sentiments du peintre et ceux d'Adélaïde subirent ces délicieuses et lentes transformations qui amènent les âmes à une parfaite entente. Aussi, de jour en jour, le regard par lequel Adélaïde accueillait son ami devint-il plus intime, plus confiant, plus gai, plus franc; sans s'être encore confié leur amour, les deux amants savaient qu'ils s'appartenaient l'un à l'autre. (I, 432)

As part of this everyday complicity, Schinner wants to be taught to play piquet. Coincidentally, to pursue the notion of risk, Barthes uses a gambling metaphor for the fortuitousness of the lover's *rencontre*: 'je suis comme un joueur dont la chance ne se dément pas et qui lui fait mettre la main sur un petit morceau qui vient du premier coup compléter le puzzle de son désir' (p. 234). But the Schinner who is lucky in love is correspondingly unlucky at cards: 'comme le vieillard, il perdit presque toutes les parties' (I, 432). Being a novice, his losses are not surprising. However, by the end of two months, not only has he effectively taken Kergarouët's place at the card table, but he is still losing: 'Le vieux gentilhomme vint moins souvent, le jaloux Hippolyte l'avait remplacé le soir, au tapis vert, dans son malheur constant au jeu.' (I, 434) Is there a psychic short circuit between the progress of Schinner's passion and his appropriation of Kergarouët's losing habit?

As the first evening visit progresses, Schinner manages to maintain a minimal conversation at the same time as giving himself up entirely to admiration of 'la belle tête de jeune fille par laquelle il était charmé' (I, 429). By alluding to 'une singulière faculté de notre âme dont la pensée peut en quelque sorte se dédoubler quelquefois' (I, 430), Balzac evidently informs the reader that part of Schinner's mind registers everything of which he seems unaware. So absorbed is he in contemplation of Adélaïde's face that he fails even to notice that mother and daughter have started to play cards with their elderly visitor. The artist is brought out of his trance by Du Halga's echo of Kergarouët's exclamation: ' "Et diantre! il est onze heures." ' (I, 430) This is the tailpiece of a minor display of ham acting whereby Kergarouët's pretended anger at another loss is accompanied by two theatrical gestures: 'Le gentilhomme tira sa bourse, et jetant deux louis sur le tapis, non sans humeur: "Quarante francs, juste comme de l'or." ' (I, 430) Some two months later, Schinner, who has been playing piquet against Adélaïde to the accompaniment of increasingly distressing suspicions, waits for the two men to leave, repeats Kergarouët's action of taking out his purse — 'tira sa bourse, afin de payer Adélaïde' (I, 436) — but is distracted by his thoughts into putting the purse down on the card table, falling into an agitated reverie, moving close to Mme de Rouville to peer into her face ('[pour] mieux scruter ce vieux visage' (I, 436)), leaving without his purse and thereby forgetting to pay. That the fact of forgetting his purse adds up to a fine *acte manqué* is supported, perhaps, by the manner in which Schinner's delusion — confirmed for him by a sharp retrospective vision of 'sa bourse étalée sur le tapis' (I, 437) — is finally dissolved. A week's madness later, Schinner will return to Mme de

Rouville's apartment, ashamed of his behaviour and blaming the loss of his purse on 'quelque hasard inconnu' (I, 441). Her predictable suggestion of a game of cards, with its allusion to Kergarouët — '"Faisons-nous notre petite partie? dit-elle, car mon vieux Kergarouët me tient rigueur."' (I, 441) — reactivates Schinner's anxiety and once more he looks hard at her face. Reassured, this time, by its expression of honest good will, 'Il se mit alors à la table de jeu' (I, 442); inevitably, he and Adélaïde, playing together, find themselves in Mme de Rouville's debt. As if the film of Schinner's mental aberration had been rewound to its starting point, the action will pick up where it had been suspended a week earlier; going to his fob to pay, Schinner sees, as it were, his purse just where he had left it:

> En voulant chercher de la monnaie dans son gousset, le peintre retira ses mains de dessus la table, et vit alors devant lui une bourse qu'Adélaïde y avait glissée sans qu'il s'en aperçût; la pauvre enfant tenait l'ancienne, et s'occupait par contenance à y chercher de l'argent pour payer sa mère. (I, 442)

By conjuring up two purses where formerly there had been only one, Adélaïde enters into Schinner's delusion the better to effect a cure. As the artist spots the new purse on the table in front of him, Adélaïde self-consciously goes through the motions of looking for money in the old one. In short, she acts out a pantomime of stealing from Schinner's own purse, reconstructing the delusive scenario even as she takes it apart.[10]

In this she prefigures to some extent Zoë Bertgang, the real Gradiva of Jensen's fictional Pygmalion phantasy; similarly, Schinner bears some resemblance to Norbert Hanold, whose magnificent delusion was famously analysed by Freud. A delusion is defined by Freud as a pathological mental state whereby a phantasy, without directly affecting the body, commands belief and influences behaviour. He describes the ease with which the intellect is willing to accept an absurdity, as long as it satisfies 'powerful emotional impulses', and the more so 'if some of the mental processes concerned are linked with unconscious or repressed motives'. What he calls, in a fine metaphor, 'this mental cobweb' is structured by a displacement of conviction from 'unconscious truth' to 'conscious error':

> If a patient believes in his delusion so firmly, this is not because his faculty of judgement has been overturned and does not arise from what is false in the delusion. On the contrary, there is a grain of truth concealed in every delusion, there is something in it that really deserves belief, and this is the source of the patient's conviction, which is therefore to that extent justified.[11]

Clearly, Schinner's 'conscious error' is his belief that his purse has been stolen, and this is the so-called comedy plotline to which *La Bourse* is so often reduced. The complexity of the text derives from Balzac's creation of a psychic hinterland: the emotional impulses and repressed intuitions that conceal something more worthy of belief. Schinner's mental cobweb is woven around the small cast of characters who congregate in Mme de Rouville's *salon*, and he weaves himself into the web by joining in the nightly game of piquet. Presiding over this scene is an absent presence: the M. de Rouville who, in his crumbling pastel incarnation, hangs opposite the mirror until the artist, on the afternoon following his first visit, removes him upstairs to his studio. He will remain there for the two months it takes Schinner to transfer his likeness from paper to canvas. It is the return of M. de Rouville, varnished and framed, to his rightful setting that will trigger Schinner's delusion on the very evening of the domestic *vernissage*.

Schinner's first view of the portrait follows his realization that the *salon* also serves as Mme de Rouville's bedroom: 'le peintre vit une fente et les cassures produites dans le papier par les portes d'une alcôve où Mme Leseigneur couchait sans doute, et qu'un canapé placé devant déguisait mal' (I, 423). His eyes then travel over 'le portrait d'un militaire de haut grade que le peu de lumière ne permit pas au peintre de distinguer' (I, 423); since he can recognize the uniform, as well as the shoddy quality of the drawing, it is the face that he cannot make out at this stage. Between this initial sighting and the more careful inspection that leads to Schinner's offer to copy the portrait, Balzac inserts his lengthy reflection on the difficulty for an observer of interpreting the apartment — 'cette misère fardée comme une vieille femme qui veut faire mentir son visage' (I, 423) — and on the equally challenging ambiguity of Mme de Rouville's face: 'Il en était du visage de cette vieille dame comme de l'appartement qu'elle habitait' (I, 425).[12] What starts as a simile becomes a metonym and the mother's face remains throughout the story a focus of Schinner's anxiety. For the moment, rather than resolve whether she is 'une ancienne coquette habituée à tout peser, à tout calculer, à tout vendre', or 'une femme aimante, pleine de noblesse et d'aimables qualités' (I, 425), he gazes instead at her daughter's noble features and breathes in 'les suaves et modestes parfums de la vertu' (I, 425). However, in the very next sentence, Balzac makes him turn the conversation to portraiture to justify further examination of 'l'effroyable pastel': '"Vous tenez sans doute à cette peinture en faveur de la ressemblance, mesdames, car le dessin en est horrible?"' (I, 425). The allusion to 'la ressemblance' seems a tactful way of inquiring into the identity of the model. Yet the painter's probing is visual as well as biographical. The passage has been constructed so as to juxtapose the faces of mother, husband and daughter and it is at Adélaïde that Schinner looks — 'dit-il en regardant Adélaïde' — as he addresses to both women what is implicitly a more anxious questioning of family resemblance. If Schinner chooses for now to read in Mme de Rouville's expression 'les vestiges d'un deuil éternel' (I, 425–26), his offer to eternalize on canvas this '"figure qui vous est chère"' (I, 426) is a painter's solution to a problem deferred.

(iii) '"Il paraît que nous sommes en famille ce soir"'

Schinner's collection of the portrait produces a reticent first love scene, not least because he had not expected to find Adélaïde alone. In a parallel with *Catherine Lescault*'s famously fetishistic foot, Adélaïde's *pudeur* is provoked by the realization that she cannot reach the portrait 'sans mettre le pied sur la commode' (I, 431); it is increased by Schinner's recognition that this is her reason for asking him to take down the picture himself: 'En voyant que le peintre l'avait devinée, Adélaïde baissa les yeux par un mouvement de fierté dont le secret appartient aux vierges.' (I, 431) Intimidated and lost for words, Schinner takes refuge in solemn examination of the portrait: 'le peintre prit alors le tableau, l'examina gravement en le mettant au jour près de la fenêtre, et s'en alla sans dire autre chose à Mlle Leseigneur que: "Je vous le rendrai bientôt."' (I, 431) By the time, two months later, that the painting is finally finished, such timidity seems a thing of the past: 'Il complota joyeusement avec Adélaïde de mettre le portrait en place pendant une absence de Mme de Rouville.' (I, 434) Thus it is that Adélaïde, during her mother's regular afternoon walk in the Tuileries, 'monta seule, pour la première fois, à l'atelier d'Hippolyte' (I, 434). This first return to the studio since the opening scene may seem the ideal setting for a mutual declaration of love. In the event, the episode follows the pattern of that of the portrait's collection. Neither of the lovers dares express their feelings in words and Adélaïde, 'trop émue' when the hand she has extended to Schinner is covered in kisses, takes refuge in 'un regard plein de naïveté' and the exclamation: '"Vous allez rendre ma mère bien heureuse!"' (I, 434). The artist's question ('"Quoi! Votre mère seulement?"') is similarly side-stepped by an ambiguous response ('"Oh! moi, je le suis trop"') which leaves him 'effrayé de la violence des sentiments que l'accent de cette phrase réveilla dans son cœur' (I, 434–35). Strangely inhibited by the situation in which they find themselves, they go down to the apartment and hang the portrait in its place without more ado.[13]

Even so, the minor celebration that follows appears to prepare the ground for a proposal of marriage. The painter is invited to dinner for the first time and Mme de Rouville, 'tout en pleurs, voulut l'embrasser' (I, 435). But Kergarouët, whose evening visits had become less frequent, turns up during the *vernissage* like some inexorable return of the repressed: 'Le soir, le vieil émigré, ancien camarade du baron de Rouville, fit à ses deux amies une visite pour leur apprendre qu'il venait d'être nommé vice-amiral.' (I, 435) As Mme de Rouville had told Schinner when accepting his offer to copy the portrait, not only was her husband, *capitaine de vaisseau*, killed in naval combat, but her recently renewed request for a pension has been turned down on the grounds he would still be alive had he emigrated, and 'serait sans doute aujourd'hui contre-amiral' (I, 427).[14] The *vieil émigré* on the other hand, now described for the first time as her husband's 'ancien camarade', has just been promoted: 'Ses navigations terrestres à travers l'Allemagne et la Russie lui avaient été comptées comme des campagnes navales.' (I, 435) Not only has Kergarouët usurped, as it were, M. de Rouville's promotion, he now tries to pay for his old friend's portrait and to match it with one of himself: '"Ma foi! [...] je donnerais bien cinq cents pistoles pour me voir aussi ressemblant que l'est mon vieux Rouville."' (I, 435) It is Mme de Rouville's reaction to her friend's proposition ('la baronne regarda son ami, et sourit en laissant éclater sur son visage les marques d'une soudaine reconnaissance' (I, 435)), that confirms Schinner in his determination to take offence:

> Hippolyte crut deviner que le vieil amiral voulait lui offrir le prix des deux portraits en payant le sien. Sa fierté d'artiste, tout autant que sa jalousie peut-être, s'offensa de cette pensée et il répondit: 'Monsieur, si je peignais le portrait, je n'aurais pas fait celui-ci.' (I, 435)

In this transformed atmosphere, the card game that hastily follows ('L'amiral se mordit les lèvres et se mit à jouer' (I, 435)) is fertile territory for a delusion triggered by Kergarouët's clumsy offer. The eroticization of Mme de Rouville's passionate gambling — 'Jamais cette vieille baronne n'avait encore manifesté un désir si ardent pour le gain, ni un plaisir si vif en palpant les pièces d'or du gentilhomme' (I, 435) — draws Schinner's attention, in three easy steps, to a newly observed complicity between the pair:

> Ce vieillard paraissait être assez fin pour ne pas se laisser impunément prendre son argent. Quel intérêt l'attirait dans cette maison pauvre, lui riche? Pourquoi, jadis si familier près d'Adélaïde, avait-il renoncé à des privautés acquises et dues peut-être? Ces réflexions involontaires l'excitèrent à examiner le vieillard et la baronne, dont les airs d'intelligence et certains regards obliques jetés sur Adélaïde et sur lui le mécontentèrent. 'Me tromperait-on?' (I, 435–36)

The short cut from an unconscious paternity scenario to the 'conscious error' of the 'stolen' purse is very clearly spelled out here: '"Me tromperait-on?"' is described as 'une dernière idée, horrible, flétrissante' (I, 436) and it is his need to confirm it by scrutiny of Mme de Rouville's face that leads him to forget his purse.[15]

In the best illustration of Schinner's delusion controlling his actions as well as the mind, he gets up early after a sleepless night and 'alla se promener sous les frais ombrages des Tuileries, absorbé par ses idées, oubliant tout dans le monde' (I, 438). If Schinner, in this mechanical walk in the nearby Tuileries, is not quite Norbert Hanold propelling himself from Germany to Pompeii, the mechanism is nevertheless similar. The *portière* had first sown the image of Adélaïde as someone who attracted male attention in the Tuileries — '"Ah! quand elles vont aux Tuileries, mademoiselle est bien flambante, et ne sort pas de fois qu'elle ne soit suivie de jeunes gens"' (I, 419) — and, as Schinner knows, it was to the Tuileries that Mme de Rouville had gone when he collected and reinstalled her husband's portrait. When, supposedly by chance, Schinner runs into a close friend, we can be sure he will hear confirmed the details of which he has gone in search: '"Sa mère est une baronne! [...] Nous voyons ici, dans cette allée, la vieille mère tous les jours; mais elle a une figure, une tournure qui disent tout. Comment! Tu n'as pas deviné ce qu'elle est à la manière dont elle tient son sac?"' (I, 438).[16] When other high-spirited artists turn up to add 'des observations, des rires, des moqueries innocentes et empreintes de la gaieté familière aux artistes' (I, 438), Schinner blames these friends for 'sa passion déchirée, mise en lambeaux' (I, 438) as if they, rather than himself, had betrayed his intimate secret. But he exacts still further proof, and Balzac's symbolic trio — Souchet, Bridau and Bixiou are sculptor, painter and caricaturist — obliges with a further barrage of jokes, of which Bixiou's has the authority of an artistic argument: '"Ah! la mère a, entre autres vertus, une certaine robe grise que je regarde comme un type."' (I, 439)

It remains for Schinner to pass to a new phase of a psychic logic that accommodates such degrading beliefs even as it refuses to give up its deep-seated love. As he passes the famous brown door on the way to his studio, he feels an unmistakable pain: 'Il aimait Mlle de Rouville si passionnément que, malgré le vol de sa bourse, il l'adorait encore' (I, 439). And as proof that Schinner's 'malgré' masks an equally powerful 'à cause de', he wallows in a classical, Freudian rescue phantasy that is mediated by the visual image of Manon Lescaut's degradation: 'Son amour était celui du chevalier des Grieux admirant et purifiant sa maîtresse jusque sur la charrette qui mène en prison les femmes perdues. [...] "Pourquoi l'abandonner au mal et au vice, sans lui tendre une main amie?"' (I, 439)[17] It is in this frame of mind — 'Cette mission lui plut. L'amour fait son profit de tout.' (I, 439) — that he arrives at his studio where, in a clear parallel with the opening scene, he is described as absorbed in immobile contemplation of his canvas:

> Hippolyte s'assit dans son atelier, contempla son tableau sans y rien faire, n'en voyant les figures qu'à travers quelques larmes qui lui roulaient dans les yeux, tenant toujours sa brosse à la main, s'avançant vers la toile comme pour adoucir une teinte, et n'y touchant pas. La nuit le surprit dans cette attitude. (I, 439)

Where once the figures came alive in the twilight, now they are veiled by his tears; awakened by darkness from his reverie, and setting off to visit his neighbours, it is no longer a 'délicieuse tête de jeune fille' that he sees. In this regression to the prostitution prelude of the Pygmalion myth (the 'loathsome Propoetides'), a predictable vision of Kergarouët greets Schinner on the stairs: 'il descendit, rencontra le vieil amiral dans l'escalier, lui jeta un regard sombre en le saluant, et s'enfuit' (I, 439).

Schinner's flight marks the end of a detailed delusion sequence which has effectively filled twenty-four hours (from Kergarouët's arrival at the *vernissage* to one of his regular visits the following evening). The week that Schinner stays away from Adélaïde is summarized in five lines of text. We are not told how many times he crosses the fourth-floor landing but, as he leaves his studio one evening, and in a further echo of the opening episode, he finds the brown door ajar: 'Une personne y était debout, dans l'embrasure de la fenêtre.' (I, 440) On the first evening visit, a long evocation of the 'amphibious' antechamber had culminated in a description of this same embrasure, 'où les précédents locataires avaient signé leur présence par diverses incrustations, espèces de fresques domestiques' (I, 422). The incrusted frescoes, concealed behind carefully draped percale curtains, sum up the more visible 'stigmates de misère' — 'des tons noirs et gras, des teintes huileuses, des taches et autres accessoires assez désagréables qui décoraient les boiseries' (I, 420) — and act as a fine image for the projection onto the shabby dining room décor of the layers of Schinner's mental life. The sight of Adélaïde, doubly framed in the doorway and the window embrasure, becomes therefore a veritable *mise en abyme* of the artist's *fantasme*. As if it were not enough for this Pygmalion to have turned the living girl back into stone, the climax of his pathological behaviour is to inflict on her the imaginary hurt done to himself, as well as the real hurt done to his mother: 'La disposition de la porte et de l'escalier ne permettait pas au peintre de passer sans voir Adélaïde, il la salua froidement en lui lançant un regard plein d'indifférence' (I, 440). However, such are his shifting identifications that, at once subject and object, he experiences the pain with Adélaïde: 'mais, jugeant des souffrances de cette jeune fille par les siennes, il eut un tressaillement en songeant à l'amertume que ce regard et cette froideur devaient jeter dans un cœur aimant' (I, 440). It is a jolt of recognition that causes him to look at his behaviour from the outside and that thereby sets in train the dissolution of his delusion.

Is *La Bourse* simply the story of a 'délire d'artiste' that has been laid out with the same psychological acuity as Sarrasine's 'passion d'artiste'? Nowhere in the story is Schinner's unconscious belief explicitly confirmed, yet nothing in the text contradicts it (indeed neither Adélaïde, her mother or the narrator ever refer to M. de Rouville as her father).[18] The nub of Schinner's delusion — the 'grain of truth' that is displaced to his 'conscious error' — is a mental juxtaposition of two portraits: M. de Rouville's likeness, which he has transferred from paper to canvas ('un de ses meilleurs ouvrages' (I, 434)), and its phantom double, the likeness of Kergarouët ('"me voir aussi ressemblant que l'est mon vieux Rouville"' (I, 435)) that he has declined to undertake. If the repressed linking remains unconscious for Schinner, for the reader it has powerful retroactive effect. Rouville's faded pastel portrait had aroused Schinner's interest on the first evening visit; no sooner had the artist's offer to paint a copy been accepted by Mme de Rouville — and the narrative of her husband's death been cut short on Adélaïde's advice — than enter Kergarouët with his own phantom double.

In the sustained caricatures that follow, the relation between Kergarouët and Du Halga is summed up by the image of 'la première et dernière épreuve d'une litho-graphie' (I, 428). Kergarouët, for all his anachronistic eccentricity ('ce prétentieux *voltigeur de Louis XIV*' (I, 428)), exudes health and vitality: 'Tout en accusant le caractère loyal et franc des vieux émigrés, sa physionomie dénotait aussi les mœurs libertines et faciles, les passions gaies et l'insouciance de ses mousquetaires, jadis si célèbres dans les fastes de la galanterie.' (I, 428) He is followed by 'une figure vraiment fantastique' whose secondary status is nevertheless stressed: 'pour la bien peindre il faudrait en faire l'objet principal du tableau où elle n'est qu'un accessoire' (I, 428). Indeed, Du Halga is described only in relation to Kergarouët, of whom he is in every way a flaccid shadow or reflection:

> L'habit, neuf chez l'un, se trouvait vieux et flétri chez l'autre. La poudre des cheveux semblait moins blanche chez le second, l'or des fleurs de lys moins éclatant, les attentes de l'épaulette plus désespérées et plus recroquevillées, l'intelligence plus faible, la vie plus avancé vers le terme fatal que chez le premier. (I, 428)

It is a Balzacian *morceau de bravoure* that proceeds to a set of rhetorical questions designed to suggest the nature of their tie: 'Était-ce un ami, un parent pauvre, un homme qui restait près du vieux galant comme une demoiselle de compagnie près d'une vieille femme? [...] Avait-il sauvé la fortune ou seulement la vie de son bienfaiteur? Était-ce le *Trim* d'un autre capitaine Tobie?' (I, 428–29) Though the specific identities of the two elderly comrades were only introduced into the Furne edition of 1842 (by which time Du Halga's life-defining love affair with Kergarouët's wife had been recounted in *Béatrix*), no reader of *Physiologie du mariage*, and probably no reader at all, could have failed to decipher this quintessentially homosocial friendship: 'Qui pouvait, sous la Restauration, se rappeler l'attachement qui liait avant la Révolution ce chevalier à la femme de son ami, morte depuis vingt ans?' (I, 429) Curiously, we are specifically told that Du Halga 'fut un mystère pour le peintre, et resta un mystère' (I, 428). But that this should be so lends narrative authenticity to this 'secondary' relationship, just as its secondary status surely implies that it mirrors the structure of a more central triangle: that what Du Halga is to Kergarouët, Kergarouët must have been to another of his former comrades-in-arms.

A second pictorial allusion leads to the same conclusion: what for Schinner may

remain an unconscious belief feeding an absurd conscious error, for the reader
is the grain of narrative truth without which the story cannot work. It follows
immediately in the text:

> Le personnage qui paraissait être le plus neuf de ces deux débris s'avança
> galamment vers la baronne de Rouville, lui baisa la main, et s'assit près d'elle.
> [...] Adélaïde vint appuyer ses coudes sur le dossier du fauteuil occupé par le
> vieux gentilhomme en imitant, sans le savoir, la pose que Guérin a donnée
> à la sœur de Didon dans son célèbre tableau. Quoique la familiarité du
> gentilhomme fut celle d'un père, pour le moment ses libertés parurent déplaire
> à la jeune fille. (I, 429)

Should the visual intertext for Adélaïde's painterly pose distract us from Balzac's
own carefully composed group (Mme de Rouville, Kergarouët and Adélaïde), the
detail that follows ('la familiarité d'un père') has been planted with the calculated
obviousness of Poe's purloined letter. From the moment of Kergarouët's entry, when
the sound of a kiss exchanged in the dining room makes Schinner anxious to see
'celui qui traitait Adélaïde si familièrement' (I, 427), Balzac exploits the semantic
ambiguity of *familier* to build into his narrative the two interlinked scenarios: on the
one hand, the *libertés* that, fitting the portrait of Kergarouët as an unreconstructed
galant, will make Schinner jealous and will feed into his fear that the old *émigré* is
protecting Adélaïde in return for sexual favours; on the other, the literal meaning
that is brazenly displayed in 'la familiarité d'un père', and that will reverberate
retroactively from the disingenuous closing line of the story: '"Il paraît que nous
sommes en famille ce soir."' (I, 443)

I suggested earlier that the reappearance of the purse allowed normal action to
resume where it had been frozen on the evening of the *vernissage*. The postponed
demande en mariage is set in train as Schinner, 'par un mouvement irrésistible', seizes
Adélaïde in his arms and 'lui ravit un baiser; [...] "Je vous la demande pour femme",
s'écria-t-il en regardant la baronne.' (I, 442) This sudden release from inhibition
leaves Adélaïde almost offended and her mother briefly at a loss for words. In a
stroke of inventive genius, Balzac fills the gap between Schinner's question and
Mme de Rouville's answer with a psychic *coup de théâtre*. When 'cette scène' (I, 442)
is interrupted by the sound of the doorbell, the reader is hardly surprised by the
arrival of Kergarouët. But this time it is not just Du Halga who follows him, for 'le
vieux vice-amiral apparut suivi de son ombre et de Mme Schinner' (I, 442). The
entry of Schinner's mother in the company of Kergarouët allows the ripples of her
son's psychic projections to play themselves out in the last paragraph of the story.
Moreover, from the point of view of the now omniscient reader, her entry in the
company of Kergarouët and Du Halga allows her to represent the missing pole of
their triangle by standing in for Kergarouët's long dead wife. In this kaleidoscope
of identifications and substitutions, she thus serves as a pivot between two 'grains
of truth': that which gives psychological coherence to Schinner's delusion, and
that which, through the staggering of two adulterous triangles, gives narrative
coherence to the text as a whole.[19] With the full phantasmatic cast assembled for a
final bow — 'Lorsque Mme Schinner eut salué Mme de Rouville, celle-ci regarda
le comte de Kergarouët, le chevalier du Halga, l'ancien ami de la feue comtesse de

Kergarouët, Hippolyte, Adélaïde' (I, 443) — Mme de Rouville's cleverly delayed reply, '"Il paraît que nous sommes en famille ce soir"' (I, 443), means more than its overt assent to her daughter's marriage.[20]

While Schinner's anxiety over Adélaïde's paternity is an inner psychological drama that subsides without practical consequence for his marriage, it nevertheless takes the form of a neurosis that circles around the spectre of the deceased father-in-law. The real family structures that contextualize the artist's delusion are interesting and relatively complex; moreover, in *La Bourse*, unusually it is two mothers — the one widowed, the other never married — who exchange their children. In *La Vendetta*, the neurosis is reversed in that an incestuously possessive father refuses to admit a son-in-law into the family unit. When the daughter, in order to exchange herself in marriage, has recourse to the provisions of the Civil Code, the tight-knit family structure implodes. As will be seen in the next chapter, the result is a psychodrama that is melodramatic in mode, but historically and socially precise in its effects.

Notes to Chapter 2

1. *La Bourse*, ed. by Jean-Louis Tritter, in *La Comédie humaine*, I, 405–43, (p. 413).
2. See '*La Maison du Chat-qui-pelote*', *suivi de* '*Le Bal de Sceaux*', '*La Vendetta*', '*La Bourse*', ed. by Anne-Marie Baron (Paris: Flammarion, 1985), pp. 22–23. Baron's reference for Laure Surville's comment is Marie-Jeanne Durry, *Un début dans la vie*, les Cours de Sorbonne, 1953, p. 153. As I shall argue, to put matters this way round (first the cruel doubts, then the idyllic love) is to miss the psychological force, stressed in Balzac's text, of a delusion that takes hold at the very moment a love idyll reaches its climax: 'Couronner les plus douces fêtes qui aient jamais réjoui deux âmes pures par un dédain de huit jours, et par le mépris le plus profond, le plus entier?... affreux dénouement!' (I, 440).
3. See 'Introduction par Félix Davin aux *Études de mœurs au XIXe siècle*' (1835), ed. by Anne-Marie Meininger, in *La Comédie humaine*, I, 1143–72 (p. 1168). The preface was closely reworked by Balzac and sections of it are in his hand alone. However, there is no clue in Meininger's notes as to the exact authorship of this painterly evaluation of *La Bourse*.
4. See *La Peinture dans la création balzacienne: Invention et vision picturales de 'La maison du Chat-qui-pelote' au 'Père Goriot'* (Geneva: Droz, 1969), p. 31. Further page references are included in the text.
5. Barthes, *Fragments d'un discours amoureux* (Paris: Seuil, 1977), p. 227. Further page references are included in the text.
6. Bonard argues that the exposition of *La Bourse*, formed of a sequence of pictures, does not simply trigger the *drame* as it does in *La Maison du chat-qui-pelote* and *La Vendetta*: 'elle envahit le drame, elle devient le drame lui-même, au point que l'élément d'intrigue sur lequel toute la nouvelle est construite, l'épisode de la disparition de la bourse de Schinner, devient en somme accessoire' (pp. 35–36).
7. '"Je suis bien sûr, dit André Wurmser, que Delacroix n'a jamais pleuré avec une femme peinte, ni ri, ni causé."' (Bonard, p. 32, quoting Wurmser, *La Comédie inhumaine* (Paris: Gallimard, 1964), p. 398).
8. As Naomi Schor neatly puts it, describing a 'mytho-pathology' common in nineteenth-century literature, 'before the statue could be transformed into woman, woman had to be turned into stone'. See 'Smiles of the Sphinx: Zola and the Riddle of Femininity', in *Breaking the Chain: Women, Theory and French Realist Fiction* (New York: Columbia University Press, 1985), pp. 29–47 (p. 45). According to Didi-Huberman, 'l'amour que porte Pygmalion à son œuvre [...] exige la catalepsie de l'objet, sa non-réponse, la non-réciprocité' (p. 80).
9. According to Baron, 'la faute féminine' is the 'péché originel de l'imaginaire balzacien' (*Balzac, ou les hiéroglyphes de l'imaginaire*, p. 69).
10. Adélaïde's therapeutic willingness to understand Schinner's thoughts — 'Il y a des secrets que les âmes jeunes entendent si bien!' (I, 441) — is truly a 'témoignage de tendresse' (I, 442). As such,

it subsumes the gift of the ornately decorated purse she has stoically embroidered in Schinner's cruel absence. By restoring to its proper place this 'ouvrage de femme' (I, 441), she lends herself, more willingly than Gillette, to the male castration fantasy that was first lightly set in motion by the wound to Schinner's forehead.

11. Freud, *Delusions and Dreams in Jensen's 'Gradiva'* (1907), in *Art and Literature*, Pelican Freud Library, XIV, trans. by James Strachey, ed. by Albert Dickson (Harmondsworth: Penguin, 1985), pp. 27–118 (p. 94, p. 103).

12. In her brief comments on this passage, Régine Borderie appears to detect a more permanent ambiguity: 'au moins temporairement, [...] l'hésitation réintroduit du possible dans la vie de la vieille dame'. See *Balzac peintre du corps: 'La Comédie humaine' ou le sens du détail* (Paris: SEDES, 2002), p. 204.

13. In what, to my knowledge, is the only critical discussion to cast doubt on Adélaïde's paternity, Massol picks out this exchange: 'une exclamation ambiguë d'Adélaïde, à la vue du portrait de Rouville refait par le peintre, peut donner à penser que l'officier n'est pas son père'. She also refers to the mystery sown by the *portière*, who tells Schinner that daughter and mother have different names: 'Il est clair, ou à peu près, que le mystère sert à entretenir le doute sur la bonne moralité de la baronne, suspectée, par exemple, d'avoir un enfant adultérin.' Surprisingly, she adds: 'Mais plus aucune interrogation ne suivra'. See *Une poétique de l'énigme: Le Récit herméneutique balzacien* (Geneva: Droz, 2006), p. 177.

14. Until the Furne edition, the still anonymous Kergarouët is described as 'le contre-amiral' in the closing paragraph of the story (I, 1318). A rear-admiral is a rank below a vice-admiral; however, Tritter's choice of variants is insufficient to establish whether the ranks of Kergarouët and Rouville (achieved and potential) might have been intended by Balzac to be the same.

15. Freud's 'Contributions to the Psychology of Love' are richly suggestive for a reading of *La Bourse*. 'A Special Type of Object Choice Made by Men' (1910) (*On Sexuality*, Pelican Freud Library, VII, trans. by James Strachey, ed. by Angela Richards (Harmondsworth: Penguin, 1977), pp. 227–42) deals with a set of behavioural characteristics deriving from an infantile fixation on the mother. While 'the adult's conscious thought likes to regard his mother as a person of unimpeachable moral purity' (p. 237), it is part of the 'psychical constellation connected with the mother' (p. 236) that the object choice should have the qualities of a prostitute and should provoke jealousy on behalf of the father as injured third party. (He will also feel betrayed on his own account, perceiving the mother's intercourse with the father as infidelity to himself.) It is easy to see that the illegitimate Schinner has placed M. de Rouville in the position of an injured third party, and that the resentment against Kergarouët, perceived to be Adélaïde's biological father but also standing in for his own real father ('un homme riche qui ne se piquait pas d'une grande délicatesse en amour' (I, 417) will be overdetermined.

16. When Souchet suggests in conclusion 'viens ici vers quatre heures, et analyse un peu la marche de la mère et de la fille' (I, 439), his advice is superfluous: Schinner has already followed the two women's trail to the Tuileries and has completed his mental detective work.

17. See Freud, 'A Special Type of Object-Choice', p. 234, p. 239.

18. There are no clues as to Balzac's intentions in variants for *La Bourse* or in other texts of *La Comédie humaine*.

19. What is more, Kergarouët has confided in Mme Schinner. The wording is ambiguous enough to support the suggestion that he has explained his motivation as well as his method: 'Animé par son courroux, l'amiral avait appris à Mme Schinner le secret des pertes volontaires qu'il faisait au jeu, puisque la fierté de la baronne ne lui laissait que cet ingénieux moyen de la secourir.' (p. 443)

20. Both Franc Schuerewegen and Tim Farrant attribute the punch line of the story to Mme Schinner rather than, as is surely the case, to Mme de Rouville. Schuerewegen interestingly notes the exchange of a new-for-old picture for a new-for-old purse, while Farrant sees the portrait and the purse as symbolic representations of the missing paternal element. Although Farrant does not question Adélaïde's biological paternity, his brief but dense reading of *La Bourse* shares common ground with my own. I disagree, however, that 'Schinner has faith in Adélaïde and is rewarded' (I have argued that lack of faith is intrinsic to his neurosis). See Farrant, *Balzac's Shorter Fictions: Genesis and Genre* (Oxford: Oxford University Press, 2002), pp. 144–45, and Schuerewegen, 'La Toile déchirée: Texte, tableau et récit dans trois nouvelles de Balzac', *Poétique*, 65 (1986), 19–27 (p. 25).

CHAPTER 3

❖

La Vendetta

(i) 'A travers la crevasse'

Whereas, in *Sarrasine*, Girodet's *Le Sommeil d'Endymion* is the end point of the chain of representations that structure the narrative, in *La Vendetta* it is the starting point of 'l'étrange aventure' set in the studio of the artist Servin. Balzac's use of Girodet's painting is overdetermined; it is the beginning of a chain of copies and is also the implicit referent of a *tableau vivant* whereby Ginevra di Piombo, herself attentively observed, gazes down at the sleeping Luigi Porta through a narrow crevice in a closet partition. In her detailed interrogation of Balzac's fascination with *Le Sommeil d'Endymion*, Baron reads its 'hieroglyphic' — 'cette union symbolique entre l'amoureuse Séléné et le jeune garçon, sous les yeux complices d'un amour'[1] — as a primal scene, to be looked at illicitly and, by definition, without the awareness of the 'parental' protagonists. As such, the picture satisfies a scopic drive as much as any aesthetic ideal. In *La Vendetta*, the young man asleep in the closet acts as a magnet for the collective curiosity of Servin's female art pupils. By the end of the first week, of fifteen young women, only Ginevra's friend Laure will have resisted the temptation to look at Luigi through the crevice, and will have distanced herself from the shared certainty that Servin is hiding Ginevra's lover in his closet during their classes. Although Luigi is actually a political proscript (it is late July 1815) none of the girls will realize this; what is more, and as if not by chance, the plot of the Napoleonic proscript-in-hiding fizzles out when the girls' mothers take them away from the studio. In short, the open secret that is Luigi's presence in the studio closet makes him the vanishing point of other proscribed sights.[2]

'"Envoyez-la chez Servin!"' is the word from the salons when the daughters of cautious mothers want to learn to paint or draw.[3] 'La peinture féminine' is this art teacher's trademark, and it is recognized that 'une jeune femme qui avait pris des leçons chez Servin pouvait juger en dernier ressort les tableaux du Musée, faire supérieurement un portrait, copier une toile et peindre son tableau de genre. Cet artiste suffisait ainsi à tous les besoins de l'aristocratie.' (I, 1041) The irony of the last sentence implies that it is precisely 'sa prudence, la supériorité avec lesquelles il initiait ses élèves aux secrets de l'art' (I, 1040) that have established his virtuous reputation: the secrets he imparts are reliably partial. In order to attract and keep a distinguished clientele, 'il se refusait même à prendre les jeunes filles qui voulaient devenir artistes et auxquelles il aurait fallu donner certains enseignements sans lesquels il n'est pas de talent possible en peinture' (I, 1040).[4] There can be no naked models in an art class for well-bred young women. On the walls of the studio, 'une foule de caricatures, de têtes faites au trait, avec de la couleur ou la pointe d'un couteau, [...] prouvaient, sauf la différence de l'expression, que les filles les plus distinguées ont dans l'esprit autant de folie que les hommes peuvent en avoir' (I, 1041). However, these lively female minds must derive their artistic knowledge from the standard paraphernalia of a studio: *écorchés*, manikins, skeletons, skulls, plaster casts of heads and hands, a weeping Niobe, a smiling Venus, the 'tête d'Antinoüs' (I, 1043) at which one languorous pupil casts furtive glances. At best, they may copy representations of the male body, such as Girodet's *Le Sommeil d'Endymion*. In this context, Ginevra's sketch of Luigi, conceived as a warning to Servin that she has discovered the secret in his closet, turns the proscript into the life model that is taboo for a female artist. Balzac conflates this transgressive vision with the image of Ginevra, herself spied on by Amélie Thirion, gazing down from on high at the sleeping Luigi, and reproducing as she does so the composition of Girodet's painting. In this *pose mythologique* à la Canler (see Chapter I), two female curiosities, the sexual and the artistic, are merged. What Baron calls the 'hystérisation du regard' (p. 52) — and its mediation in this text by the male model of Ginevra's drawing — is captured in an extraordinary description of Amélie, who intercepts Luigi's image even as Ginevra commits it to paper: 'il y eut un moment où elle n'aperçut pas le lorgnon que son impitoyable ennemie braquait sur le mystérieux dessin en s'abritant derrière un grand portefeuille. Mlle Thirion, qui reconnut la figure du proscrit, leva brusquement la tête, et Ginevra serra la feuille de papier.' (I, 1053)[5]

In his concern to market his teaching studio as a strictly female enclave, Servin has walled up the outer door: 'Pour parvenir à cette retraite, aussi sacrée qu'un harem, il fallait monter par un escalier pratiqué dans l'intérieur de son logement' (I, 1041). The male teacher is himself absent — he works on his own painting elsewhere — when the brightly lit stage of the studio is first animated by its female pupils. In the dazzling midday sun, strong shadows, cast by the blinds that filter the light from the vast sash-windows, produce 'de piquants effets de clair-obscur' (I, 1042), and the narrator's delicate brush strokes — 'celle-ci [...], celle-là [...], une autre [...], sa voisine' (I, 1042–43) — transform the girls themselves into 'le plus beau de tous les tableaux de l'atelier': 'Assises ou debout, ces jeunes filles, entourés de leur boîtes à couleurs, jouant avec leurs pinceaux ou les préparant, maniant leurs éclatantes palettes, peignant, parlant, riant, chantant, abandonnées à leur naturel, laissant voir leur caractère, composaient un spectacle inconnu aux hommes.' (I, 1042) The exceptional narrative texture of the studio sequence will depend on its juxtaposition of layers of female voyeurism; however, the fact that this tableau of the girls at work portrays 'un spectacle inconnu aux hommes' betrays the male voyeurism that the representation of a collective female phantasy also invites.

The phantasy is orchestrated by Amélie Thirion, who mediates it for the reader. Amélie's expulsion of Ginevra's easel, stool and paintbox, along with a picture by Prud'hon that her absent classmate is currently copying, is overtly motivated by political spite (it is the very beginning of the Second Restoration and Ginevra's father is 'un des serviteurs de Napoléon qui avaient coopéré le plus efficacement au retour de l'île d'Elbe' (I, 1045)). Moreover, this historically contextualized revenge is prepared by the information that the art class — 'un groupe d'anges assis sur un nuage dans le ciel' — is divided into bourgeois and aristocratic factions. But the fact that Amélie is responsible for Ginevra's privileged proximity to the closet, makes her, from the outset, complicit in the voyeurism she objectifies, imitates and relays to her companions, and gives psychological subtlety to a jealous curiosity that will remain focused on Ginevra rather than Luigi. In the first of the suspenseful silences that will punctuate this opening episode, 'le parti de la banque' (I, 1044) watches Amélie strike her blow; a second hush descends in anticipation of Ginevra's entry: 'le bruit des pas d'une personne qui montait l'escalier retentit dans la salle. Ce mot: "La voici!" passa de bouche en bouche, et le plus profond silence régna dans l'atelier.' (I, 1044–45) Ginevra's manifest unawareness of 'la curiosité insolite qu'excitait sa présence', as she mechanically prepares to start painting, makes her an even more intense focus of attention: 'Toutes les têtes du groupe des bourgeoises étaient tournées vers elle. Si les jeunes personnes du camp Thirion ne mettaient pas tant de franchise que leurs compagnes dans leur impatience, leurs œillades n'en étaient pas moins dirigées sur Ginevra.' (I, 1047) The class is rewarded by the sight of Ginevra's mysterious gymnastics as she climbs up on a chair, pretends to adjust the blinds, gets down to fetch a table upon which she then puts the chair, almost topples from the top of this precarious scaffolding — 'toutes les jeunes filles regardèrent l'imprudente qui chancelait' (I, 1048) — before recovering her balance, removing the blind, pushing the table and chair away from the partition and silently preparing her paints. Her indifference to her physical banishment is so uncharacteristic that the curiosity of her receptive audience increases still further:

> La belle Italienne devint donc le centre de tous les regards, et fut épiée par ses amies comme par ses ennemies. Il est bien difficile de cacher la plus petite émotion, le plus léger sentiment, à quinze jeunes filles curieuses, inoccupées, dont la malice et l'esprit ne demandent que des secrets à deviner, des intrigues à créer, à déjouer, et qui savent trouver trop d'interprétations différentes à un geste, à une œillade, à une parole, pour ne pas en découvrir la véritable signification. (I, 1050)

In this orgy of active curiosity, Amélie, with 'cette finesse qui accompagne toujours la méchanceté' (I, 1049–50), is by far the most vigilant interpreter of Ginevra's enigmatic absorption; she notes Mme Servin's glance at the closet door when she arrives to apologize for her husband's absence, Ginevra's determination to continue her work when it is time to go home, and her attentive listening to a sound that nobody else can hear. Thus it is Amélie who stealthily returns to discover (and to focalize for the reader), Ginevra perched once more on her improvised scaffolding and gazing through her spyhole. By the next class, having managed to arrive before everyone else, Amélie, who crucially does not see Luigi's Napoleonic uniform, has observed his 'tête ravissante' and 'se perdit alors en conjectures'. She therefore recognizes the face of the mysterious, sleeping man as the subject of Ginevra's sketch and 'se mit, pour ainsi dire, en tiers dans les émotions qui agitèrent le maître et l'écolière' (I, 1053). In a bizarre cat-and-mouse tussle she fails to gain possession of Luigi's sepia portrait: '[Amélie] essaya d'ouvrir le portefeuille où elle avait vu mettre le lavis. Ginevra saisit le carton et le plaça devant elle sans mot dire.' (I, 1053) However, by the end of this second day's class, when Servin's alertness forestalls Amélie's return to the studio, the teacher's suspicious behaviour, combined with the overheard creaking of the closet door, allows her to consider her investigations complete: 'elle avait déjà inventé tout ce qui devait être' (I, 1055). At the next class, the phantasmatic secret of this literal closet is put into circulation: 'Mlle Thirion apprit sous le secret à toutes ses compagnes que Ginevra di Piombo était aimée d'un jeune homme qui venait, pendant les heures consacrées aux leçons, s'établir dans le cabinet noir de l'atelier' (I, 1060). Amélie's pathological surveillance refuels that of the class as a whole and, from then on, Ginevra's every move is watched with 'une attention diabolique':

> On écouta ses chansons, on épia ses regards. Au moment où elle ne croyait être vue de personne, une douzaine d'yeux étaient incessamment arrêtés sur elle. Ainsi prévenues, ces jeunes filles interprétèrent dans leur sens vrai les agitations qui passèrent sur la brillante figure de l'Italienne, et ses gestes, et l'accent particulier de ses fredonnements, et l'air attentif avec lequel on la vit écoutant des sons indistincts qu'elle seule entendait à travers la cloison. (I, 1060)

None of them needs to have been literally present at the phantasmatic scene in which Luigi's wound, and his naked arm, are uncovered by Servin before Ginevra's eyes. Only when the girls confide in their mothers — 'par hasard, par caquetage ou par pruderie, toutes les autres jeunes personnes instruisirent leurs mères de l'étrange aventure qui se passait à l'atelier' (I, 1061) — will Servin and Ginevra finally realize that their secret has long been an open one. Well might it emerge from the closet, for no one is left in the studio to take pleasure from spying upon it.

(ii) 'L'étrange aventure qui se passait à l'atelier'

For the reader who sees events with Ginevra, as well as looking at her in the ways described so far, the love affair taking place in the studio is another Pygmalion narrative. Ginevra, an amateur artist of talent, will marry the Napoleonic proscript whom she has discovered in the studio and whose portrait she has sketched. Like other Pygmalions, prior to her phantasmatic *rencontre* in the studio, the twenty-four-year-old Ginevra had sublimated her erotic life in art: 'Elle s'était refusée au mariage, par amour pour son père et sa mère, en se sentant nécessaire à leurs vieux jours. Son goût pour la peinture avait remplacé les passions qui agitent ordinairement les femmes.' (I, 1047) Parts of the Pygmalion plot are filled in retrospectively, so that chronologically its starting point is the copy that Ginevra had made, a few days before the opening studio scene, of *Le Sommeil d'Endymion*. It is followed by her chance interception, a day or two later, of the sound of someone breathing in the closet used to store old canvases and broken plaster casts ('le léger bruit qui avait si fortement excité sa curiosité et fait parcourir à sa jeune imagination le vaste champ des conjectures' (I, 1048)). The overheard breathing, in itself a key component of a primal scene, is what prompts Ginevra, now watched by her classmates, to spy so energetically through the crevice in the partition dividing off the dark closet: 'le regard qu'elle y jeta ne peut se comparer qu'à celui d'un avare découvrant les trésors d'Aladin' (I, 1048). But what she discovers more than satisfies her curiosity and transforms its phantasmatic substance: 'A travers la crevasse, elle avait entrevue l'aigle impériale et, sur un lit de sangles faiblement éclairé, la figure d'un officier de la Garde.' (I, 1049) In the same way that breathing is proof for Frenhofer that *Catherine Lescault* is a living woman — ' "il te semblerait voir le sein de Catherine rendre le mouvement de sa respiration" ' (x, 432); ' "Mais elle a respiré, je crois! [...] Elle va se lever, attendez." ' (x, 435) — in *La Vendetta*, breathing is a stage in the metamorphosis of the painted, sleeping Endymion into the living, but as yet still sleeping, Luigi. From her fortuitously positioned easel, Ginevra distinctly hears 'la respiration forte et régulière de l'homme endormi qu'elle venait de voir' (I, 1048); at the end of the lesson, believing herself alone, she again clambers up to the crevice to gaze down at him. So intense is her contemplation that, though interrupted, she leaves the studio 'en emportant gravée dans son souvenir l'image d'une tête d'homme aussi gracieuse que celle d'Endymion, chef-d'œuvre de Girodet qu'elle avait copié quelques jours auparavant' (I, 1051–52).

The engraving is metaphorical, but it is an important link in the chain of copies whereby Luigi gradually emerges from *Le Sommeil d'Endymion*. When, two days later, Ginevra urgently needs to convey to Servin that she has discovered his secret, the image of the proscript, so vividly stamped upon her memory, is transferred to a sepia likeness that will cause her teacher to go pale: 'La tête de l'officier fut jetée sur le papier au milieu d'un tressaillement intérieur qu'elle attribuait à la crainte, et dans lequel un physiologiste aurait reconnu la fièvre de l'inspiration.' (I, 1052–53) In fact, so inspired is the hasty portrait that Servin cannot resist proclaiming aloud his aesthetic admiration — ' "Ceci est un chef-d'œuvre digne de Salvator Rosa" ' — and the ensuing stampede to Ginevra's easel will rouse the proscript from his slumbers. Awoken by the impact of his own portrait, as it were, the living Luigi, released from his hiding place at the end of the day, will step out from the frame of the open door: 'L'Italienne vit paraître un jeune homme grand et bien fait dont l'uniforme impérial lui fit battre le cœur. L'officier avait un bras en écharpe, et la pâleur de son teint accusait de vivres souffrances.' (I, 1055) His emergence coincides almost literally with cries from the street below reporting the death sentence on Labédoyère. At this news, Luigi sinks down onto Ginevra's stool and leans on the very easel where she had earlier that day sketched the likeness of his head: 'il saisit d'une main et par un geste de désespoir les touffes noires de sa chevelure, et appuya son coude sur le bord du chevalet de Ginevra' (I, 1056). The sepia portrait, now hidden in Ginevra's portfolio, has given way to the real head of its model.

However, Ginevra's love for Luigi, although it is mediated by pictures, is not initially an artist's investment in an aesthetic image. We are specifically told that it is not the beauty of Luigi that arouses Ginevra's senses: 'quoique l'inconnu fût beau, son aspect n'avait point ému la jeune fille' (I, 1057). In the first instance, it is the political danger that excites Ginevra:

> 'Proscrire un homme si jeune! Qui donc peut-il être, car ce n'est pas le maréchal Ney?'
> Ces deux phrases sont l'expression la plus simple de toutes les idees que Ginevra commenta pendant deux jours. (I, 1052)

What was set in motion by the sight of the imperial eagle, glimpsed through the chink in the closet wall, crystallizes two days later around Luigi's declared desire to avenge the impending death of Labédoyère:

> La douce pitié que les femmes trouvent dans leur cœur pour les misères qui n'ont rien d'ignoble avait étouffé chez Ginevra toute autre affection; mais entendre un cri de vengeance, rencontrer dans ce proscrit une âme italienne, du dévouement pour Napoléon, de la générosité à la corse...? (I, 1057)

For the first time, we are told, 'un homme lui faisait éprouver un sentiment si vif' (I, 1057). But only when Luigi bursts into Corsican dialect — 'Ce proscrit était un enfant de la Corse, il en parlait le langage chéri!' (I, 1058) — is the process of psycho-erotic investment in an image complete: 'la jeune fille resta pendant un moment immobile, retenue par une sensation magique; elle avait sous les yeux un tableau vivant auquel tous les sentiments humains réunis et le hasard donnaient de vives couleurs' (I, 1058). As Servin dresses the 'chairs meurtries' (I, 1059) of Luigi's forearm, Ginevra identifies with his pain, shudders at the sight of 'la longue et large plaie faite par la lame d'un sabre' (I, 1058) and lets out an involuntary moan. But Luigi's face, as he looks at Ginevra, already reveals more pleasure than pain. A last ray of sunlight cuts through the enveloping darkness of the studio and Luigi's image is aesthetically, as well as psychically, consecrated:

> Une artiste devait admirer involontairement cette opposition de sentiments, et les contrastes que produisaient la blancheur des linges, la nudité du bras, avec l'uniforme bleu et rouge de l'officier. En ce moment, une obscurité douce enveloppait l'atelier; mais un dernier rayon de soleil vint éclairer la place où se trouvait le proscrit, en sorte que sa noble et blanche figure, ses cheveux noires, ses vêtements, tout fut inondé par le jour.[6]

With no class the next day and the studio to themselves, Luigi woos the Bonapartist Ginevra — 'sa voix fut une musique pour l'Italienne' — with an elegiac narrative of his sufferings, from 'la déroute de Moscou' to the 'grand désastre de Waterloo' (I, 1059). This most narcissistic of loves finds its expression not only in the reflected 'douceur' of Luigi and Ginevra's eyes, but in the frozen tableau of the lovers locked in mutual contemplation across the mirror of Ginevra's easel:

> Les yeux attachés sur l'officier et la bouche légèrement entreouverte, elle écoutait, se tenant toujours prête à donner un coup de pinceau qu'elle ne donnait jamais. [...] Puis, elle peignait ensuite avec une attention particulière et pendant des heures entières, sans lever la tête, parce qu'il était là, près d'elle, la regardant travailler. (I, 1059–60)

Their passion is encouraged by the benevolent Servin in whose studio it has been born, almost as if, Venus-like, he had conjured up the ideal spouse for the female Pygmalion who is his favourite pupil: '"Vous vous marierez, mes enfants? [...] Soyez heureux, je vous unis"' (I, 1064). The first days of their marriage are given over to mutual absorption — 'Luigi restait des heures aux pieds de sa femme, admirant [...]; Ginevra caressait la chevelure de son Luigi sans se lasser de contempler' [...] (I, 1092) — and when they seek paid work, Ginevra's copies of old paintings are joined by Luigi's handwritten copies of legal documents. Appropriately, their first wedding anniversary is celebrated by Ginevra's gift to Luigi of her self-portait: 'A part une ressemblance parfaite, l'éclat de sa beauté, la pureté de ses sentiments, le bonheur de l'amour y étaient rendus avec une sorte de magie. Le chef-d'œuvre fut inauguré.' (I, 1094)

According to Baron, 'la légende de Pygmalion est une version opposée à celle d'Endymion, avec le mythe d'un amour qui crée la vie au lieu de donner la mort' (p. 57). Just two or three years after the installation of Ginevra's portrait, the Pygmalion myth will be absorbed back into that of Endymion, from whose death-like sleep Luigi had first emerged. The passage of Ginevra and Luigi through hardship to indigence — 'la Pauvreté se levait comme un squelette au milieu de cette moisson de plaisir' (I, 1094) — is accelerated by the collapse of their respective markets for copying. The birth of a child, '*beau comme le jour*' (I, 1096), reanimates them only briefly; as if their vital resources were draining away, 'parfois ils s'abandonnaient à une apathie semblable à ces sommeils qui précèdent la mort' (I, 1097). With the arrival of 'la Misère dans toute son horreur' (I, 1097), Ginevra's self-portrait serves only to register by contrast the approaching death of its model:

> Sept ou huit mois après la naissance du petit Bartholoméo, l'on aurait eu de la peine à reconnaître dans la mère qui allaitait cet enfant malingre l'original de l'admirable portrait, le seul ornement d'une chambre nue. Sans feu par un rude hiver, Ginevra vit les gracieux contours de sa figure se détruire lentement, ses joues devinrent blanches comme de la porcelaine et ses yeux pâles comme si les sources de la vie tarissaient en elle. (I, 1097)

The day he realizes that Ginevra is literally dying of hunger, 'Luigi l'embrassa par un de ces baisers de désespoir qui se donnaient en 1793 entre amis à l'heure où ils montaient ensemble à l'échafaud' (I, 1098). He then mirrors Ginevra one last time by following up his sale of her portrait — the paltry sum obtained had 'prolong[é] l'agonie du ménage pendant quelques moments' (I, 1097) — with the exchange of himself for a handful of gold: 'il résolut de se vendre, de s'offrir comme remplaçant pour le service militaire' (I, 1098). He returns to a twilight tableau: 'Les derniers rayons du soleil pénétrant par la lucarne venaient mourir sur le visage de Ginevra qui dormait assise sur une chaise en tenant son enfant sur son sein.' (I, 1099) The baby is dead ('la pose de son enfant qui dans ce moment conservait un éclat surnaturel' (I, 1099)) and the death of its mother follows in a matter of lines. In the melodramatic closing scene of the story, a single light is about to go out in his parents–in–law's vast salon: 'sans les flammes pétillantes du foyer, ils eussent été dans une obscurité complète' (I, 1100). The Luigi who bursts through the door, looming up like an apparition with his wife's long, black *chevelure*, is 'un homme dont le visage n'avait plus rien d'humain' (I, 1101). In Balzac's overblown *Liebestod* plot, the two lovers are not only artist and her model, artist and her spouse, but two childhood escapees from death by vendetta who had been granted a mere stay of execution: ' "*Morte!* Nos deux familles devaient s'exterminer l'une par l'autre, car voilà tout ce qui reste d'elle" ' (I, 1101).[7]

(iii) '"Sors donc, malheureuse"'

'"Il paraît que la peinture passe devant nous"' (I, 1070), declares the jealous Bartholoméo di Piombo, when his twenty-four-year-old daughter starts coming home from her art class a little later than usual. The day after he learns the identity of the husband Ginevra has found for herself there, he blocks her path to Servin's studio: 'Ginevra, qui voulut sortir à l'heure où elle avait coutume de se rendre à l'atelier, trouva la porte de l'hôtel fermée pour elle' (I, 1080). So energetically had Piombo not wanted this particular son-in-law — '"je ne veux pas qu'un Porta soit mon gendre"' (I, 1079) — that he has taken the precaution, like some cruel character in Greek myth wishing to forestall the inevitable, of attempting to exterminate him as a young child. However, it seems likely that anyone wishing to marry his daughter would have met with similar hostility, for Piombo's vendetta with the Porta family — '"qui n'épouse pas ma vengeance, n'est pas de ma famille"' (I, 1079) — is a fine excuse for the possessiveness he freely proclaims even before Luigi's identity is discovered: '"vous faites mal, vous, ma fille, d'aimer un autre homme que votre père"' (I, 1071).[8] Balzac clearly intends to depict Piombo's excesses as pathological, but also to make Ginevra's complicity with them part of the problem. Their power struggles are a dangerous game for which her father has trained her, and his masochistic pleasure in giving in to her is spelled out:

> Ginevra ne pardonnait rien à son père et il fallait qu'il lui cédât. [...] Au milieu de ces tempêtes que Bartholoméo aimait à exciter, un mot de tendresse, un regard suffisaient pour apaiser leurs âmes courroucées, et ils n'étaient jamais si près d'un baiser que quand ils se menaçaient. (I, 1068)

In their battle over Ginevra's determination to marry Luigi, father and daughter are simply playing for higher stakes: 'Ils s'encourageaient l'un et l'autre dans leur colère et fermaient les yeux sur l'avenir. Peut-être aussi se flattaient-ils mutuellement que l'un céderait à l'autre.' (I, 1081) The climax of this pattern of behaviour occurs in the episode of the *actes respectueux* whereby Ginevra, reaching the age of twenty-five, may marry without her parents' consent as long as she fulfils the legal requirement of formally seeking their advice.[9] Realizing that he has been outmanoeuvred by his daughter's recourse to the law, Piombo's violent approach with his dagger is met by Ginevra's 'air de triomphe' (I, 1084) as she kneels with provocative passivity. Piombo's '"Non! non! je ne saurais"' (I, 1084) leads to a declaration of filial love that is a hyperbolic variant on their familiar script: '"Ô mon père, jamais je ne vous ai tant aimé"' (I, 1084). However, from her father's point of view, it is invalidated by the second half of Ginevra's sentence — '"accordez-moi Luigi?"' — and what retrospectively will be referred to as 'la malédiction paternelle' (I, 1088) takes the form of the melodramatic decree: '"Je n'ai plus de fille! Je t'abandonne, et tu n'as plus de père. [...] Sors donc, malheureuse [...], sors et ne reparais plus devant moi."' (I, 1084)

It is the sort of scene that inclines critics to dismiss *La Vendetta* as embarrassing melodrama. Bonard, for example, who greatly admires the painterly qualities of the studio scene, describes the text as 'ce petit roman, auquel la violence des sentiments donne quelquefois un pathétique un peu forcé' (p. 23). Pierre-Georges Castex deplores the exaggerated dialogues between father and daughter and the crude narrative clichés that accompany them at the expense of naturalness and truth: 'de semblables indications s'apparentent à celles qu'on rencontre dans les mélodrames et dans les romans populaires de l'époque' (p. 209). Yet Balzac is doubtless aiming in *La Vendetta* at sentimental, bourgeois melodrama in the mode of Diderot and Greuze, and perhaps the best way to recuperate the interest of the text as a whole is to resist using 'melodrama' as a negative value judgement.[10] Michael Fried makes Greuze a central figure in his influential study *Absorption and Theatricality*; accepting the taste and sensibility that made Greuze a phenomenon at a particular historical moment, he analyses his paintings for their exploitation of visual perspective as a compositional device cutting across form and subject matter. Whereas the early Greuze interests Fried on account of his representation of states of absorption, the two 'dramatic masterpieces' of 1777 and 1778 — *Le Fils ingrat* (*La Malédiction paternelle*) and *Le Fils puni* — illustrate a shift to the 'representation of heroic or grandly pathetic action and expression'.[11] Anita Brookner relates the overwhelming success of the two *Fils* paintings to a sensibility that was 'approaching its decadence and craving stronger stimulants'. She is especially interesting on the reception and nineteenth-century legacy of Greuze, whose 'unfortunate distinction of being plagiarized both in his lifetime and after his death' is well illustrated by the continuity of the theme of *la malédiction paternelle* and the modifications introduced by subsequent generations. The title of Boilly's painting, *'Je te donne ma malédiction'*, nicely sums up the trend.[12]

According to Brookner, 'whereas the ungrateful son was the stock figure of the eighteenth century, the nineteenth preferred the fallen girl who eventually became embellished with an illegitimate child and a blinding snowstorm outside the window'. This account of the nineteenth-century posterity of the motif suggests that Balzac, in *La Vendetta*, may have exploited a melodramatic commonplace without ironic purpose as to its manner, but with the intention of inverting its perceived moral message.[13] When Piombo, somewhat late in the day, concedes defeat in his power struggle with Ginevra — '"Ô mon enfant chéri! Tu m'as vaincu."' (I, 1101) — his wife imagines their daughter cold, hungry and unable to breastfeed her baby. It is midnight, and 'la bise chassa si violemment les flocons de neige sur les persiennes, que les deux vieillards purent en entendre le léger bruissement' (I, 1101). But this is a legitimate baby, and Ginevra's only transgression is to have sought the protection of the Civil Code in order to get married, rather than remain the plaything of a tyrannical father. In Greuze's *La Malédiction paternelle*, the 'fils ingrat' is cursed by his violent-looking father for abandoning his family to join the army; he becomes 'le fils puni' of the narrative sequel when he returns to find his father on his deathbed. The ending of *La Vendetta* depicts the punishment, not of the daughter for abandoning her father, but of the father for banishing his daughter. However, such is the grip of moral stereotypes, that the claim of Davin's preface is often taken at face value: 'l'auteur a montré qu'un enfant avait tort de se marier en faisant les actes respectueux prescrits par le Code. Il est d'accord avec les mœurs contre un article rarement appliqué.' (I, 1024)[14] And such is the allure of statements of intent, that Castex, disapproving of this supposed moral lesson, is ironically bemused — 'Il faut avouer qu'une histoire aussi édifiante ne nous touche guère' (p. 209) — and ultimately rebellious: 'Comment justifier humainement qu'une fille doive obéir à son père, lorsque le père n'oppose à la pureté de son amour que le préjugé le plus absurde et le plus révoltant?' (p. 210).

Melodramatic as Balzac's *malédiction paternelle* is clearly intended to be, its interest is precisely that it is performed in the legal context of the *actes respectueux*. Indeed, 'deux notaires accompagnés de plusieurs témoins' form an audience for the extraordinary family dynamics of the 'trois principaux acteurs de cette scène' (I, 1081). The reactions of the lawyers and witnesses are carefully charted, and though this may be thought a narrative device for heightening the dramatic tension ('cette scène devint si effrayante que les témoins étrangers tremblèrent' (I, 1083)), it also introduces a significant shift in perspective: '"As-tu jamais vu des clients fabriqués comme ceux-là?"' (I, 1083). Roguin's own theatricality — the 'manœuvre oratoire' (I, 1081) of his calculated pauses, his 'masque de bienveillance, dont le mécanisme est si facile à saisir' (I, 1082) — is part of his strategy as Ginevra's legal representative: '"Je produis de l'effet!"' (I, 1082). But Roguin overplays his part, and the expression on the silent Piombo's face is transformed from anger to 'un air de cruauté indéfinissable' (I, 1083). In the end it is the irritatingly calm voice of the Civil Code — 'M. Roguin lut un papier timbré contenant un procès-verbal rédigé à l'avance et demanda froidement à Bartholoméo quelle était sa réponse' (I, 1083) — that will trigger Piombo's leap for the paternal dagger. In an almost comical inversion of moral perspectives, 'les figures que Piombo voyait lui semblèrent échappées de l'enfer' (I, 1083) and the Corsican patriarch produces his stereotypical reply: 'Il sauta sur un long poignard suspendu par un clou au-dessus de sa cheminée et s'élança sur sa fille.' (I, 1084)

Decidedly, Piombo's ontological dignity is invested in his phallic dagger. In the earlier argument that determines Ginevra's recourse to the *actes respectueux*, the dagger lays claim to symbolic authority in what may seem a classic instance of the Name-of-the-Father:

> — Telle est ma sentence. Qu'il ne soit plus question de ceci entre nous. Je suis Bartholoméo di Piombo, entendez-vous Ginevra?
> — Attachez-vous quelque sens mystérieux à ces paroles, demanda-t-elle froidement.
> — Elles signifient que j'ai un poignard, et que je ne crains pas la justice des hommes. (I, 1079–80)

In Lacan's oft-quoted formulation, 'c'est dans le *nom du père* qu'il nous faut reconnaître le support de la fonction symbolique qui, depuis l'orée des temps historiques, identifie sa personne à la figure de la loi'.[15] In that the *nom du père* is also the *non du père*, Piombo's dagger, according to his own perception of his authority, mediates the legislative and punitive functions. Hence his indignant lament to Roguin: '"il y a donc en France des lois qui détruisent le pouvoir paternel"' (I, 1083). But there are two laws in conflict here, and Ginevra is well aware that her father's version of Roman law (which includes the right of life and death over his daughter) has no legitimacy under the Napoleonic Code: '"Eh bien! dit la fille en se levant, je suis Ginevra di Piombo, et je déclare que dans six mois je serai la femme de Luigi Porta. Vous êtes un tyran, mon père."' (I, 1080) In fact, Piombo's refusal to exchange his daughter in marriage flouts the Lacanian Name-of-the-Father, which supposedly exists to forbid Oedipal desires and thereby maintain the incest taboo.

If the Name-of-the-Father ironically alludes to the Christian liturgy, in 1815, even after Waterloo, the place of the father can only be taken by Napoleon, and that of the liturgy by the Napoleonic Code. When Piombo declares to Ginevra that, being Corsican, he has no need to fear human justice ('"nous autres Corses, nous allons nous expliquer avec Dieu"'), he knows very well that this is not the case: '"Ah! nous sommes à Paris"' (I, 1080). Just as Piombo's Corsican vendetta serves the interests of his incestuous possessiveness, so the Corsican connection provides narrative motivation for the opening encounter, set in 1800, between Piombo and the First Consul, the function of which surely exceeds that of laying the ground for the re-emergence of Luigi Porta. It is in Napoleon that Balzac invests the historically relevant *nom/non du père*, with its legislative prerogative — '"Je suis devenu le chef d'une grande nation, je commande la république et doit faire exécuter les lois"' — and its prohibitory, punitive function: '"Mais plus de *Vendetta*! [...] Si tu joues du poignard, il n'y a pas de grâce à espérer. Ici la loi protège tous les citoyens"' (I, 1039). In this sense, Piombo is a rebellious *fils ingrat* of his benefactor Napoleon and, at the end of the story, he becomes the *fils puni* for his disobedience.

The opening scene portrays the indifference of Napoleon and Lucien Bonaparte to the quarrels of their Corsican past, and Balzac makes Napoleon mutter under his breath: '"le préjugé de la *Vendetta* empêchera longtemps le règne des lois en Corse [...]. Il faut cependant le détruire à tout prix."' (I, 1039) In the case of Piombo, the hypercathexis of family represented by his stubborn vendetta is part and parcel of his refusal of exogamy. Appropriately, the First Consul who muses about bringing Corsican customs into line with French law is also the Napoleon who will bequeath to France the Civil Code with its carefully imbricated regulation of family, marriage and the transmission of property. Cursed by her father, Ginevra's marriage to Luigi will be blessed by a Bonapartist artist ('"Soyez heureux, je vous unis"' (I, 1064)) and a Napoleonic soldier ('"Dieu les bénisse"' (I, 1090)); we also learn that Napoleon (strategic matchmaker par excellence, both for himself and for his extended family) had personally proposed advantageous alliances for Piombo's daughter. By disobeying her father, Ginevra is paradoxically obeying the letter and spirit of the Code, and both mother ('"nous sommes mises au monde pour nous marier"' (I, 1074)) and daughter ('"un époux qui me protège après vous"' (I, 1072)), try to persuade Piombo of the benefits of its conjugal ideology: '"nous serons deux à vous aimer, [...] vous connaîtrez l'homme aux soins duquel vous me laisserez!"' (I, 1072).[16] By making Piombo's behaviour seem socially as well as psychologically pathological, the melodrama that is *La Vendetta* may seem to normalize the homosocial exchange between fathers and sons-in-law that is inscribed in the 1804 Civil Code. For all Balzac's exploitation of pathos, and his exaggeration of plot and character, is this an instance of mimetic writing at the service of a conservative patriarchal ideology?[17] If so, that ideology is contradicted by *La Maison du chat-qui-pelote*, which critically portrays the role of marriageable daughters in the transmission of property and does so in a more conventionally realist register. It is my third example of a nineteenth-century artist story in which a painter marries his or her painting; like *La Bourse* and *La Vendetta*, it will be discussed in the first instance as a Pygmalion narrative.

Notes to Chapter 3

1. *Balzac, ou les hiéroglyphes de l'imaginaire*, p. 53 (further references are given in the text).
2. For an overview of voyeuristic scenes in *La Comédie humaine*, see Max Milner, 'Les Dispositifs voyeuristes dans le récit balzacien', in *Balzac: Une poétique du roman*, ed. by Vachon, pp. 157–71.
3. Balzac, *La Vendetta*, ed. by Meininger, in *La Comédie humaine*, I, 1021–1102 (p. 1040).
4. In an earlier version of this passage, Balzac had specified that Girodet, Gérard or Gros would provide the education refused by Servin (I, 1540).
5. In an earlier version, Amélie trains her lorgnette on the drawing 'sans pudeur'. See Balzac, *La Maison du Chat-qui-pelote, Le Bal de Sceaux, La Vendetta*, ed. by Pierre-Georges Castex (Paris: Garnier, 1963), p. 370 (further references to this edition are given in the text).
6. The passage is a key one for Maurice Samuels's analysis of voyeurism, narcissism and fetishism as mediators, in *La Vendetta*, of 'la dimension historique de l'érotisme et la dimension érotique de l'histoire'. See 'L'Érotique de l'histoire: *La Vendetta* et l'image de Napoléon au XIXe siècle', in *L'Érotique balzacienne*, ed. by Lucienne Frappier-Mazur and Jean-Marie Roulin (Paris: SEDES, 2001), pp. 105–16 (p. 116).
7. As children, both escape murder by the other's family on the same day; Luigi is the only one of his regiment to survive the retreat from Moscow and to cross the Berezina, and he has narrowly eluded arrest with Labédoyère after the Hundred Days. The lovers' meeting in the shadow of the latter's death sentence might suggest that Ginevra falls in love with Luigi because of who he is, with the same inexorable logic that draws Sarrasine to Zambinella ('*en Zambinella, c'est le castrat que j'ai aimé*', as Barthes puts it in *S/Z* (p. 193)).
8. Had Piombo, like Frenhofer, been an artist, he could have fashioned his love-object from stone or paint and kept her safely shut up in his studio. As it is, his only defence is to try to keep his daughter away from the studio where it is she who has transformed a portrait into a husband. The underlying incest theme of the Pygmalion myth is interestingly displaced, in *La Vendetta*, to the relation between father and daughter (Samuels convincingly suggests that Ginevra falls in love with Luigi 'parce qu'il est à la fois son propre reflet et celui de son père' (p. 108)).
9. For fuller details, see Marie-Henriette Faillie, who interestingly notes that Ginevra is the only heroine of the *Comédie humaine* to turn to the Civil Code for protection of her rights. See *La Femme et le code civil dans 'La Comédie humaine' d'Honoré de Balzac* (Paris: Didier, 1968), pp. 69–70. The relevant clauses (Articles 152 and 153) are reproduced in Faillie's Appendix (p. 202). The age of majority was twenty-one for women and twenty-five for men, while the age at which they could marry without parental consent was twenty-five and thirty respectively. The *acte respectueux* had to be renewed twice, at monthly intervals, and a month later the marriage could take place whatever the formal answer. It is for this reason that Roguin tries to persuade Piombo of the pointlessness of withholding his consent.
10. To take Balzac's use of melodrama seriously is Christopher Prendergast's strategy in *Balzac: Fiction and Melodrama* (London: Edward Arnold, 1978). His main context is popular fiction of the 1830s and 1840s which he derives from the Gothic novel, rather than the sentimental visual melodrama of painting and theatre in Diderot's period. Linzy Erika Dickinson, in an excellent study of theatre in *La Comédie humaine*, argues that Balzac's use of painting metaphors 'strengthens rather than detracts from the impression that through metaphor Balzac is expressing dramaturgy after the manner of Diderot', and that Balzac's frequent use of the word *drame* 'expresses his own dramaturgy which is that of a realistic and intimate *drame bourgeois*'. See *Theatre in Balzac's 'La Comédie humaine'* (Amsterdam: Rodopi, 2000), p. 221, p. 226.
11. See *Absorption and Theatricality: Painting and Beholder in the Age of Diderot* (Berkeley and Los Angeles: University of California Press, 1980), p. 70. The studio scene in *La Vendetta* contains many of the absorption motifs identified by Fried, most notably avid contemplation, reverie

and sleep. The text as a whole would seem to embody a literary version of both the early and late Greuzian modes between which Fried distinguishes. In *Courbet's Realism*, which contains a useful overview of the concepts of absorption and theatricality (pp. 6–8), Fried returns to the difficult issue of evaluating Greuze's aesthetics. He notes the rapid shift from the 'documented ability' of *La Piété filiale* to 'hold contemporary audiences spellbound and even to move them to tears' to the way Greuze's art, in the space of a few decades, 'wholly lost its power to persuade and move', and did so in a way that coincides with its late twentieth-century reception (pp. 13–14). For Fried, the issue turns on the 'peculiar instability of historical determinations of what is and is not theatrical' (p. 15). To describe *La Vendetta* as 'melodramatic' in today's pejorative sense would equate to calling it 'theatrical' in Diderot's negative sense. I think it likely, however, that Balzac conceived *La Vendetta* as 'anti-theatrical' in the spirit of Fried's analysis of the relations between painting and beholder in Greuze. Earlier sketches of *La Malédiction paternelle* and *Le Fils puni* were enthusiastically described by Diderot in his 1765 *Salon* (see *Œuvres esthétiques*, ed. by Paul Vernière (Paris: Garnier, 1965), pp. 547–52).

12. See Brookner, *Greuze: The Rise and Fall of an Eighteenth-Century Phenomenon* (London: Elek, 1972), p. 122, p. 138, p. 149.

13. *La Vendetta* was originally divided into chapters with titles suggesting a cautionary tale: *L'Atelier*, *La Désobéissance*, *Le Mariage*, *Le Châtiment* (see I, 1536–38).

14. Meininger, for example, uses the Davin preface to support her claim that *La Vendetta*, along with other *Scènes de la vie privée*, had been written 'pour avertir les jeunes filles sur les conséquences fatales des illusions et des fautes de la passion' (I, 1034).

15. Jacques Lacan, *Écrits*, 2 vols (Paris: Seuil (Points), 1966), I, 157–58.

16. Balzac was familiar with Greuze's well-known *La Piété filiale*, in which the paralysed father has just been fed by his visibly loving and respectful son-in-law. Diderot's enthusiastic description makes this relation the emotive centre of the painting (see *Salon de 1763*, in *Œuvres esthétiques*, p. 525, p. 527).

17. For a sustained discussion of the ideology of mimesis in the nineteenth-century French novel, see Prendergast, *The Order of Mimesis: Balzac, Stendhal, Nerval, Flaubert* (Cambridge: Cambridge University Press, 1986).

CHAPTER 4

❖

La Maison du chat-qui-pelote

(i) 'Ce jeune marbre'

La Maison du chat-qui-pelote ends with an evocation of a marble cippus in the cimetière Montmartre. Its inscription informs the reader, as well as the passer-by, that 'madame de Sommervieux' died at the age of twenty-seven:

> Dans les simples lignes de cette épitaphe un ami de cette timide créature voit la dernière scène d'un drame. Chaque année, au jour solennel du 2 novembre, il ne passe jamais devant ce jeune marbre sans se demander s'il ne faut pas des femmes plus fortes que ne l'était Augustine pour les puissantes étreintes du génie.[1]

Augustine's early death is the logical denouement of the drama of her marriage to a famous artist, and her epitaph might well have included the resonant line from Poe's *The Oval Portrait*: 'And evil was the hour she saw, and loved, and wedded the painter.'[2] But this is no Gothic melodrama, and the Pygmalion elements of Augustine's story — brought alive by a painted likeness, she will return to a death in marble — are mapped onto the realist canvas that Balzac would retrospectively choose as the entry point to *La Comédie humaine*. Whereas, in *Sarrasine*, the story of a painting turns out to contain that of a statue — a statue that will survive the sculptor's violent attempt to destroy it, along with its model Zambinella — in *La Maison du chat-qui-pelote*, the 'jeune marbre' conceals the parallel life stories (from conception to destruction) of a painting and a marriage.

The passion of the aristocratic Sommervieux for a draper's daughter is explained by his recent return, sexually and aesthetically satiated, from seven years in Rome:

> Son âme nourrie de poésie, ses yeux rassasiés de Raphaël et de Michel-Ange, avaient soif de la nature vraie, après une longue habitation du pays pompeux où l'art a jeté partout son grandiose. [...] Abandonné longtemps à la fougue des passions italiennes, son cœur demandait une de ces vierges modestes et recueillies que, malheureusement, il n'avait su trouver qu'en peinture à Rome. (I, 53)

It is in this state of mind that, in the rue Saint-Denis, the painter chances upon 'un tableau qui aurait arrêté tous les peintres du monde' (I, 52). It is the privileged Pygmalionesque moment of nightfall and, once again, a chiaroscuro effect turns the 'real' interior of the Chat-qui-pelote, seen from the street through Sommervieux's eyes, into a virtual painting:

> Le magasin, n'étant pas encore éclairé, formait un plan noir au fond duquel se voyait la salle à manger du marchand. Une lampe astrale y répandait ce jour jaune qui donne tant de grâce aux tableaux de l'école hollandaise. Le linge blanc, l'argenterie, les cristaux formaient de brillants accessoires qu'embellissaient encore de vives oppositions entre l'ombre et la lumière. (I, 52)

Sommervieux's new-found sensibility is enthused by the modest domestic scene, the figures of which form an appealingly naive composition. The tableau is unposed — its actors are unaware they are being watched — and one could imagine the narrator's description as an ekphrasis lifted from one of Diderot's *Salons*:

> La figure du père de famille et celle de sa femme, les visages des commis et les formes pures d'Augustine, à deux pas de laquelle se tenait une grosse fille joufflue, composaient un groupe si curieux; ces têtes étaient si originales, et chaque caractère avait une expression si franche; on devinait si bien la paix, le silence et la modeste vie de cette famille, que, pour un artiste accoutumé à exprimer la nature, il y avait quelque chose de désespérant à vouloir rendre cette scène fortuite. (I, 52–53)

While it is specified that Sommervieux's aesthetic and moral enthusiasm is a reaction to this 'tableau naturel' as a whole, the whole contains its part, and the painter 'passa naturellement à une profonde admiration pour la figure principale' (I, 53). This is the pensive Augustine, a painter's virgin but also a real young women who happens to meet the needs of Sommervieux's jaded heart. Augustine's 'formes pures' are sculptural, and the light from the ceiling lamp, falling directly upon her, makes them hover between art and life: 'Son buste semblait se mouvoir dans un cercle de feu qui détachait plus vivement les contours de sa tête et l'illuminait d'une manière quasi surnaturelle. [...] Une sensation presque inconnue, un amour limpide et bouillonnant inonda son cœur.' (I, 53) The next morning Sommervieux goes straight to his studio, and leaves it only when he has 'déposé sur une toile la magie de cette scène dont le souvenir l'avait en quelque sorte fanatisé. Sa félicité fut incomplète tant qu'il ne posséda pas un fidèle portrait de son idole.' (I, 53) Augustine's portrait is effectively an enlarged detail of the naive interior of the Chat-qui-pelote; indeed, Sommervieux will enter the shop in disguise 'afin de voir de plus près la ravissante créature que Madame Guillaume couvrait de son aile' (I, 53). This last image, combined with an eight-month withdrawal from the world that seems close to a period of gestation — 'adonné à son amour, à ses pinceaux, il resta invisible pour ses amis les plus intimes' (I, 53) — suggests that Augustine has been incubated at the Chat-du-pelote, and will be ready to emerge into life when she recognizes herself in the 'toile vivante' of Sommervieux's completed portrait.

The brilliantly conceived 'scène du Salon' (I, 58), in which painter, portrait and unknowing model are brought together in the midst of the thronging crowds at the Louvre, allows an art-historical overview that integrates Sommervieux's fictional paintings into the real world of early nineteenth-century French art:

> La scène d'intérieur fit une révolution dans la peinture. [...] Quant au portrait, il est peu d'artistes qui ne gardent le souvenir de cette toile vivante à laquelle le public, quelquefois juste en masse, laissa la couronne que Girodet y plaça lui-même. Les deux tableaux furent entourés d'une foule immense. (I, 54)

For all that Sommervieux's paintings have become a cultural talking point in Paris, such is the social isolation and unworldliness of the Chat-qui-pelote ('la petite Thébaïde de la rue Saint-Denis' (I, 55)) that it is sheer chance that Augustine should turn up at the Salon with her mother's cousin. If Castex is right that the Salon in question is that of 1810,[3] there were apparently so many paintings that year that the portraits were exhibited in a separate room. The crowds were indeed extraordinary (the Salon was a would-be democratic institution and entry was free), and a one-way system was in operation to control the circulation of so many visitors.[4] Thus it is entirely convincing that Augustine should become separated from Mme Roguin, and that, when she refinds her cousin, who is still attempting to fight her way to the portrait, the two women should be swept by the crowd right up to the 'petit tableau de chevalet'. Recounted from Augustine's point of view, however, it is an extraordinary sequence, somewhere between a bewildering dream and a fairy tale.[5] Her recognition of herself as the subject of the famous portrait triggers the first symptom of a bodily reaction ('un frisson la fit trembler comme une feuille de bouleau' (I, 55)); it overwhelms her as the episode progresses and builds up to a climax ('cette pantomime jeta comme un braiser dans le corps de la pauvre fille' (I, 56)) in which terror and joy are increasingly indistinguishable. Tearing herself away the portrait and from the 'figure enflammée' (I, 55) of the artist, she is carried by the unpredictable surges of the crowd to the painted interior of the Chat-qui-pelote. It is a second recognition scene that begins to make sense of the first:

> L'exclamation de surprise que jeta la femme du notaire se perdit dans le brouhaha et les bourdonnements de la foule; quant à Augustine, elle pleura involontairement à l'aspect de cette merveilleuse scène, et par un sentiment preque inexplicable, elle mit un doigt sur ses lèvres en apercevant à deux pas d'elle la figure extatique du jeune artiste. (I, 55–56)

In an extension of the Pygmalion motif that brings art to life, the pictures merge for Augustine with the visitors to the Salon, and this literal mêlée of 'figures vivantes ou peintes', of dazzling costumes and gold frames, produces an intoxicating kaleidoscope of colours that might well have made her faint, 'si, malgré ce chaos de sensations, il ne s'était élevé au fond de son cœur une jouissance inconnue qui vivifia tout son être' (I, 56). Recognizing the desires she has been brought up to believe sinful, Augustine experiences a veritable 'moment de folie'. Her metamorphosis is complete when, giving in to her feelings, she allows herself to look at the painter: 'jamais l'incarnat de ses joues n'avait formé de plus vigoureux contrastes avec la blancheur de sa peau' (I, 56). The living qualities of the portrait — 'cette toile vivante' — are now incarnated in its model: 'L'artiste aperçut alors cette beauté dans toute sa fleur, cette pudeur dans toute sa gloire.' (I, 56)

Sommervieux's withdrawal of his pictures from the Salon, immediately after Augustine's visit, is seen by her as 'la révélation d'une délicatesse de sentiment que les femmes savent toujours apprécier' (I, 58). The plot requires, of course, that neither Mme Roguin nor Augustine's parents (who go to the Louvre the next day in search of the picture of their house) should know that Augustine is the subject of the equally famous portrait. However, Sommervieux had already refused to sell his paintings at any price, or to permit copies or engravings, as if (despite exhibiting

Augustine to *le tout-Paris*) he was jealously guarding possession of a unique representation of a unique object of passion. Ironically, the Salon does turn out to be the only public appearance of Augustine's portrait, for all the lasting impression it is deemed to have made on the artists of the day; within just a few years it will have been destroyed, leaving no copy. First, this unique, supposedly inalienable portrait of Augustine will be handed over to the painter's mistress; next, when the Duchesse de Carigliano, tiring of Sommervieux, sees in the picture a cynical means of sending him back to his wife — via whom, with malicious foresight, she returns it — he will smash the painting to pieces in Augustine's presence. So much, then, for Augustine's momentous discovery at the Salon that she is loved by '[celui] dont le talent donnait l'immortalité à de passagères images' (I, 56). As it turns out, the portrait is no more immortal than the model, for neither has unique or lasting value for Sommervieux.

An unfaithful Pygmalion seems not to have been programmed by Ovid. In the many literary variations on the theme, the artist is often metaphorically adulterous, preferring his painting to his wife or sexual partner (typically the model, as in Zola's *L'Œuvre*), while in generically fantastic stories, such as Henry James's *The Last of the Valerii* or Mérimée's *La Vénus d'Ille*, the trouble-making work of art is often a statue. Sommervieux, by contrast, is a real adulterer who is unfaithful to his wife with a flesh-and-blood woman; however, he is also a serial Pygmalion, for whom one work of art makes way, albeit somewhat parodically, for another. I am thinking not so much of the portrait he conceives to humiliate the mistress who is abandoning him in her turn — '"je la peindrai! oui, je la représenterai sous les traits de Messaline sortant à la nuit du palais de Claude"' (I, 92)[6] — as of the tableau that greets the astonished Augustine when she visits her rival, 'non pas pour lui redemander le cœur de son mari, mais pour s'y instruire des artifices qui le lui avaient enlevé' (I, 84):

> Au fond de ce frais boudoir, elle vit la duchesse voluptueusement couchée sur une ottomane en velours vert placée au centre d'une espèce de demi-cercle dessiné par les plis moelleux d'une mousseline tendue sur un fond jaune. Des ornements de bronze doré, disposés avec un goût exquis, rehaussaient encore cette espèce de dais sous lequel la duchesse était posée comme une statue antique. La couleur foncée du velours ne lui laissait perdre aucun moyen de séduction. Un demi-jour, ami de sa beauté, semblait être plutôt un reflet qu'une lumière. (I, 86)

When 'cette artificieuse duchesse' (I, 87) who, as Augustine immediately understands, is as false as this scenario in which she poses as a statue, leads the spurned wife to her portrait, Balzac juxtaposes this painting with its model for the second time in the story. The painting hangs in 'une somptueuse galerie' (I, 90), but this recognition scene — 'A cet aspect, Augustine jeta un cri' — is a murky sequel to the magical episode in the Louvre:

> — Je savais bien qu'il n'était plus chez moi, dit-elle, mais... ici!
> — Ma chère petite, je ne l'ai exigé que pour voir jusqu'à quel degré de bêtise un homme de génie peut atteindre. Tôt ou tard, il vous aurait été rendu par moi, car je ne m'attendais pas au plaisir de voir ici l'original devant la copie. (I, 90–91)

The duchess's insincere painting metaphor — 'l'original devant la copie' — returns Augustine to her status as a painting, even as it underlines that she could, after all, circulate as a copy. Armed with the supposed talisman of her portrait, but in fact an unsuspecting go-between, Augustine returns home with no better plan for winning back her husband than to put the portrait in her bedroom and wait for Sommervieux's return.

Is it the duchess's metaphor, or her seductive pose as a glowing statue, that gives Augustine the imprudent idea of turning herself back into her portrait, thereby staging a Pygmalion scenario for the benefit of the artist-husband who no longer loves her: 'Elle eut l'idée de faire une toilette qui la rendît semblable en tout point au portrait. Puis, connaissant le caractère inquiet de son mari, elle fit éclairer son appartement d'une manière inusitée, certaine qu'en rentrant la curiosité l'amènerait chez elle.' (I, 92) If her artificially illuminated bedroom is a reminder, for the reader, of the unusual light effects of the interior that first stopped Sommervieux in his tracks, it is the 'scène du Salon' that she now tries to recreate in her bedroom: 'elle s'élança au cou de son mari et lui montra le portrait' (I, 92). Her naive plan is successful to the extent that she lures the painter into playing his part, but her attempt to reverse cause and effect (to look just like the portrait) has a predictable outcome. As Sommervieux takes in the fact that the portrait is in Augustine's possession, and even as he absorbs the connoted message from his mistress, he does indeed reconnect the portrait with his wife: 'L'artiste resta immobile comme un rocher, et ses yeux se dirigèrent alternativement sur Augustine et sur la toile accusatrice.' (I, 92)[7] As a result, the destructive violence of 'un artiste en proie aux tortures de la vanité blessée' (I, 92) falls equally upon the returned portrait and upon its human double. What happens exactly is not described in the text: 'il serait odieux de peindre toute cette scène à la fin de laquelle l'ivresse de la colère suggéra à l'artiste des paroles et des actes qu'une femme moins jeune qu'Augustine aurait attribués à la démence' (I, 92–93). However, it is clear that both painting and model have been violated when, the next morning, 'madame Guillaume surprit sa fille pâle, les yeux rouges, la coiffure en désordre, [...] contemplant sur le parquet les fragments épars d'une toile déchirée et les morceaux d'un grand cadre doré mis en pièces' (I, 93).

Throughout this bedroom scene, from the moment Augustine first reads the symptoms of her husband's impending violence, colour and life drain from her ('la timide épouse demi-morte [...] crut sentir son sang se figer dans ses veines' (I, 92–93)). Now, in the presence of her mother, 'Augustine, que la douleur rendait presque insensible, montra ces débris par un geste empreint de désespoir.' (I, 93) In a final recall of the scene in the Louvre, where she implicitly accepted the painter's love by placing a warning finger to her lips ('mit un doigt sur ses lèvres' (I, 55)), she repeats that gesture — though her lips are now drained of blood — in an attempt to stem the flow of her mother's platitudes: 'Augustine mit un doigt sur ses lèvres pâlies, comme pour implorer de sa mère un moment de silence.' (I, 93) At this point, Balzac introduces into his narrative a temporal ellipsis of some five years. However, by the very next paragraph, Augustine and her portrait have metamorphosed into the modest marble column that marks her grave.[8]

(ii) ' "N'est-ce pas elle... que... j'aime?" '

In *Art and Illusion*, E. H. Gombrich devotes a marvellous chapter ('Pygmalion's Power') to 'belief in the power of art to create rather than to portray'. It is a function of art he presents as both 'earlier and more awe-inspiring' than the 'imitation of nature' he has addressed so far; his engaging examples, such as what happens when we build a snowman ('We do not say, "Shall we represent a man who is smoking?" but "Shall we give him a pipe?" ') are as conceptually challenging as they are wilfully naive. In this spirit, or perhaps because he does not really like Ovid's 'erotic novelette', he quotes as an epigraph a fairy tale of the Guiana Indians:

> Once there was an old man whose name was Nahokoboni. He was troubled in his mind because he had no daughter, and who could look after him if he had no son-in-law? Being a witch doctor, he therefore carved himself a daughter out of a plum tree.[9]

Gombrich makes no comment on this curious instance of a Pygmalion myth where creation is predicated upon the need to acquire a son-in-law. In my analysis of *La Vendetta*, I suggested that the violent refusal of exogamy that underpins Piombo's behaviour is presented as so pathological — socially as well as psychologically — that it risks normalizing the exchange of daughters that is institutionalized in the Civil Code. In Augustine's father, M. Guillaume, Balzac has created an exemplary anti-Piombo, dedicated to handing on the Maison du chat-qui-pelote to a capable son-in-law, in the same way that it had been transmitted to him when he married the daughter of his late employer Chevrel. Just as the son-in-law has long since been chosen, so too has the daughter who will be handed over to Joseph Lebas with the business, for Guillaume (more fortunate in this respect than Nahokoboni) has the luxury of possessing two daughters. In the Sunday-morning dialogue between Guillaume and his future son-in-law, Balzac exploits the device of a comic quid pro quo to pinpoint what is at stake when one man transmits his property to another through a conjugal alliance:

> — Comment, monsieur? [...] vous sauriez qui j'aime?
> — Je sais tout, vaurien, lui dit le respectable et rusé marchand en lui tordant le bout de l'oreille. Et je te pardonne, j'ai fait de même.
> — Et vous me l'accorderiez?
> — Oui, avec cinquante mille écus, et je t'en laisserai autant, et nous marcherons sur nouveaux frais avec une nouvelle raison sociale. [...] Vois-tu, mon gendre, il n'y a que le commerce! (I, 62)

When Joseph's emotional outpouring (' "je l'aime tant, tant" ') reaches its enthusiastic climax (' "Mademoiselle Augustine, mademoiselle Augustine!" ' (I, 63)), the reality of the transaction is rapidly absorbed by the future son-in-law:

> — Qu'est-ce que fait donc Augustine dans cette affaire-là? demanda Guillaume dont la voix glaça sur-le-champ le malheureux Joseph Lebas.
> — N'est-ce pas elle... que... j'aime? dit le commis en balbutiant. (I, 63)

As we have seen, as sexual partner and as work of art, Augustine will turn out, after marriage, to remain open to exchange. In her days as a marriageable daughter she was not only exchangeable, but also interchangeable: '"Joseph, reprit le négociant avec une dignité froide, je vous parlais de Virginie."' (I, 63)

The handover from Chevrel to Guillaume of both Mlle Chevrel and the business is presented in the story as the defining moment of Guillaume's life. The relation between father- and son-in-law, which frames the famous image of the 'chat qui pelotait', is inscribed for all to read:

> A droite du tableau, sur un champ d'azur qui déguisait imparfaitement la pourriture du bois, les passants lisaient GUILLAUME; et à gauche, SUCCESSEUR DU SIEUR CHEVREL. Le soleil et la pluie avaient rongé la plus grande partie de l'or moulu parcimonieusement appliqué sur les lettres de cette inscription, dans laquelle les U remplaçaient les V et réciproquement, selon les lois de notre ancienne orthographe. (I, 41)

Marriage to Chevrel's daughter has allowed Guillaume permanently to mingle his weathered letters with those of his revered employer — the Vs of Guillaume with the U of Chevrel — while their relation is re-flagged in what is presumably a daily ritual: an ancient retainer ('vraisemblablement contemporain de l'enseigne') opens the shop door and, with trembling hand, 'y attacha le morceau de drap carré sur lequel était brodé en soie jaune le nom de *Guillaume, successeur de Chevrel*' (I, 43). Guillaume's discourse is punctuated by nostalgic references to his father-in-law and role model — '"quand j'étais chez le sieur Chevrel"' (I, 46); '"Je mourrai dans ce tracas-là, comme le vieux Chevrel"' (I, 62–63); '"ce pauvre père Chevrel!"' (I, 67) — with whom he clearly hopes to be reunited in the afterlife: '"si j'allais trouver trop tôt le père Chevrel"' (I, 71). When nobody, despite her large dowry, shows an interest in marrying his twenty-eight-year-old daughter, Guillaume's half-formulated plan — 'aussi Joseph Lebas, son premier commis, orphelin et sans fortune, était-il, dans son idée, le futur époux de Virginie' — takes concrete form through the recollection of his own marriage to Mlle Chevrel: 'Quelle belle affaire que de marier sa fille et d'acquitter une dette sacrée, en rendant le bienfait qu'il avait reçu jadis de son prédécesseur dans les mêmes circonstances!' (I, 52).

In the wonderful little scene that precedes his Sunday morning summons of Joseph, it is clear that Guillaume's nostalgia derives from the cementing of his relationship with his father-in-law, rather than that with his wife. At seven in the morning, while the rest of the house sleeps off the previous night's celebration of the *clôture* of the annual inventory, Guillaume, shaved and carefully costumed in his best attire, enters what for him is the symbolic heart of the Chat-qui-pelote, the heavily barred 'petit cabinet attenant à son magasin du premier étage' (I, 60). In an emotional and compulsive re-enactment of his past, Guillaume, self-conscious pivot of a genealogical chain, identifies with both Chevrel and Joseph as he prepares to change status from son-in-law to father-in-law: 'Le marchand resta debout la main posée sur le bras crasseux d'un fauteuil de canne doublé de maroquin dont la couleur primitive était effacée, il semblait hésiter à s'y asseoir'. (I, 60) His hesitation is explained when he succeeds in conjuring up the ghosts of the past amongst the poetically evoked paraphernalia of the drapery business: 'Il contempla les cartons numérotés, les ficelles, les ustensiles, les fers à marquer le drap, la caisse, objets d'une origine immémoriale, et crut se revoir devant l'ombre évoquée du sieur Chevrel.' (I, 61)

The modest scenario he stages recreates the precise layout of the long-past scene:

> Il avança le même tabouret sur lequel il s'était jadis assis en présence de son
> défunt patron. Ce tabouret garni de cuir noir, et dont le crin s'échappait depuis
> longtemps par les coins mais sans se perdre, il le plaça d'une main tremblante au
> même endroit où son prédécesseur l'avait mis; puis, dans une agitation difficile
> à décrire, il tira la sonnette qui correspondait au chevet de lit de Joseph Lebas.
> (I, 61)

Joseph's love for the wrong daughter introduces a crisis that turns out to be a minor
one; it is easily accommodated by the social structure it serves to uncover. In the
first instance, Guillaume tries to persuade Joseph to follow his example: '"Mlle
Chevrel n'était pas belle [...]. Fais donc comme moi."' (I, 64) However, such is
his affection for his *premier commis* that, despite his awareness of Virginie's love for
Joseph, and despite his total ignorance of the feelings of Augustine, Guillaume is
willing to contemplate Joseph marrying his younger daughter instead, as long as
her sister is somehow married first: '"Que veux-tu? Cela s'arrangera peut-être [...].
Allons, sarpejeu, mon enfant, donne ce matin le bras à Augustine pour aller à la
messe."' (I, 64) On this basis, Joseph 'songeait déjà pour Mlle Virginie à l'un de ses
amis' (I, 64); indeed, he has already tipped off his friend to 'demander Mlle Virginie
en mariage' (I, 66) when he receives the disappointing news: 'Guillaume désespéra
Joseph Lebas en lui confiant l'amour d' Augustine pour un étranger' (I, 66). While
Virginie is left in ignorance of the developments that concern her so crucially,
Guillaume conscientiously reports back to his chosen successor. By the evening, the
future of the Maison du chat-qui-pelote will have been resolved by the fortuitously
timed discovery of Augustine's romance with Sommervieux; Guillaume, who has
been presented with a means to 'se tirer d'affaire' (I, 64), 'alla trouver Joseph Lebas,
et l'instruisit de l'état des choses' (I, 70). It is inevitable that Joseph, 'qui prenait
son bonheur en patience' (I, 70), will accept the substitution of the unattractive,
unwanted Virginie for the sister whom, that very morning, he naively thought he
loved ('"N'est-ce pas elle... que... j'aime?"'). The essential relationship — '"Hein,
Joseph! Guillaume et Lebas, ces mots ne feraient-ils pas une belle raison sociale?"'
(I, 61) — had been sealed in the early-morning meeting in Guillaume's *cabinet*,
when, in an ironically worded acceptance of a contract, Joseph 'sortit du cabinet
enfumé en serrant la main de son futur beau-père' (I, 64).

A few months later, 'le maître-autel de Saint-Leu fut témoin de deux mariages
bien différents' (I, 71); the one is wordly, and exudes love, elegance and happiness,
the other is modest, domestic and subdued: 'Virginie, appuyée sur le bras de son
père, suivait sa jeune sœur humblement et dans de plus simples atours, comme une
ombre nécessaire aux harmonies de ce tableau.' (I, 72) The pictorial simile implies
a closer link between these two marriages than may superficially seem the case. As
in the case of Du Halga, the metaphorical shadow who follows Kergarouët in *La
Bourse*, a part of the picture that appears unimportant can open up the significance
of the whole. When Virginie is introduced to the reader as 'tout le portrait de sa
mère' (I, 48), the cruel caricature that follows highlights her mother's lack of appeal
('sans grâces et sans manières aimables' (I, 48)), even as it explains to the reader why
Guillaume had married her:

> Mme Guillaume, fille du sieur Chevrel, se tenait si droite sur la banquette de
> son comptoir, que plus d'une fois elle avait entendu des plaisants parier qu'elle
> y était empalée. [...] Ses gestes avaient quelque chose des mouvements saccadés
> d'un télégraphe. Son œil, clair comme celui d'un chat, semblait en vouloir à
> tout le monde de ce qu'elle était laide. (I, 48)

Virginie barely escapes her mother's looks ('l'air disgracieux que sa ressemblance
avec sa mère donnait parfois à sa figure' (I, 48)), even if the very rigours of the
maternal upbringing ('les lois despotiques de leur mère' (I, 48)) have made her
mild-tempered and patient. Whatever proportion of Mme Guillaume's ugliness
might be inherited from her own mother, doubtless her 'dévotion outrée' (I, 48),
and the prudish, soul-destroying principles that flow from it, derive from a Mme
Chevrel who does not merit any place at all in Guillaume's nostalgic returns to his
past. When, as her own brilliant marriage collapses, Augustine turns to her sister
for advice, she discovers in 'la femme du prudent Lebas' (I, 78) an exact replica of
their mother, despite the many improvements Joseph has introduced into the daily
regime: 'La sœur d'Augustine occupait au comptoir antique la place de sa mère.
[...] La femme du peintre vit que, sauf les barbes au bonnet, sa mère avait trouvé
dans Virginie un successeur qui conservait l'antique honneur du Chat-qui-pelote.'
(I, 78) But the resemblance between daughter and mother goes beyond their shared
appearance and narrow outlook, for they occupy the same structural position as
vehicles of the transmission of the family business. That they seem happy to do
so is hardly the point, no more, perhaps, than Joseph's sympathetically treated
but entirely transitory despair. Despite the words that Virginie was unfortunate
enough to overhear on the famous Sunday afternoon — 'elle apprit que Lebas
aimait Augustine' (I, 66) and had, as it were, refused her — marriage to Virginie is
the foundation of Joseph Lebas's considerable success as business man and general
luminary of the world of commerce.[10] While his future can be tracked through the
pages of *La Comédie humaine* (when he retires in the 1840s it is to take up a peerage),
one detail, which concerns the plot of *La Cousine Bette*, is especially striking. Nearly
thirty years later, in 1838, a proposed marriage between Joseph Lebas's son and
Hortense Hulot will be called off when inquiries into her father's finances reveal
that the dowry is unlikely to be paid. Not that Hortense, who only learns the
identity of this potential husband from her cousin Bette — '"il s'agit (je puis te dire
cela) d'un conseiller à la Cour royale"'[11] — has any more desire than Augustine to
find herself married off to a Lebas. Indeed, Hortense is about to contrive a *mariage
d'amour* with a talented sculptor, and one strand of a Balzacian artist story is about
to repeat itself.

(iii) 'Cette gothique façade'

Augustine's sad pilgrimage to the Chat-qui-pelote is introduced as follows:

> Un matin donc, elle se dirigea vers la grotesque façade de l'humble et silen-
> cieuse maison où s'était écoulée son enfance. Elle soupira en revoyant cette
> croisée d'où, un jour, elle avait envoyé un premier baiser à celui qui répandait
> aujourd'hui sur sa vie autant de gloire que de malheur. (I, 78)

The final words are a reminder that the story was initially published as 'Gloire et Malheur', and that its seemingly self-evident title, *La Maison du chat-qui-pelote*, was introduced by Balzac only when he positioned this text, in 1842, as the façade of *La Comédie humaine*. Rarely can a new title have been so perfectly chosen. Its artless simplicity is a subtle and artful effect that is carefully anchored in the text's opening description of the curious frontage of the house ('l'apparente simplicité de cette gothique façade' (I, 44)) and the 'peinture naïve' (I, 40) of the famous shop sign. The ancient and caricatural representation of 'un chat qui pelotait' gives its name not just to the drapery business it advertises, but to the story with which both house and business — 'la maison du chat qui pelote' — are made to coincide. Augustine's return to her childhood home takes her inside the 'humble et silencieuse maison' where she stays long enough to dine with Virginie, Joseph and the apprentices in the *salle à manger* made famous by her husband's painting. Yet it is to the 'grotesque façade' that Balzac first directs Augustine, and towards the Raphaelesque virgin's third-floor *croisée* that he makes her look up and sigh.

In a brief scene set in Sommervieux's studio, Girodet's 'lente et avide contemplation des deux chefs-d'œuvre' (I, 54) was followed by the advice, which his friend ignored, not to send the paintings to the Salon: 'Ces couleurs vraies, ce travail prodigieux ne peuvent pas encore être appréciés, le public n'est pas accoutumé à tant de profondeur. Les tableaux que nous peignons, mon bon ami, sont des écrans, des paravents.' (I, 54) The implied distinction between flatness and depth, attributed here to Girodet, is reminiscent of the anxious relation between painting and sculpture, and between writing and fullness, that lies at the heart of Barthes's reading of *Sarrasine*. Having started my analysis of *La Maison du chat-qui-pelote* with its ending — the marble cippus that metaphorically figures the deceased 'madame de Sommervieux' — I shall end with a reading of its famously pictorial opening sequence: Balzac's tour-de-force description of the metonymic façade of the Chat-qui-pelote as viewed by the artist and husband-to-be. What is the relation between the façade, Sommervieux's paintings and the narrative that fills out the space between beginning and end of this artist's story?

When Augustine, her head full of Sommervieux, asks Joseph what he thinks of painting as a profession, he responds with relative enthusiasm: '"je connais un maître peintre en bâtiment [...] qui a des écus"' (I, 65). His confusion of two sorts of painting appears a cultural gaffe on a par with that of Guillaume, who finds common ground with the artist in their shared passion for drapery: '"Vous aimez donc la draperie, [...] touchez-là, mon jeune ami."' (I, 70) Yet the discussion of drapery is motivated by Sommervieux's gift to his future parents-in-law of the painted interior of the Chat-qui-pelote, which represents not just the dining room in which the handover takes place, but also the draper's merchandise that Joseph finds so lifelike: '"Et ces étoffes dépliés, on les prendrait avec la main."' (I, 70) In short, it is an everyday commercial interior that 'fit une révolution dans la peinture' (I, 54), and Balzac's heavy wordplay reminds us that commerce, in this flagship story, is the subject matter of his own art. The precarious-looking exterior evoked in its opening paragraphs ('ce débris de la bourgeoisie du seizième siècle' (I, 39)) incorporates a shop sign described as a masterpiece of caricatural art. The façade could also be seen, broadly, as a celebration of the rough art of the joiners and painters — a first draft of the passage explicitly mentions 'le badigeonneur' (I, 1182) — who, with some help from the erosive effects of three centuries of Parisian weather, have combined to produce its visually extravagant features. Indeed, for the narrator, the façade is the ground for a set of metaphorical verbs — *barioler, tracer, dessiner, rechampir* — that tend to collapse the difference between building construction, naive architecture and art.

The opening description is different in degree of realism from that of the interior of the shop at nightfall, where it is light falling from overhead, contrasting with a foreground in darkness, that transforms the distanced family group into a living painting, even before Sommervieux has transposed it to canvas. Although the strengthening light of daybreak on a rainy March morning increases what little can be seen of the interior, the façade itself is not subject to the light effects that typically bring Balzac's interiors to life. Its portrayal, verging on the two dimensional, strays very little from its own minor deviations from its vertical plane. The distorted triangular roof projects just three feet into the street, protecting the vulnerable wooden walls of the attic, as well as the threshold of the shop door, so that when Guillaume magically materializes on the latter for his morning inspection of the rue Saint-Denis, he remains within the narrow horizontal range of the façade, as if embossed upon it with the furrows combed into his hair, the horizontal wrinkles traced on his forehead ('aussi nombreuses que les plis de son habit' (I, 45)), and the little eyes that look as if they have been pierced with a gimlet. Sommervieux is stationed on the other side of the street, and much of the description is filtered through his eyes, either directly (what he sees), or indirectly (what he fails to see or what does not attract his interest). However, this does not introduce an effect of width, partly because the house is relatively tall (three floors and an attic in addition to the ground-floor shop), and partly because the painter is close enough to be baptized by the shaving water carefully squirted from the attic by a jovial *commis*. The narrator's sculptural metaphor for the three chubby-faced apprentices turns them into part of the façade: 'trois joyeuses figures rondelettes, blanches, roses, mais aussi communes que les figures du Commerce sculptées sur certains monuments' (I, 42), before transposing them into a picture of cherubs painted into the frame of their window: 'Ces trois faces, encadrées par la lucarne, rappelaient les têtes d'anges bouffis semés dans les nuages qui accompagnent le Père éternel.' (I, 42) The sudden opening of the attic window was missed by Sommervieux due to his increasing irritation with his long wait; by the time he disdainfully shakes the soap-scented spray from his coat and looks up, the apprentices have withdrawn to the back of their attic, which is just far enough behind the window, if they stand on tiptoe, for them to observe the effects of their joke without being seen.

However, at the very moment Sommervieux raises his scornful eyes to the empty attic window, the picture of commerce gives way to one of art: 'une main blanche et délicate fit remonter vers l'imposte la partie inférieure d'une des grossières croisées du troisième étage' (I, 43). The appearance of Augustine at her window follows a similar pattern to that of the *commis*, for it culminates in her sudden withdrawal behind the plane of the façade when she spots Sommervieux looking up at her: 'la coquetterie la fit sans doute souffrir d'être vue en déshabillé, elle se retira vivement en arrière' (I, 43). The humour of this episode is underlined, should anyone be in doubt, by the sudden descent of the heavy sash window provoked by the hastiness of her retreat: 'le tourniquet tout usé tourna, la croisée redescendit avec cette rapidité qui, de nos jours, a valu un nom odieux à cette naïve invention de nos ancêtres, et la vision disparut' (I, 43).[12] The reader had been warned from the outset of the unreliability of the window mechanism ('ces coulisses dont le tourniquet laisse souvent tomber à l'improviste le lourd vitrage qu'il doit retenir' (I, 43)); however, for as long as the vision lasts, 'la vieillesse de cette fenêtre massive aux contours grossiers, dont l'appui était noir' (I, 43), forms a *repoussoir* for the youthful charms of the flower-like maiden. Her sculpted features are credited to the sleep from which she has yet fully to emerge ('la jeunesse des joues de cette figure, sur laquelle le sommeil avait comme mis en relief une surabondance de vie' (I, 43)), as are the glimpses of her body: 'Quoique couverts d'une étoffe brune, son cou, ses épaules s'apercevaient, grâce à de légers interstices ménagés par les mouvements du sommeil.' (I, 43) Predictably, Augustine has been transformed into a Raphael virgin: 'Aucune expression de contrainte n'altérait ni l'ingénuité de ce visage, ni le calme de ces yeux immortalisés par avance dans les sublimes compositions de Raphael: c'était la même grâce, la même tranquillité de ces vierges devenues proverbiales.' (I, 43) The aesthetic compartmentalization of Augustine seems to be ironically inflected here (the art-historical commonplace is acknowledged), in line with the less than poetic manner in which this all too brief vision is abolished. Moreover, it is important to stress that this is not, as some critical readings imply, Sommervieux's first vision of Augustine;[13] her portrait has long been completed and their first meeting is far enough in the past to explain the painter's frustration ('les deux amants se voyaient pour la quatrième fois depuis la scène du Salon' (I, 58)). The initial erotic investment in an aesthetic image had taken place up to a year earlier, when the painter first chanced upon the magical family tableau in the depths of the Chat-qui-pelote, and fell in love with Augustine because she was part of it. Although Balzac must have considered introducing his story with that foundational scene, he chose not to do so. Instead he restricts his opening description to the exterior of the Chat-qui-pelote, and appends an ironic cameo of Augustine — another metaphorical low relief — to the pictorial plane of its façade.

As master draper and artist inspect each other across the narrow space of the street, Balzac sets up a familiar cultural collision — 'Cet étrange jeune homme devait être aussi curieux pour les commerçants du Chat-qui-pelote que le Chat-qui-pelote l'était pour lui' (I, 42) — in which differences are comically magnified: '[Guillaume] aperçut alors le passant en faction, qui, de son côté, contemplait le patriarche de la draperie, comme Humboldt dut examiner le premier gymnote électrique qu'il vit en Amérique' (I, 44). While Guillaume concludes that 'cette sinistre figure en voulait à la caisse du Chat-qui-pelote' (I, 45), it is Joseph Lebas who, 'après avoir discrètement joui du duel muet qui avait lieu entre son patron et l'inconnu' (I, 45), notes the stranger's furtive contemplation of the third-floor windows. What was in fact already a *face-à-face* between father and would-be son-in-law, is transformed into a four-way comedy of looks between father, two sons-in-law and daughter, as Joseph first joins Guillaume on the threshold of the shop ('le plus âgé des commis hasarda de se placer sur la dalle où était M. Guillaume' (I, 46)), then boldly steps out from the plane of the façade: 'Il fit deux pas dans la rue, leva la tête, et crut avoir aperçu Mlle Augustine Guillaume qui se retirait avec précipitation.' (I, 46) Acknowledging Joseph's correct interpretation of Sommervieux's presence (if not the reason behind such astuteness), Guillaume, 'mécontent de la perspicacité de son premier commis, lui lança un regard de travers' (I, 46). Effectively exposed by his rival, Sommervieux departs the scene with affected indifference, and the façade, on which the Chevrel-Guillaume relation is already inscribed, gives way to the story of two marriages: the one with art, the other with commerce.

Uncharacteristically, Guillaume had ignored the arrival of his apprentices. Not having suspected a connection between Sommervieux and his third-floor windows, he had been trying to work out why 'le jeune homme en bas de soie et en manteau portait alternativement les yeux sur son enseigne et sur les profondeurs de son magasin' (I, 45). The quotation captures very neatly Girodet's opposition between pictures as screens and pictures with depth, and furthers my attempt to establish the relation between the façade and the story behind it. It will require a narrative flashback to explain why, as the inside of the shop becomes visible with the increasing light, 'le trop curieux étranger semblait convoiter ce petit local, y prendre le plan d'une salle à manger latérale, éclairée par un vitrage pratiqué dans le plafond' (I, 45). However, for anyone but the genuine first-time reader, the chronological priority of Sommervieux's *tableau de chevalet* and, before that, of the 'real' twilight tableau that inspired it, can be summoned up to fill out the empty interior. The shop sign, meanwhile, has been presented by the narrator as a marvellous caricature: 'Au milieu de cette large poutre mignardement sculptée se trouvait un antique tableau représentant un chat qui pelotait. [...] Il faut dire que le plus spirituel des peintres modernes n'inventerait pas de charge si comique.' (I, 40) The flair with which it has been conceived, and the skill of its execution — 'Dessin, couleurs, accessoires, tout était traité de manière à faire croire que l'artiste avait voulu se moquer du marchand et des passants.' (I, 40) — make the artist in Sommervieux smile despite himself each time he lowers his eyes from the third-floor windows to the shop: 'cette toile causait la gaieté du jeune homme' (I, 40). While Augustine, Guillaume and the apprentices are turned into metaphorical pictures by the windows and doorway that frame them, the *enseigne* of the Maison du Chat-qui-pelote is a 'peinture naïve' that hangs literally on its façade.

For a long time, influenced perhaps by illustrated editions of the text, I assumed that the words 'Chat-qui-pelote' were actually displayed on the shop sign. They are not, of course, and there is no more textual basis for my phantasy image than there is for the phantasy title, '*Chat-qui-pelote (Le)*, tableau de Théodore de Sommervieux' (XII, 1925) to be found in the Pléiade 'Index des œuvres des personnages fictifs de *La Comédie humaine*'.[14] Although the shop, throughout the story, is consistently named as the Chat-qui-pelote, 'GUILLAUME' and 'SUCCESSEUR DU SIEUR CHEVREL' are the only words literally present to be read.[15] Like the picture whose description has evolved into the name of the shop, the owners' names, with their picturesque old-fashioned spelling, adorn a façade that is covered with the metaphorical writing of its wooden struts and beams:

> Les murs menaçants de cette bicoque semblaient avoir été bariolés d'hiéroglyphes. Quel autre nom le flâneur pouvait-il donner aux X et aux V que traçaient sur la façade les pièces de bois transversales ou diagonales dessinées dans le badigeon par de petites lézardes parallèles?

Descriptions of the façade as 'gothique' and 'grotesque' (types of printing character, as Balzac would be the first to know), add to the effect of a vertical wall of writing, while the 'formidable pièce de bois' was originally supported by *jambages* (the downward strokes of writing) rather than *piliers* (I, 1182). It is tempting, too, to imagine the half-timbered façade as a woodcut, and I have already noted other engraving metaphors that evoke the effect of low relief. In short, the façade, with its asymmetrical array of beams, planks, frames, bars, sills, shutters, curtains and window panes (design and colours differ from storey to storey), not to mention the ancient and grotesque shop sign, and the figures who emerge from their respective frames to take an opening bow, is a palimpsest of metaphors that merge writing with the plastic arts.

This 'extrême évidence plastique' is very well captured in Bonard's subtle commentary on the façade: 'On s'aperçoit qu'il s'agit bien ici d'un tableau, que Balzac veut nous faire considérer comme tel, c'est-à-dire comme un objet d'art.' (p. 19, p. 20) In particular, he proposes his own image of an advent calendar, 'mignard et gaufré, dont on aurait ouvert les petites lucarnes' (p. 21). According to Bonard, the *invraisemblance* of Balzac's visually poetic description is increased by 'de subits grossissements de plans visuels', such as the 'légers interstices' in Augustine's nightwear, supposedly seen by Sommervieux from across the street: 'Le détail est trop fabriqué pour ne pas suggérer, dans la proximité où il est saisi, le mouvement d'un amateur qui s'approche d'une toile pour en scruter le "fini".' (p. 21) Certainly, the reader's inspection of the plastic qualities of the façade is mediated by Sommervieux (although I believe he has been positioned by Balzac to create the effect of somebody viewing a large upright canvas). Where I disagree with Bonard — as I have throughout my discussion of the three artist stories of the *Scènes de la vie privée* — is in his concluding espousal of Gaëton Picon's comment on the story: 'ce qui assure à *la Maison du Chat-qui-pelote* une place privilégiée dans notre mémoire, ce ne sont pas plus qu'une intrigue, des personnages ou des situations. Ce n'est pas même un décor. Très exactement, c'est un *tableau*.' (p. 23)[16] The quotation usefully highlights the critical tendency (already noted in relation to *La Bourse*), to undervalue or distort the subject matter whenever the 'painterly' — and even fictional paintings — are celebrated in Balzac. In fact, as I hope to have shown, Balzac's representation of a homosocial structure is what gives meaning to this *tableau*. If the relation of father- and son-in-law is literally written across its surface ('Guillaume successeur du sieur Chevrel'), it is the next son-in-law in line (Joseph Lebas) who briefly steps out from the frame.

As we saw in the first chapter, the tragic artists of *S/Z*, in which category I ended up by placing Barthes himself, want to pass '*dans* le modèle, *sous* la statue, *derrière* la toile', while a realist writer like Balzac, and realist critics seduced by his project, want to take their readers '*derrière* le papier' (p. 128). It is significant to my own reading of *La Maison du chat-qui-pelote* that it is a fictional artist, and not just any passer-by, who mediates our inspection of the façade, for it is Sommervieux, through the plot constructed around his two 'real' paintings, who takes us behind the metaphorical canvas and into a quintessential Balzacian analysis of the institution of marriage. In particular, the portrait that Sommervieux destroys, along with the draper's daughter who was its unknowing model, is — as are all Balzac's fictional works of art — part of that bigger picture.

Notes to Chapter 4

1. *La Maison du chat-qui-pelote*, ed. by Meininger, in *La Comédie humaine*, I, 23–94 (p. 93).

2. Unlike *La Maison du chat-qui-pelote*, *The Oval Portrait* (1845) is one of those inversions of the Pygmalion myth where (as in *The Picture of Dorian Gray*) the degree of 'life' of the portrait and its model are in inverse proportion: '"This is indeed *Life* itself!"', cries the amorous but obsessed painter, turning at that very moment 'to regard his beloved: — *She was dead!*' (Edgar Allan Poe, *The Fall of the House of Usher and Other Writings*, ed. by David Galloway (Harmondsworth: Penguin, 1986), pp. 250–53 (p. 253)). A longer first version (1842) was published as *Life in Death*.

3. The detailed internal chronology that Castex constructs for the story is based on the false premise that the 1810 Salon opened in August (in fact it opened in early November, and was visited by Napoleon and Marie-Louise later that month). The three possible Salons are those of 1808, 1810 and 1812, each of which leads to minor historical inconsistencies. Two drafts of the opening passage contain the date 1808 (see I, 1182; I, 1183), which is the year four real painters (Girodet, Gros, Gérard and Carle Vernet) received the Légion d'honneur from Napoleon at the Salon, as will the fictional Sommervieux. Balzac may have removed this date in order to send the family to a performance of *Cendrillon* (I, 60) (according to Meininger, both *La Cendrillon des écoles* and *La Chatte merveilleuse ou la Petite Cendrillon* were first staged at the Variétés in November 1810 (see I, 1197)). Guillaume's allusion to the rate at which Napoleon is reducing the nation's stock of potential husbands (I, 52) is generally thought to refer to the *sénatus-consulte* of 1812, which raised extra troops for the Russian campaign by calling up 300,000 young men from the class of 1813. Finally, it is commonly pointed out that Girodet's *Tête de vierge*, a possible intertext for Augustine's portrait, was exhibited to great acclaim at the 1812 Salon (see the catalogue entry by Danielle Oger in *Balzac et la peinture*, ed. by Jean-Pierre Boyer and Élisabeth Boyer-Peigné (Tours: Musée des Beaux-Arts de Tours/Farrago, 1999), pp. 236–37).

4. For an overview of the institutional dimension of the Salon, and its relation to the permanent collections of the Louvre, see Udolpho van de Sandt, 'Le Salon', in *L'Empire des Muses: Napoléon, les Arts et les Lettres*, ed. by Jean-Claude Bonnet (Paris: Belin, 2004), pp. 59–78. Napoleon visited all of the Empire Salons, and is made by Balzac to ask to be shown Augustine's portrait. See too Philippe Monnet, 'Balzac et les salons', in *Balzac et la peinture*, pp. 41–51.

5. The text contains a number of allusions to *Cendrillon*, not least Mme Roguin as the fairy godmother and Sommervieux's return at the stroke of midnight to destroy his wife's fairy tale.

6. See Wettlaufer, pp. 71–76 and p. 171, for the parallel with Girodet's *La Nouvelle Danaé*, painted as revenge for the rejection of *Mademoiselle Lange en Danaé* (the latter famously torn from its frame and returned to the sitter in shreds). The episode is described in detail by Crow in *Emulation: Making Artists for Revolutionary France* (New Haven: Yale University Press, 1995), pp. 269–73, p. 231, pp. 233–35.

7. Bizarrely, in Castex's edition of the text, the painter looks alternately at Augustine and 'la toilette accusatrice' (p. 98). I have not encountered any comment on what I take to be an interesting mistake.

8. The idea of destroying the portrait came to Balzac between completion of the manuscript and the first edition. Originally, he passed directly from Augustine's visit to the duchess to the final meditation on her epitaph (see I, 1207–08).

9. See *Art and Illusion: A Study in the Psychology of Pictorial Representation* (London and New York: Phaidon/Pantheon, 1960), p. 99, p. 93.

10. In particular, Joseph Lebas will become a significant voice of the Code de commerce; he serves as judge, and five times as *président*, of the Tribunal de commerce, and for ten years he is 'conseiller du département de la Seine'. For a summary, see the Pléiade index of fictional characters, XII, 1399–1400.
11. *La Cousine Bette*, ed. by Meininger, in *La Comédie humaine*, VII, 3–451 (p. 93).
12. For readings of the descent of the *fenêtre à guillotine* as a metaphorical castration, see Wettlaufer, p. 160, and Del Lungo, 'Fenêtres à l'envers (perversions, effractions, pénétrations)', in *Envers balzaciens*, ed. by Del Lungo and Alexandre Péraud (Poitiers: La Licorne, 2001), pp. 87–102 (p. 94).
13. See Bonard, p. 22, and Baron, *Le Fils prodige: L'Inconscient de 'La Comédie humaine'* (Paris: Nathan, 1993), p. 58.
14. '*Augustine Guillaume* (portrait d')' is similarly included in the list compiled by Citron and Meininger (XII, 1924–26), along with '*Rouville* (baron de), portrait par Schinner'. Curiously, the index is not comprehensive. Pierre Grassou fares better than Joseph Bridau, who has no entries at all, while Sarrasine's *Zambinella* is especially striking by its absence (statues are not excluded, as there is an entry for 'Montcornet (statue du général de) de Wenceslas Steinbock').
15. This would be in keeping with the suggestion, noted by Meininger, that the picture is a rebus: 'Chaque y pelote (chacun y trouve son profit)' (I, 1186).
16. Bonard is quoting Picon's preface to the story in *L'Œuvre de Balzac*, ed. by Albert Béguin and J.-A. Ducourneau, 16 vols (Paris: Le Club français du livre (réimpression corrigée), 1953–55), I, 160.

PART III

❖

From Model to Artist

Il faut que le peintre lui aussi copie un autre code, un code antérieur.
ROLAND BARTHES, *S/Z*

CHAPTER 5

❖

La Rabouilleuse

(i) 'Ce charmant modèle'

La Rabouilleuse is at once an artist story and an ambitious social canvas. Political events in France, as they affect one family between 1792 and 1839, provide a precise historical context for the familiar components of a Balzacian inheritance struggle: celibacy, marriage, widowhood, adultery, illegitimacy and prostitution. The novel's publication as *Un ménage de garçon en province* (1843), and its inclusion in the series *Les Célibataires*, pointed readers in this general direction.[1] At first sight, the story of Joseph Bridau's early career as a painter, and the manner and content of his art, may seem incidentally related to this wider subject matter: creators and creations do not saturate the plot as they do in some of the shorter artist stories explored so far. However, by introducing onto the Furne corrigé the title by which the novel is now conventionally known,[2] Balzac established a fertile connection between 'la Rabouilleuse' as female victim of a homosocial society, and realist representation as mode. Painting metaphors are never far away in Balzac's realist texts, and in this case they are strikingly attached to Flore Brazier, the eponymous Rabouilleuse, so called in Issoudun with ironic reference to her occupation — the child is muddying a stream for her uncle who is fishing for crayfish — when she is chanced upon by the seventy-year-old Rouget: 'Le soir, dans tout Issoudun, il ne fut question que de l'établissement d'une petite Rabouilleuse chez le docteur Rouget. Ce surnom resta dans un pays de moquerie à Mlle Brazier, avant, pendant et après sa fortune.' (IV, 390) For all that gossip circulates so rapidly in Issoudun, only the omniscient narrator has knowledge of the detail of this encounter, and it is his painterly description that first establishes the peasant child as the metaphorical model of a work of art. By calling his novel *La Rabouilleuse*, a title that espouses the local viewpoint, but is perhaps also suggestive of a statue or painting, Balzac gives wider significance to Joseph's status as a painter than might otherwise have been the case. Indeed, the familiar conjunction of artist and model — here Joseph Bridau and Flore Brazier — cuts across the seemingly disparate strands of this novel. Over twenty years later, the unworldly Joseph, newly arrived in Issoudun to rescue his uncle Jean-Jacques — and the Rouget fortune — from the clutches of the adult Flore, will be overcome by admiration for her physical beauty. His aesthetic enthusiasm, enhanced by the sight of his uncle's paintings, and by anticipated pleasure in their possession, leads him to commit what from the point of view of the inheritance is a tactical blunder, but from that of the novel as a whole is a highly charged act:

he parades joyfully through the streets of Issoudun with the Rabouilleuse on his arm. That Flore, sold by her uncle to Joseph's grandfather for the equivalent of six acres of vineyard, should end up, first as Joseph's aunt-by-marriage, then as his sister-in-law, underscores the extent to which the artist-model relation intersects, in this as in Balzac's other artist stories, with the conjugal structures depicted in *La Comédie humaine*.

In *S/Z*, along with *Sarrasine* and *Le Chef-d'œuvre inconnu*, *La Rabouilleuse* is the third text to be drawn, if briefly, into Barthes's analysis of Balzac's realism. A digression, *Le Modèle de la peinture*, interrupts Barthes's analysis of how Mme de Rochefide's examination of the elderly Zambinella implicitly frames the painterly portrait that follows. As Barthes convincingly claims, the realist writer places an imaginary frame, almost obsessively, around whatever it is he wants to describe, as if only by passing through the intermediary of a painting could material reality be allowed to accede to language: 'Ainsi le réalisme [...] consiste, non à copier le réel, mais à copier une copie (peinte) du réel: [...] code sur code, dit le réalisme' (p. 60). In this sense, still according to Barthes, the talent of Joseph Bridau is perfectly compatible with his imitation of painters of genius: 'd'une façon ou naïve ou éhontée, Joseph Bridau n'éprouve aucun scrupule à faire du Raphaël (car il faut que le peintre lui aussi copie un autre code, un code antérieur), pas plus que Balzac n'en éprouve à déclarer ce pastiche un chef-d'œuvre' (p. 61).[3] And with this Barthes arrives at the example of Balzac's first description of the Rabouilleuse:

> La circularité infinie des codes une fois posée, le corps lui-même ne peut y échapper: le corps réel (donné comme tel par la fiction) est la réplique d'un modèle articulé par le code des arts, en sorte que le plus 'naturel' des corps, celui de la Rabouilleuse enfant, n'est jamais que la *promesse* du code artistique dont il est par avance issu ('*Le médecin, assez anatomiste pour reconnaître une taille délicieuse, comprit tout ce que les arts perdraient si ce charmant modèle se détruisait au travail des champs*'). (p. 62)

As we have seen, Barthes's reading of *Sarrasine* is caught up in an ambivalent attempt to separate realist writing from any referential origin. In Barthes's reading, since beauty is a catachresis defined through an endlessly receding code of art, for Sarrasine, Zambinella is at best its illusory starting point (the long sought after *chef-d'œuvre* in living form), at worst, when the illusion is shattered, he is a 'subhuman' castrato (something less than a man). As I argued in Chapter 1, in his anxious attempt to shift the parameters of what is understood by realist writing, Barthes apparently sidesteps the possibility that the 'real' body of a Neapolitan *ragazzo*, sold for his beauty into homosexual prostitution, could be the referential starting point of sculptural, painterly and realist literary art. If only for the parallel of the eleven-year-old Rabouilleuse, similarly sold into prostitution, and precisely on account of the 'promise' of her childish body, Barthes's comments on the aesthetic coding of Flore Brazier's body may seem similarly narrow in scope. The allusion to the anatomical expertise of the doctor underscores the irony of the aesthetic alibi lent to him by the narrator; indeed, the sentence quoted by Barthes is a cynical summary of the merging in Balzac's text of two perspectives. The description of the Rabouilleuse is focalized through the doctor — 'ce malicieux et vicieux vieillard aperçut une petite fille ravissante' — but is elaborated via the narrator's aesthetic commentary: 'la petite montra soudain au docteur une des plus belles têtes de Vierge que jamais un peintre ait pu rêver' (IV, 385); 'cette nymphe avait des yeux bleus garnis de cils dont le regard eût fait tomber à genoux un peintre ou un poète' (IV, 386). If Balzac's set-piece portrait of a beautiful peasant child is built up from artistic codes in the way Barthes suggests, it is framed, however strategically, by the lecherous gaze of an old man.[4] From the point of view of *La Rabouilleuse* as a realist novel, what does each code add to the other?

In the first instance, the portrait inscribes the 'realist' sculptural aesthetic that is delegated by Balzac to his fictional artists Sarrasine and Frenhofer. Not only is the figure to be described framed as a painting, the object of representation is perceived as a statue, with all the erotic, aesthetic and epistemological potential so insistently elaborated in *S/Z*. Here, the child is disturbed in her *rabouillage* by the sound of the doctor's horse; she straightens up to emerge as a sculpted water-nymph, a figure in relief against a painted backcloth: 'l'enfant se dressa du fond d'un des ruisseaux qui, vus du haut d'Issoudun, ressemblent à des rubans d'argent au milieu d'une robe verte' (IV, 385).[5] The drafts of the passage show Balzac working on the detail of the way her skimpy ragged clothes reveal her bare body even as they serve to cover it. In the final version, 'la fille, quasi-nue, portait une méchante jupe courte trouée et déchiquetée' (IV, 385–86). There is no need here for Frenhofer's undressing of Gillette, nor for his careful excavation of Titian's art ('"j'ai analysé et soulevé couche par couche les tableaux de Titien"' (X, 424)). Flore's rags are effectively falling from her body, so that patches of white skin can be seen under her sunburn: 'sa jolie poitrine hâlée, son cou à peine couvert par un fichu en loques, qui jadis fut un madras, montrait des places blanches au-dessous du hâle' (IV, 386). Her skirt, which has been passed through her legs and pinned up to her waist, acts as an improvised bathing costume, and Balzac leaves it to the reader to imagine what was more clumsily spelled out in his earliest draft: 'Elle avait sa jupe passée entre les jambes, relevée à mi-corps en sorte qu'elle [était nue *rayée*] s'en était fait une espèce de caleçon de nageur qui laissait voir tout ce que laissent voir les nageurs.' (IV, 1270) Similarly, her bare feet and legs are visible through the transparent screen of the clear water, and what is revealed is a statue on display for, interchangeably, an artist, a poet, or an anatomically knowledgeable and 'vicieux' old man:

> Les pieds, les jambes, que l'eau claire permettait d'apercevoir, se recommandaient par une délicatesse digne de la statuaire au Moyen Âge. Ce charmant corps exposé au soleil avait un ton rougeâtre qui ne manquait pas de grâce. Le cou et la poitrine méritaient d'être enveloppés de cachemire et de soie. (IV, 386)

Like Pygmalion dressing and undressing his statue, Rouget, as an ironically appropriate enticement, offers the Rabouilleuse nice clothes: '"Veux-tu venir avec moi? tu seras [...] bien habillée, et tu auras de jolis souliers..."' (IV, 387). Later that day, the potential masterpiece that is a barefooted peasant child will be handed over, in exchange for two years' advance payment, in the setting of Rouget's grand panelled reception room. A description of the Rabouilleuse's reflection, which is literally framed in a mirror over the marble fireplace — 'une grande glace sans trumeau supérieur et dont la bordure sculptée était dorée' (IV, 388) — gives way to the first mention in the text of Rouget's magnificent collection of paintings:

une Sainte Famille de l'Albane, un Saint-Jérôme du Dominiquin, une tête de
Christ de Jean Bellin, une Vierge de Léonard de Vinci, un Portement de croix
du Titien [...]; un Lazare de Paul Véronèse, un Mariage de la Vierge du Prêtre
Génois, deux tableaux d'église de Rubens et une copie d'un tableau de Pérugin
faite par le Pérugin ou par Raphaël; enfin, deux Corrège et un André del Sarto.
(IV, 388–89)

Rouget has estimated the child's worth, both economic and aesthetic-cum-sexual,
to her uncle and to himself. But no one in Issoudun, Rouget included, has an
inkling of the value, economic or aesthetic, of the paintings amongst which she
takes her place.

All that is missing so far is a real artist. The discovery, purchase and installation
of the Rabouilleuse is recounted as an explanatory flashback; it takes place in 1799,
the year of Joseph Bridau's birth. If Flore's future is effectively determined as she
approaches the age of twelve, Joseph — 'l'un des grands peintres de l'École française
actuelle' (IV, 287) — will discover his vocation at thirteen. Balzac manipulates the
early details of the plot so that the widowed Agathe Bridau, and her sons Philippe
and Joseph, find themselves living in a narrow stretch of the rue Mazarine, in a
dark top-floor flat that not only includes 'un immense grenier sans destination'
(IV, 284), but overlooks part of the Palais de l'Institut, at this time home of the
École des Beaux-Arts. Indeed the Bridau family can look directly into the barred
loges of those 'animaux féroces' otherwise known as *rapins*, periodically engaged
in frenetic preparations for the *concours de Rome*: 'qui sculpteur, le modèle en terre
glaise d'une statue; qui peintre, l'un des tableaux que vous pouvez voir à l'École des
Beaux-Arts' (IV, 283). Already an obsessive observer of reality — the intensity of the
child's 'profonde attention' (IV, 289) is described as almost pathological — Joseph's
future is set in train by the chance sighting of a student drawing a chalk caricature
of a teacher on a wall. The very next day, from a window of the flat, he watches
the art students going into the Institut through the entrance in the rue Mazarine.
In an initiation scene reminiscent of Poussin's infiltration of Porbus's studio in *Le
Chef-d'œuvre inconnu*, Joseph 'descendit furtivement et se coula dans la longue cour
de l'Institut où il aperçut les statues, les bustes, les marbres commencés, les terres
cuites, les plâtres qu'il contempla fiévreusement; car son instinct se révélait, sa
vocation l'agitait' (IV, 289). That vocation is confirmed once and for all when he
wanders into the studio of the sculptor Chaudet, sees a group of students making
drawings of a statue, and is subjected — ' "il faut souffrir pour être artiste" ' (IV, 290)
— to a hoax initiation test. The young boy must pose without moving for fifteen
minutes, one arm in the air and the other poised to strike a blow with the fist, as
if he himself were the model for a statue: ' "L'Empereur Napoléon est bien resté
pendant un mois comme tu le vois là", dit un élève en montrant la belle statue de
Chaudet.' (IV, 290) The arrival of Chaudet puts an end to the physical ordeal of 'le
martyr de l'atelier' (290); indeed, the Napoleonic credentials of the name Bridau
(' "Mon papa, qui est mort, était un ami de l'Empereur" ' (IV, 291)) act as the *open
sesame* to the world of art symbolically figured by the studio. The child may come
there as often as he likes, portfolio, paper and pencils are to be found for him; above
all, his integration into the confraternity of artists is celebrated with a feast of treats

that the *rapin* who had tormented him is sent out to buy: 'Joseph fut alors caressé tout aussi bien qu'il avait été mystifié. Cette scène, où la plaisanterie et le cœur des artistes se révélaient et qu'il comprit instinctivement, fit une prodigieuse impression sur l'enfant.' (IV, 291)

Instinctively, too, he keeps this escapade, and his subsequent visits to Chaudet's studio, a secret from his mother. In this he is covered for by his great-aunt Descoings, who actively encourages his passion by supplying his needs — 'des crayons, de la sanguine, des estompes et du papier à dessiner' — and who takes him to the Salon, where 'l'attention profonde que le petit bonhomme donnait aux tableaux tenait du miracle' (IV, 292).[6] By the time the unintelligent Mme Bridau is advised, by Chaudet as well as by a teacher at Joseph's school, of her son's extraordinary potential — '"des dispositions comme les siennes sont rares, elles ne sont dévoilées de si bonne heure que chez les Giotto, les Raphaël, les Titien, les Rubens, les Murillo; car il me semble devoir être plutôt peintre que sculpteur"' (IV, 293) — her attempts to ban him from the studio are reinforced by a puritanical reaction when she sees Chaudet's frenzied manner of working on his statue and, worse, realizes that he works from a nude model. Like Frenhofer at work on Porbus's *Marie égyptienne*, the sculptor 'maniait son ébauchoir et sa glaise par des mouvements saccadés qui parurent à l'ignorante Agathe être ceux d'un maniaque' (IV, 292); when the sculptor, infuriated by Agathe's stupidity, tells his model he has finished for the day, 'Agathe leva les yeux et vit une femme nue assise sur une escabelle dans un coin de l'atelier, [...] ce spectacle la fit sortir avec horreur' (IV, 293). For Mme Bridau, the artist's studio is a sexualized space: '"Vous ne savez pas ce qui se passe dans ces ateliers! Les artistes y ont des femmes nues."' (IV, 296) Her attitude is mocked by the 'asymbolic' riposte of Mme Descoings: '"Mais ils y font du feu, j'espère"' (IV, 296). Indeed, unlike the unruly Sarrasine, whose route to Bouchardon's studio involved obscene carvings and expulsion from school, Joseph's attraction to art has no obviously erotic dimension: 'Au Lycée impérial, le futur artiste croquait ses maîtres, il dessinait ses camarades, il charbonnait les dortoirs, et fut d'une étonnante assiduité à la classe de dessin.' (IV, 292) It is his mother's attitude that turns the studio into a place that is somehow transgressive; if only because she has ordered him to stay away, the *rapins* delight — and succeed — in enticing Joseph into it.

Thus Mme Bridau is the vehicle of an idea familiar from *Sarrasine* and *Le Chef-d'œuvre inconnu*: that art and prostitution are linked, and that the link is the artist's model.[7] In this novel, that relation is incarnated in the Rabouilleuse. True to his promise, Rouget has dressed the child in expensive clothes and has given her jewellery and a gold watch 'pour encourager ses études' (IV, 391). Although her lessons in reading, writing and arithmetic are abandoned as a bad job, Rouget, a grotesque Pygmalion, perseveres in an education designed to fashion the child — 'qu'il décrassait, instruisait et formait avec des soins d'autant plus touchants qu'on le croyait incapables de tendresse' (IV, 391) — to his own ends. Thus for five years, from 1800 to 1805, 'le docteur eut les plaisirs de l'éducation de Flore', and 'la petite Rabouilleuse était si contente, en comparant sa situation chez le docteur à la vie qu'elle eût menée avec son oncle Brazier, qu'elle se plia sans doute aux exigences de son maître, comme eût fait une esclave en Orient' (IV, 392). The end product is a fifteen-year-old Flore who passes 'pour une fille très *délurée*' (IV, 393), for all that the new coldness with which Rouget treats her, in the two years that precede his death, is interpreted by others as 'un certificat d'innocence' for the girl of seventeen (IV, 393). The facts of the matter remain unclarified by the conflicting conjectures of small-town gossip.[8] When the dying Rouget, with characteristic malice, refuses to make any provision for Flore in his will — '"Elle est bien assez riche de sa beauté!"' — his *notaire* detects 'la haine concentrée d'un homme chez qui la nature avait trompé les calculs de la débauche, une vengeance contre l'innocent objet d'un impuissant amour' (IV, 393).

(ii) 'Une magnifique Cariatide!'

Some nine years later Mme Hochon persuades Agathe, her god-daughter, to travel with Joseph to Issoudun to attempt to destroy the influence of 'une concubine de laquelle [votre frère] est le très humble serviteur' (IV, 354). Not only has Jean-Jacques Rouget inherited the entirety of his father's estate (including his sister's 'legal' share), he has also — and this the doctor had not foreseen — inherited the Rabouilleuse. The thirty-seven-year-old bachelor, so pathologically timid that he seems imbecilic, has secretly nourished a passion for Flore that is an interesting variant of that of his domineering father. The idea of taking her over from his dead father brings the first stirrings of expression to Jean-Jacques's previously blank features; however, 'quelle que fût l'éducation que la Rabouilleuse tenait du docteur' (IV, 394), she is slow to understand his intention. Incapable of speaking to a woman, let alone paying court, Jean-Jacques has enough sense to see Flore's sexual availability as an advantage: 'Loin d'être jaloux de son père, il fut enchanté de l'éducation qu'il donnait à Flore' (IV, 396). A description of the Rabouilleuse, though not explicitly focalized by Jean-Jacques, is framed on both sides by his direct speech and, since he has asked the servant to leave them alone, implicitly shaped by his desire: 'Flore conservait encore cette finesse de taille et de traits, cette distinction de beauté qui séduisirent le docteur' (IV, 394). However, she is already revealing 'une tendance à l'embonpoint' (IV, 394), so that her body is now sculpted with fuller forms: 'Son corsage était développé. Ses épaules grasses et blanches dessinaient des plans riches et harmonieusement rattachés à son cou qui se plissait déjà. Mais le contour de sa figure restait pur, et le menton était encore fin.' (IV, 394) Jean-Jacques's desire is visual to the point of voyeurism. When the Rabouilleuse belonged to his father she was 'la seule femme [...] qu'il pût voir à son aise, en la contemplant en secret, en l'étudiant à toute heure' (IV, 396). Following the doctor's death, 'il tourn[a] autour d'elle et la regardât sournoisement avec des expressions de concupiscence' (IV, 396); three weeks after the funeral, Flore wakes up one night to hear the sound of human breathing at her door, 'et fut effrayée en reconnaissant sur le palier Jean-Jacques couché comme un chien, et qui, sans doute, avait fait lui-même un trou par en bas pour voir dans la chambre' (IV, 396–97). When Jean-Jacques finally manages to speak, it is to confess that his desire was determined once and for all by the vision of a barefooted Rabouilleuse handed over by her uncle in the setting of the Rouget *salle*: '"Voyons? Êtes-vous la même que quand vous étiez là, pieds nus, amenée par votre oncle?"' (IV, 397); '"je vous aime, et vous ai toujours aimée depuis le moment que vous êtes entrée, ici, là, pieds nus"' (IV, 398).

'"Vous êtes précisément en face de l'ennemi"' (IV, 429), says Mme Hochon, some fifteen years later, as she embarks on the 'horrible et vulgaire histoire' whereby *un ménage de garçon en province* has absorbed Flore's lover Max Gilet and turned into *un ménage à trois*. By positioning the Hochons' house directly opposite 'la salle de la maison Rouget' (IV, 429), Balzac ensures that inspection of the Rabouilleuse can take place through the Hochons' window. In the first instance it is Jean-Jacques who is doubly framed: 'Joseph vit sur la porte de la maison en face Jean-Jacques Rouget planté sur ses deux pieds; il le montra naturellement à sa mère' (IV, 434). Agathe's attempt to recognize her prematurely decrepit brother frames 'une scène évidemment calculée', the staging of which is credited by the narrator to Max and Flore: 'Une chaîne d'or ruisselait sur le corsage de la Rabouilleuse, qui apportait à Jean-Jacques son bonnet de soie noire afin qu'il ne s'enrhumât pas' (IV, 435). What Agathe sees is the uncovered hair, the elaborate dress, shawl and jewellery of an expensively kept woman:

> Elle [...] vit derrière le vieillard Flore Brazier coiffée en cheveux, laissant voir sous la gaze d'un fichu garni de dentelles un dos de neige et une poitrine éblouissante, soignée comme une courtisane riche, portant une robe à corset en grenadine, une étoffe de soie alors à la mode, à manches dites à gigot, et terminées au poignet par des bracelets superbes. (IV, 435)

Arguably, Agathe's perspective is not so different from that of her father who, sizing up the child's potential for prostitution, had gauged that her neck and chest deserved to be clothed — as now they are — in cashmere and silk. Where once the body of the sun-tanned Rabouilleuse was easily visible through the holes of the rags that covered her, now it is 'la gaze d'un fichu garni de dentelles', rather than 'un fichu en loques' (IV, 386), that both envelops and reveals 'un dos de neige et une poitrine éblouissante'. But whereas the sexual and aesthetic evaluations were ironically conflated in the description of 'la Rabouilleuse enfant' — 'le médecin, assez anatomiste pour reconnaître une taille délicieuse' (IV, 386) — here they are split into the contrasting perceptions of Mme Bridau, who sees 'une courtisane riche', and her artist-son, who sees a potential model in this beautifully formed woman: '"Voilà, s'écria Joseph, une belle femme! et c'est rare!... Elle est faite, comme on dit, à peindre! Quelle carnation! Oh! les beaux tons! Quels méplats, quelles rondeurs, et des épaules!... C'est une magnifique Cariatide! Ce serait un fameux modèle pour une Vénus-Titien."' (IV, 435)

The codes marshalled by Joseph, as he looks at the Rabouilleuse through the window, are at once sculptural and painterly; indeed, the painterly feeds off the sculptural. In the first place, Flore's see-through shawl reveals her 'dos de neige' as well as her 'poitrine éblouissante'. Citron may be right to detect here a *lapsus* on Balzac's part: is not this rear view of the Rabouilleuse 'impossible' from Agathe's position?[9] Yet the slip is a revealing one that again recalls Frenhofer's 'realist' obsession with seeing all sides of *Catherine Lescault*. For Joseph, it is because the Rabouilleuse is a magnificent caryatid, because her face and her body are beautifully shaped ('"quels méplats, quelles rondeurs, et des épaules!..."') that she is the perfect model for a future painting. Yet for Mme Hochon and Agathe, Flore is simply a prostitute ('"cette vermine"' (IV, 355) or '"cette créature"' (IV, 435)): '"Vous trouvez belle une fille qui vous enlève une fortune?"' (IV, 435). The polarized evaluations of the Rabouilleuse are captured in Joseph's response ('"Ça ne l'empêche pas d'être un beau modèle!"') and his mother's comic attempt to cut short his aesthetic commentary ('"précisément assez grasse, sans que les hanches et les formes soient gâtées..."') by reminding him that he is not in his sexually permissive studio: '"Mon ami, tu n'es pas dans ton atelier, [...] et Adolphine est là..."' (IV, 435). Even without Joseph's defence of his uncle — '"Je ne le trouve plus si crétin du moment où il a l'esprit de se réjouir les yeux par une Vénus de Titien"' (IV, 435) — Mme Bridau's reference to Joseph's studio keeps to the fore the idea of Flore as a metaphorical artist's model.

The theme is maintained, as well as a certain complicity with his uncle's perspective, when Joseph, later that day, accepts the enemy's invitation to dinner.

> — Madame, dit Joseph à Flore, avec l'entrain d'un artiste, j'enviais, ce matin, à mon oncle le plaisir qu'il a de pouvoir vous admirer tous les jours!
> — N'est-ce pas qu'elle est belle? dit le vieillard dont les yeux ternis devinrent presque brillants.
> — Belle à pouvoir servir de modèle à un peintre. (IV, 440)

The dining room in which Joseph is entertained is also the picture gallery in which the Rabouilleuse was first received as a barefooted child, her reflected image in the mirror confirming her place amongst the masterpieces on the walls. Just as, in that first description, Flore's description precedes that of the paintings — indeed the latter was motivated by the way the child and her uncle, 'toujours pieds nus, regardaient la salle du docteur avec des yeux hébétés' (IV, 388) — once more the vision of Flore, this time through Joseph's eyes, heralds that of the paintings. It is when Flore leaves the room to dress for their walk, and to put on the very cashmere shawl that the child's beautiful neck had cried out for, that 'Joseph se leva soudain à la vue des tableaux, comme si quelque enchanteur l'eût touché de sa baguette. "Ah! vous avez des tableaux, mon oncle?"' (IV, 441). He then examines, transfixed in admiration, the collection of masterpieces already described to the reader in the earlier scene. These fine paintings, '"la défroque des maisons religieuses et des églises du Berry"' (IV, 441), bought up at the time of the Revolution, had been chosen by the Descoings either because they were framed under glass, or for the sheer magnificence of the frames themselves. Through his bright idea of buying off Joseph with a gift of pictures assumed to be worthless, Max Gilet sets in train the thread of the plot that will indirectly determine the hasty departure from Issoudun of both Joseph and his mother. In itself, the episode draws comic mileage from the cultural ignorance of Issoudun — and the Rouget *ménage à trois* in particular — whereby the frames (which might indeed have been very valuable) are prized more than the masterpieces they contain, and nice new copies more than the old paintings they replace:

> — Eh bien, dit Jean-Jacques, si ces tableaux peuvent te servir à quelque chose dans ton état, je te les donne... mais sans les cadres. Oh! les cadres sont dorés, et puis ils sont drôles; j'y mettrai...

> — Parbleu, mon oncle, s'écria Joseph enchanté, vous y mettrez les copies que
> je vous enverrai et qui seront de la même dimension. (IV, 441)

By agreeing, eventually ('"quatre mille francs et les tableaux, c'est trop"') to accept four thousand francs for producing these copies ('"Eh bien, j'accepte"'), Joseph seals a scene which, with its comic stress on the frames and the copies, reads as a parody of Barthes's *modèle de la peinture*. The episode is rendered still more richly symbolic by the public parade of artist and model ('Aussi l'artiste eut-il un air joyeux en sortant et en donnant le bras à la Rabouilleuse') which is watched, moreover, from the doorways of Issoudun and thus implicitly framed: '[Flore] se promena très orgueilleusement au bras du neveu de son maître, en bonne intelligence avec lui, devant toute la ville ébahie. On se mit aux portes pour voir le triomphe de la Rabouilleuse sur la famille.' (IV, 442) News of the gift of the pictures, and the commission of copies that has been brokered by Flore, seems to have spread already, and draws attention to the underlying theme in the novel of the exchange value of both real and metaphorical works of art. By the end of *La Rabouilleuse* the collection of paintings has passed through as many hands as Flore Brazier: from the churches and abbeys of Berry via the Descoings to Rouget, from Rouget to his son, from Jean-Jacques to Joseph and back again, from Jean-Jacques to Flore herself, then to Philippe Bridau before returning, in the penultimate paragraph, to Joseph, who inherits them from his brother: 'Ce qui fit le plus de plaisir au peintre, fut la belle collection de tableaux.' (IV, 540)

These 'real' paintings outlive the Rabouilleuse, of course, in the novel as well as in fictional reality. Though ten years will pass between the death of Flore and Joseph's reacquisition of the paintings, within the text, thanks to a compressed chronology, the two episodes are separated by only a few pages. Flore and the painting collection maintain the same structural relation throughout the novel: for the third time, a set-piece description of the Rabouilleuse precedes an appearance of the paintings. However, the Rabouilleuse is no longer the same Flore Brazier who cried out to be framed as a masterpiece. Control of her destiny has been wrested from Max Gilet by Philippe Bridau, who succeeds in exploiting her value (getting hold of the Rouget fortune) where Max had failed. The dying Flore, who has been sent back to prostitution after enforced marriages with Jean-Jacques and Philippe in turn, will be framed one last time by the gaze of the artist, now her brother-in-law: 'Quoique Joseph, qui avait vu Flore si belle, s'attendît à quelque affreux contraste, il ne pouvait pas imaginer le hideux spectacle qui s'offrit à ses yeux d'artiste.' (IV, 536) In this renewed encounter of Joseph and the Rabouilleuse, the physically distressing vision of Flore in a wretched *mansarde* is an ironic return to the leitmotif of the model in the artist's studio. Flore, who at the height of her mature beauty was pleasingly plump, is now 'maigre comme l'est une étique deux heures avant sa mort' (IV, 536). If this last description inscribes grotesque echoes of the first portrait of the Rabouilleuse, it is because anatomy is again foregrounded: 'Quant à ce corps, jadis si ravissant, il n'en restait qu'une ignoble ostéologie' (IV, 536).[10] Where once the child's body could be admired through her ragged shawl and the holes in her brown and white striped skirt, now 'Flore serra sur sa poitrine un lambeau de mousseline qui avait dû être un petit rideau de croisée, car il était bordé de rouille par le fer de la tringle' (IV, 536); where once a makeshift paper head-scarf covered the child's beautiful blond hair, now a 'méchante rouennerie à carreaux' covers 'sa tête dépouillée de cheveux' (IV, 536). In a last feeble gesture towards the sculptural code, this withered 'cadavre infect' ('"Est-elle assez desséchée?"') manages to raise its arms 'qui ressemblaient à deux morceaux de bois sculpté' (IV, 536). But the lingering aesthetic perspective is reabsorbed by Bianchon's medical enthusiasm ('"l'abus des liqueurs a développé chez elle une magnifique maladie qu'on croyait perdue"' (IV, 537)), an alternative, desexualized version of the anatomical code that had initially structured the gaze of the lecherous Rouget. Finally, in death, Flore Brazier is not even the Rabouilleuse, for 'F. B.' — Comtesse de Brambourg and daughter-in-law of the late Dr Rouget — is at best an anonymous item of interest in the *Gazette des Hôpitaux*.

(iii) '*Un homme doit avoir du caractère!*'

Thus the Rabouilleuse, meant for a 'Vénus-Titien', will meet the predictable end of a 'Vénus des carrefours'. The fate of this double Venus, a bundle of bones and rags dying in a wretched attic, is the logical conclusion of the contempt in which she is held by Philippe Bridau, for whom prostitutes in general, and his wife in particular, are vehicles of a vengeful misogyny:

> Mariette fut le seul amour de ce garçon; aussi la trahison de cette danseuse lui endurcit-elle beaucoup le cœur. Quand par hasard il réalisait des gains inespérés, ou s'il soupait avec son vieux camarade Giroudeau, Philippe s'adressait à la Vénus des carrefours par une sorte de dédain brutal pour le sexe entier. (IV, 323–24)

Misogyny is the basis of his advice to his uncle on how to regain control of the Rabouilleuse: '"Les femmes sont des enfants méchants, c'est des bêtes inférieures à l'homme, et il faut s'en faire craindre, car la pire condition pour nous est d'être gouvernés par ces brutes-là!"' (IV, 489). Philippe's declaration of power over Flore is a symbolically violent gesture:

> — Vous êtes donc le maître? dit Flore avec ironie.
> — Avec votre permission, répondit Philippe en serrant la main de Flore dans la sienne comme dans un étau. (IV, 498)

His threats are reinforced, moreover, by a barrage of sexist insults:

> 'Ma toute belle, [...] je connais à Paris des Rabouilleuses qui sont, sans vous faire tort, plus jolies que vous, car elles n'ont que dix-sept ans [...]. Il n'y a qu'une seule manière de tuer un homme sans que la justice ait le plus petit mot à dire, c'est de se battre en duel avec lui; mais j'en connais trois pour se débarrasser d'une femme. Voilà, ma biche!' (IV, 499)

By ousting Max, Philippe usurps the latter's control of Jean-Jacques by means of Flore, his mental and physical subjection of the Rabouilleuse replacing the obedient passion Max Gilet had inspired in her. The marriage he engineers between Flore and his uncle, as well as his own with the soon-to-be widow — '"Je vous ai fait ma tante pour pouvoir vous épouser un jour"' (IV, 518) — is conceived, alongside the transfer of a fortune, as an exercise in intimidation and humiliation. It is experienced as such by Flore who, despite her awareness of Philippe's motives, allows herself to be terrorized into submission by 'ce soldat, qui la traitait avec la brutalité la plus polie' (IV, 519). Their wedding is a legal formality; indeed, all that counts is the contract: 'Par le contrat, Mme veuve Rouget, dont l'apport consistait en un million de francs, faisait donation à son futur époux de ses biens dans le cas où elle décéderait sans enfants. Il n'y eut ni billets de faire-part, ni fête, ni éclat, car Philippe avait ses desseins' (IV, 521).

For all that Philippe tends to be positioned by critics as a quite exceptional moral monster, Balzac very plainly traces a pattern of behaviour repeated across three generations of one family. Initially, the narrator pretends to justify Dr Rouget's ill-treatment of his wife: 'il obéissait tout bonnement à de mauvais penchants que beaucoup de gens abritent sous ce terrible axiome: *Un homme doit avoir du caractère!*' (IV, 272). But the next sentence takes the justification apart — 'Cette mâle sentence a causé le malheur de bien des femmes' — and this most gendered of proverbs is ironically repeated, a few pages later, to sum up a life of debauchery: 'Ce médecin, plein de caractère, mourut en 1805.' (IV, 276) Rouget is followed in the genealogical chain by Jean-Jacques, who 'ressemblait à son père, mais en mal, et le docteur n'était pas très bien ni au moral ni au physique' (IV, 274), and by Philippe, who 'eut tout le moral du docteur Rouget, son grand-père' (IV, 277). In the absence of anything resembling a conventional love plot,[11] Balzac's cynical sexual-political analysis emerges with unusual starkness, and the behaviour of Rouget, Jean-Jacques, Max Gilet or Philippe, to take only these obvious examples, is not difficult to place: as sexual partner in turn to grandfather, son and grandson, Flore Brazier is passed down three generations of the same family and is abused by prostitution and marriage alike. Within the novel, it is female ignorance and alienation — of which Balzac invents so many fictional examples — that causes such well-meaning women as Mme Bridau (clearly despised by her elder son), and Mme Hochon (clearly despised by her husband), to view Flore as a debased creature and the active villain of the piece. In critical discussion of the novel, Herbert J. Hunt, who describes the Rabouilleuse as 'a classical example of the "servante-maîtresse" type, ignorant, unintelligent, sensual, callous, but servile at bottom', is aware that Balzac 'had never before gone so far [...] in studying the victimizer in her alternative role of victim'. However, Hunt's conclusion, that the Rabouilleuse is 'nothing better than a peasant drab, who in happier circumstances might have been harmless and even blameless', keeps him on the territory of a moral evaluation.[12] Yet Flore's 'bad character' is surely incidental to Balzac's fierce critique of a gendered social structure. In *La Rabouilleuse*, this critique is hardly limited to the domestic *huis clos* of one bourgeois family, nor even to Balzac's depiction of the stagnating provincial town of Issoudun, where puerile codes of male honour and loyalty determine the behaviour of former Napoleonic soldiers. It is self-evident, for example, that the Chevaliers de la Désœuvrance should avenge the slight on their leader's honour when Fario publicly alludes to the fact that Max Gilet lives off Flore. Yet in this novel, as everywhere in *La Comédie humaine*, what Balzac often dubs the *Code-Homme* is obeyed by a wide range of characters, whatever their social class and historical positioning.[13] Thus, not only will Étienne Lousteau lend a helping hand to the male cause, accepting a monthly allowance in return for addicting Philippe's wife to the pleasures of Paris (so she will turn to prostitution to fund them) (IV, 535), but Maxime de Trailles, de Marsay and Rastignac — the emblematic homosocial trio of *La Comédie humaine* who, for all their Adonis-like good looks, 'ne sont pas très bien au moral' — will offer the 'comte de Brambourg' crudely misogynistic advice when his plans for an aristocratic second marriage fall through:

> — Tu peux trouver mieux, lui disait Maxime.
> — Quelle fortune faudrait-il pour épouser une demoiselle de Grandlieu? demanda Philippe à de Marsay.
> — À vous?... on ne donnerait pas la plus laide des six à moins de dix millions, répondit insolemment de Marsay.
> — Bah! dit Rastignac, avec deux cent mille livres de rente, vous auriez Mlle de Langeais, la fille du marquis; elle est laide, elle a trente ans, et pas un sou de dot: ça doit vous aller. (IV, 538–39)

Joseph, whose wealthy marriage of convenience is suddenly introduced on the last page of the novel, may seem more ambivalently positioned within its glaringly homosocial structures. If it is true that Flore's 'character' is incidental to her fate as the Rabouilleuse, are the 'good' qualities of Joseph similarly irrelevant to consideration of his homosocial advantages? As we have seen, Joseph never despises the Rabouilleuse, and is able to empathize with her behaviour:

> 'Ce garçon est très bien, se dit Joseph en admirant comme peintre la figure vive, l'air de force et les yeux gris spirituels que Max tenait de son père le gentilhomme. Mon oncle doit être bien embêtant, cette belle fille a cherché des compensations, et ils font ménage à trois. Ça se voit!' (IV, 440)

In that Flore and her lover are fodder for his tolerant artist's gaze, Joseph is happy to position himself within this *ménage*, his enjoyment of his uncle's dinner, and his chumminess with Max, underscoring his uncritical complicity with the male side of this problematic equation: 'Au dessert, à neuf heures, le peintre, assis entre Flore et Max vis-à-vis de son oncle, était devenu quasi-camarade avec l'officier' (IV, 443). When the visit to Issoudun reaches its disastrous conclusion, Joseph consoles himself by drawing from his experience the following moral lesson: '"Gredin! tu n'as que ce que tu mérites, en venant chercher une succession au lieu d'être à peindre dans ton atelier..."' (IV, 465) Painting and inheritances, it seems, belong to two distinct spheres, and Joseph would do better to stick to the former. However, seventeen years later, notwithstanding his lack of concern for money, he has married — 'par la protection du comte de Sérizy' — the daughter of a provincial millionaire and has taken his place in a wealthy bourgeois genealogy: 'Joseph, à qui son beau-père, espèce de Hochon rustique, amasse tous les jours des écus, possède déjà soixante mille livres de rente' (IV, 540). What is more, with the death of Philippe on an Algerian battlefield, which occurs in the same year as this marriage, Joseph inherits the inalienable Brambourg estate and *hôtel*, as well as his brother's title: 'Par suite d'une clause de l'érection du majorat, il se trouve comte de Brambourg, ce qui le fait souvent pouffer de rire, au milieu de ses amis, dans son atelier.' (IV, 540) It is in his studio that Joseph, surrounded by his male friends, is to be found making fun of

— though hardly refusing — the patriarchal privileges that are raining upon him. It is implied that he would have preferred artistic to social consecration ('Quoiqu'il peigne de magnifiques toiles et rende de grands services aux artistes, il n'est pas encore membre de l'Institut' (IV, 540)) and, as we already know, what most pleases him in this inheritance is 'la belle collection de tableaux'. Of his wife, other than the wealth that she brings him, we learn precisely nothing; indeed, we can only wonder whether she, like her good-natured artist husband, finds her role in these structures of inheritance a joke to be shared with her friends. Curiously, Pierre Laubriet treats Joseph's marriage as a chance occurrence on a par with his brother's death: 'il ne cherche d'ailleurs pas l'argent, pas davantage que d'Arthez, et comme lui il ne sera riche que par hasard, ayant épousé une fille riche et héritant de son frère, comme l'écrivain a hérité de son oncle'.[14] Yet the fortune, title, *hôtel* and the picture collection were only in Philippe Bridau's hands thanks to the cycle of male exploitation of the aesthetic and sexual charms of the Rabouilleuse. In the chapter that follows, I shall contextualize Joseph's structural complicity by making him the point of intersection of painting, prostitution and marriage in texts of *La Comédie humaine* where he plays a less obviously central role.

Notes to Chapter 5

1. The novel was originally published in two parts: the Parisian *Les Deux Frères* in 1841, and the largely provincial *Un ménage de garçon en province* in 1842.

2. On 11 April 1841, Balzac signed a contract with Souverain for four novels, one of which was entitled *La Rabouilleuse*; this title recurred in Balzac's correspondence, alternating with others, throughout 1841 (see the introduction to Honoré de Balzac, *La Rabouilleuse*, ed. by Citron (Paris: Garnier, 1966), p. xliii). According to Guise, Balzac abandoned this title through fear of perceived imitation of Eugène Sue's contemporaneous creation, la Goualeuse, in *Les Mystères de Paris* (see *La Rabouilleuse*, ed. by Guise, in *La Comédie humaine*, IV, 247–541 (p. 252)). Citron suggests that Balzac returned to the title *La Rabouilleuse* for its evocative power ('aller au fond des choses en remuant la vase') (p. xcvi).

3. Though Joseph Bridau will accept commissions for copies of old masters in order to support himself financially (IV, 327; IV, 349), he fosters his own talent by absorbing their methods in the process ('aussi sa brosse est-elle une des plus savantes' (IV, 327)), to the extent that his first major work, 'un des chefs-d'œuvre de la peinture moderne' (IV, 326), is mistaken by Gros for a Titian, and is accused by others of being a pastiche. However, unless Barthes has mistakenly conflated several of Joseph's paintings, he is presumably referring to the mature portrait of the artist's mother ('qui existe encore dans l'atelier de Bridau'), of which 'plus d'un artiste [...] demande aujourd'hui à notre grand peintre: "Est-ce la copie d'une tête de Raphaël?"' (IV, 277).

4. The similarity of the lecher's and the artist's initial evaluation of a beautiful body is also emphasized in *Les Marana*: 'avec cette science de vision qui donne à un débauché, aussi bien qu'à un sculpteur, le fatal pouvoir de déshabiller pour ainsi dire une femme, d'en deviner les formes par des inductions et rapides et sagaces, [Montefiore] vit un de ces chefs-d'œuvres dont la création exige tous les bonheurs de l'amour.' (*Les Marana*, ed. by Citron, in *La Comédie humaine*, X, 1015–94 (p. 1045).) In *Balzac, peintre de corps*, Borderie notes of this passage: 'Le désir, même dégradé, donne donc une perspicacité particulière.' (p. 170)

5. For Balzac's exploitation of the myth of Flora (goddess and nymph), see Takao Kashiwagi, *La Trilogie des célibataires* (Paris: Nizet, 1983), pp. 130–31.

6. This would be the 1812 Salon, the last to take place during the Empire. On the editorial choice of *estompe* rather than *estampe*, see IV, 1226.

7. On the perception (and reality) of the model as prostitute, see Lathers, *Bodies of Art*.

8. Even for the reader, the details remain somewhat opaque. However, the opening overview of

Rouget's marriage and widowhood is entirely unambiguous: 'Après la mort de sa femme, le docteur mena toujours une vie débauchée; mais il la régla pour ainsi dire et la réduisit au huis-clos du chez soi.' (IV, 276) It seems likely that periodic recourse to qualification and equivocation was one of Balzac's strategies for conveying fairly explicit information about sexual behaviour whilst attempting to evade censorship. On Balzac's oblique but obvious references to sexuality, see Jacques Cellard, 'Le *Vicaire* et la *Rabouilleuse*: Autocensure et sexualité dans la *Comédie humaine*', in *Censures: De la Bible aux larmes d'Éros. Le livre et la Censure en France*, ed. by Martine Poulain and Françoise Serre (Paris: Centre Pompidou / BPI, 1987), pp. 140–45.

9. See Citron, p. 256, and Kashiwagi, who points out that Balzac reread the sentence carefully enough to add the words 'de neige' to his copy of the Furne edition (p. 176).

10. As previously seen, Barthes's *modèle de la peinture* moves from 'Zambinella centenaire' to 'la Rabouilleuse enfant'. I am struck by the similarity of detail in Balzac's descriptions of the dying Flore and the withered, skeletal Zambinella (see VI, 1051–52). In both cases two portraits are contrasted, one of the artist's model sculpted to perfection, the other of physical decline represented as a bundle of bones and concavities. However, in terms of the gendered sexual politics governing the destinies of these two beautiful children, both sold into prostitution, the resemblance stops there. One dies of poverty and squalor, the other is a multi-millionaire cosseted by his descendants. Which is not to say there are not female equivalents to Zambinella's wealth and success (see the next chapter for discussion of Josépha in *La Cousine Bette*), as well as beautiful young males heading for the sorry fate of the Rabouilleuse. See Canler's *Mémoires* (pp. 316–39) for information on male prostitution, of which Idamore Chardin, who has a fleeting role in *La Cousine Bette*, is an interesting example.

11. See Balzac's well-known comment on the novel: 'un ouvrage fait sans l'élément amour, ce qui est d'un difficile!' (letter of 11–16 November 1842, in *Lettres à Madame Hanska*, ed. by Roger Pierrot, 2 vols (Paris: Robert Laffont, 1990), I, 611).

12. See Hunt, *Balzac's Comédie humaine* (London: The Athlone Press, 1964), p. 341, p. 343.

13. See, for example, *La Député d'Arcis*, ed. by Colin Smethurst, in *La Comédie humaine*, VIII, 697–813 (p. 804): 'Pour cet homme [Maxime de Trailles], les femmes ne furent jamais que des moyens, il ne croyait pas plus à leurs douleurs qu'à leurs plaisirs; il les prenait, comme feu de Marsay, pour des enfants méchants. [...] Le comte Maxime de Trailles savait seul combien de désastres il avait causés; mais il s'était toujours mis à l'abri du blâme en obéissant aux lois du Code-Homme.'

14. See Laubriet, *L'Intelligence de l'art chez Balzac: D'une esthétique balzacienne* (Geneva: Slatkine Reprints, 1980 [first pub. 1961]), p. 222.

CHAPTER 6

❖

The Joseph Bridau Cycle

(i) 'L'art était représenté par Joseph Bridau'

One of the most interesting scenes of *La Rabouilleuse* is staged in Joseph's studio. Agathe has manipulated Joseph into agreeing to seek out his brother Philippe, who will pose for a portrait representing his moment of military glory, 'en uniforme des Dragons de la Garde impériale' (IV, 347). The tolerant Joseph, who avoids moral judgements, is typically complicit with the semi-pathological desire of his mother: '"C'est ta passion, à toi, ce garçon! dit-il, et nous avons tous notre passion malheureuse"' (IV, 346). Whereas Agathe was always anxious to excuse Philippe's behaviour and, such was her desire not to displease him, would support him financially and accede to his endless demands, she has finally banished him from the home for causing the death of her aunt Descoings. Is it for this reason, or for the pleasure of a *mise en scène* devised by herself, that her presence during the sitting will be kept from Philippe? Agathe will hide in the studio and, in a specific and powerful echo of the voyeurism of her brother Jean-Jacques, will spy through a hole she has made in a screen.[1] Thus Philippe will pose in what, for his mother, is clearly a psychically charged *tableau vivant*. Not only does Joseph's complicity extend this far, he will also, as the artist, knowingly enact his role. What the reader sees is a layering of representations, set in the artist's studio, as the mother peers through her chink to watch one of 'les deux frères' — the initial title of the first part of the novel — painting the other in the interests of her 'passion'. Within the tableau created for her, the model is posed on a stuffed horse that has been hired by Joseph for the purpose (the painted horse already exists, '"un beau cheval d'après Gros"' (IV, 346) that was awaiting a suitable destination). Philippe is decked out in the uniform he had sent round the previous day (and which the fetishistic Agathe, when it arrived, 'ne put s'empêcher d'embrasser' (IV, 347)); at the end of the painting performance, which has lasted for four hours (with an 'interval' for lunch), 'le dragon reprit ses habits ordinaires' (IV, 348).[2] One is reminded yet again of the Pygmalion-in-a-brothel scene that Canler describes himself watching through a chink in the wall, not least because this careful conflation of artist and model — of theatrical props, a costume, voyeurism and satisfied desire — has a relatively weak function in the plot. Agathe cannot resist revealing her presence at the end of the sitting, so that the session the following Sunday is an altogether more straightforward affair ('Cette fois sa mère assista visiblement à la séance. Elle servit le déjeuner et put questionner le dragon.' (IV, 348)), while Philippe's subsequent theft of what he mistakes for an original Rubens (in fact a copy made by Joseph), brings matters to a premature close:

> — J'achèverai sa maudite figure de mémoire, il y manque peu de chose.
> — Laisse-la comme elle est, il me ferait trop de mal à voir. (IV, 350)

Given that the painting will not be finished, or mentioned again in the text, the episode seems to have been used by Balzac to motivate a powerful scenario in which Joseph poses as a painter even as he paints. As a child, in order to accede to the status of future artist, he was hoaxed into posing as the model for a statue in Chaudet's studio. Now that he has become that artist is Joseph, one of the vehicles of representational writing in *La Rabouilleuse*, also an object of Balzac's realist gaze?

Critical discussions of Joseph tend to veer off into the question of real life models for the artist and his art: was he based on Delacroix, or on Delacroix and a few others besides? For Antoine Adam, discussing the addition of Joseph to the Cénacle in *Illusions perdues*, 'Il y eut sans doute divers modèles et le Bridau de *Pierre Grassou* n'est pas celui de *La Rabouilleuse*, ni celui d'*Un début dans la vie*.'[3] Pierre Citron finds Joseph 'saisissant de vérité dans *La Rabouilleuse*', but elusive and lacking coherence once placed in the overall context of *La Comédie humaine*: 'figure d'une immense fresque dans *Illusions perdues*, personnage de drame ici, rapin de comédie dans *Un début dans la vie*, il assume des rôles divers, en rapport chaque fois avec la nature de l'œuvre où il apparaît; les raccords faits par Balzac ne suffisent pas à lui assurer une rigoureuse unité'.[4] What Citron fails to find across these incarnations is the psychological and aesthetic unity of a consistently complex character. For me, Joseph Bridau's coherence within *La Comédie humaine* can be read at the level of a structure that repeatedly links the figure of the artist to his model. This structure is a simple one; however, as we have seen in the case of *La Rabouilleuse*, it is embedded in the complex social realities of *La Comédie humaine* and is invariably a useful focus for their sexual politics. For example, in *Illusions perdues*, a conversation between Joseph and Lucien de Rubempré is an artificial *raccord* of the sort Citron finds ineffectual. Yet the Joseph who speaks is so much the Joseph of *La Rabouilleuse* that the passage reads as a parody:

> — Coralie est bien admirablement belle, s'écria Joseph Bridau. Quel magni-fique portrait à faire!
> — Et bonne, répondit Lucien. [...] mais tu feras son portrait; prends-la, si tu veux, pour modèle de ta Vénitienne amenée au Sénateur par une vieille femme.[5]

In *La Rabouilleuse*, Joseph has indeed borrowed Coralie to model for his young girl being sold into prostitution. The painting that results, often referred to in the text as Bridau's first work of genius, acts as an indirect pictorial allusion to Flore's delivery by her uncle to the elderly doctor. The Lucien who jumps in to offer Joseph his eighteen-year-old mistress as a model has none of the scruples, authentic or feigned, of Nicolas Poussin in *Le Chef-d'œuvre inconnu*. Coralie is already a prostitute who had been sold by her mother to de Marsay when she was fifteen; abandoned by the latter, she has found a wealthy protector in Camusot, a fifty-six-year-old silk merchant with four children from two marriages, and partner in lechery of his elderly father-in-law.[6] Camusot is willing to turn a blind eye to Lucien as long as Coralie will go on sleeping with him, a situation that Lousteau, who shares Coralie's friend Florine with Matifat, easily persuades Lucien to accept: '"C'est comme si vous aimiez une femme mariée, voilà tout."' (v, 377) As in *La Rabouilleuse*, prostitution is as commonly structured as marriage by the *ménage à trois*. The parallel fates of Coralie and Flore are allusively compressed in a single fictional painting for which they are, respectively, the literal and metaphorical models of a young girl sold by her family into prostitution. In short, Joseph's aesthetic admiration for Coralie as a potential model provides the sort of link, however clumsy, upon which Balzac's wide-ranging social analysis depends. Throughout *La Comédie humaine*, significance tends to emerge, less from an increasing inner coherence of reappearing characters, than from Balzac's vast assemblage of schematic but mutually reinforcing parts. Although *Un début dans la vie* and *Pierre Grassou* are very different from *La Rabouilleuse* in scope and tone, my analysis of Joseph Bridau — which explores the relation between his status as artist and his position within the social codes that structure marriage and inheritance — has been furthered by reading the three texts in conjunction.[7]

Balzac's earliest description of Joseph, to be found in *Illusions perdues*, is so unlike those that follow that it acts as a useful foil. In the page-long portrait to be found in *Un grand homme de province à Paris*, Joseph is introduced as a member of the Cénacle: 'L'Art était représenté par Joseph Bridau' (v, 316). His talent, however, is apparently uneven for a reason unrecognizable to readers of *La Rabouilleuse*: Joseph allows his capricious personality, and especially his capricious love affairs, to interfere with his painting:

> Il a le dessin de Rome et la couleur de Venise; mais l'amour le tue et ne traverse pas que son cœur: l'amour lui lance ses flèches dans le cerveau, lui dérange sa vie et lui fait faire les plus étranges zigzags. [...] Il est éloquent et sait aimer, mais avec ses caprices, qu'il porte dans ses sentiments comme dans son *faire*. (v, 316)

In *La Rabouilleuse*, there is no mention whatsoever of any love affairs in the life of the cheerful and even-tempered Joseph. Not that he fits Barthes's analysis in *S/Z* of the asexual Sarrasine, shut away from the world with his muse: 'Sarrasine ne fait jamais l'amour, il est en état d'*aphanisis* (ou perte de sexualité); Sarrasine, tel Pygmalion, couche avec des statues, il investit son érotisme dans son art.' (p. 109) Joseph does not appear to relate erotically to his painting, and if there is an ironic Pygmalion in *La Rabouilleuse*, it is Dr Rouget. Despite his aesthetic enthusiasm for Flore Brazier, Joseph does not idealize her as 'perfect woman'; he is not sexually attracted to the metaphorically sculpted figure he perceives as a Titian Venus, nor does he attempt to transform her into an actual work of art. After accepting his uncle's picture collection and parading through Issoudun with the Rabouilleuse, Joseph returns late and somewhat drunk, and sleeps until midday. If he has dreamed, it is more likely of the paintings than the Rabouilleuse, for Balzac makes him wake up to the sight of canvases piled up in his room: 'De son lit, il aperçut les toiles mises les unes sur les autres, et apportées sans qu'il eût rien entendu.' (iv, 443) To find a Joseph in love we must turn to *Un début dans la vie*, published between the two *feuilleton* sequences of *La Rabouilleuse*. However, as if to prove a point, this amorous Joseph is an assumed persona; indeed, he is as much a joke as the story he chooses to tell.

The coach journey that takes Joseph to Presles in the company of, amongst others, the comte de Sérisy and père Léger — his future marriage broker and his future father-in-law — follows, in fictional time, the hasty departure from Issoudun that is narrated in *La Rabouilleuse*. It is not only the episode of Joseph's false arrest, and his close escape from the angry Issoudun mob, that is repeated in parodic mode in his Dalmatian *mystification*; what precedes his near lynching in the town of Zara is an equally parodic recall of his very recent encounter with the Rabouilleuse. If the close resemblance of the two crowd scenes has generated scholarly editorial notes,[8] the similarities in events leading up to the arrests have passed, to my knowledge, without critical comment. What leaps from the page, in Joseph's tale of an abortive adulterous passion, is the conflation of the aesthetic and the sexual that is so strikingly absent, in *La Rabouilleuse*, from his relation to art. His fanciful alter ego (relayed via the assumed identity of Schinner), is an artist in whom a clichéd aesthetic ideal — a classical Greek beauty encountered in a Venetian state — immediately arouses a clichéd desire:

> 'j'aperçois une femme, oh! mais une femme! une Grecque, c'est tout dire, la plus belle créature de toute la ville: des yeux fendus en amande, des paupières qui se dépliaient comme des jalousies, et des cils comme des pinceaux, un visage d'un ovale à rendre fou Raphaël, un teint d'un coloris délicieux, les teintes bien fondues, veloutées... des mains... oh!...'[9]

Like the Rabouilleuse, 'Zéna' lives on the other side of a narrow street, a location chosen, no doubt, so that the artist can frame her in his window: '"Il serait trop long de vous peindre le plus délicieux temps de ma vie, à savoir, les trois jours que j'ai passés à ma fenêtre"' (I, 792). Like Flore, in what is presented, however, as a quaint and positively un-French custom — '"dans ce pays-là, on achète sa femme, et sans voir..."' — she has been sold to a lecherous old man: '"Pour épouser Zéna, le mari, vieil infâme, a donné trois cent mille francs aux parents, tant était célèbre la beauté de cette fille vraiment la plus belle de toute la Dalmatie, Illyrie, Adriatique, etc."' (I, 791). Moreover, as in the case of Flore, the old man's wealth is the cause of her misfortune: '"l'immense fortune du damné pirate causait tout le malheur de ma Zéna"' (I, 793). Finally, if 'Schinner', unlike the 'real' Joseph, still dreams of this beautiful woman — '"il y a des nuits où mon sommeil est éclairé par les yeux de Zéna"' (I, 791) — he rounds off his story on a bathetically predictable note: '"J'irai faire son portrait, car dans quelques années tout sera oublié."' (I, 793–94)

The context of Joseph's story, a parody of the artist falling in love with his aesthetic ideal, is also a palimpsest of pastiches. Joseph is pretending to be his friend Schinner, a more famous artist, while Mistigris, with his suggestion that the anecdote is apocryphal, trumps Sérisy — who apparently knows its source — concerning the truth value of Joseph's Dalmatian arrest :

> — Comment, dit naïvement Oscar, ça vous est arrivé?
> — Pourquoi ce ne serait-il pas arrivé à monsieur, puisque c'était arrivé déjà une fois pendant l'occupation française en Illyrie à l'un de nos plus beaux officiers d'artillerie? dit finement le comte.
> — Et vous avez cru l'artilleur? dit finement Mistigris au comte. (I, 794)

Moreover, as is well known, Balzac's text, first published as *Le Danger des mystifications*, is a rewriting (in places very close to the original) of *Le Voyage en coucou*, a story supplied by his sister.[10] Although Nadine Satiat assumes that Laure must have given her brother her manuscript as well as her subject, she claims, misleadingly in my view, that Joseph is a 'personnage quasi inexistant dans la nouvelle de Laure Surville'.[11] Unlike Balzac's Joseph, Laure's Jules Dubois is blond and good looking, and his 'lie' is limited to pretending to be a painter who has ' "concour[u] pour le grand prix de Rome" ' (whereas, in reality, he has been forced by his father's death to give up trying to become an artist, and now supports his mother by painting imitation marble). However, not only has Laure chosen for one of her main characters a future great artist, she has also invented the painter's symbolically paternal protection by a count who will further his career. In *Le Voyage en coucou*, le comte Maurice recognizes Jules's moral superiority over the other boastful travellers and, once the identities are out and Jules's apology has been kindly received, offers there and then, like a self-conscious fairy godfather, to ensure his success as a painter. The structure of *Un début dans la vie*, in which a repeat coach journey takes place seventeen years later, also derives from *Le Voyage en coucou*; when Laure's travellers are reunited after a gap of just six years, 'Jules Dubois, par la puissante protection du comte devenu son ami, voyait donc la fortune et la célébrité lui sourire au début de sa carrière' (I, 1466). Thus Laure has contributed the basic homosocial structure that leads, in Balzac's hands, to Joseph's marriage to the daughter of a provincial millionaire: ' "C'est un mariage que M. le comte de Sérisy a bien voulu préparer pour moi, je lui devais déjà beaucoup comme artiste; et avant de mourir, il a voulu s'occuper de ma fortune, à laquelle je ne songeais point..." ' (I, 885).[12] Balzac appears to have grafted Laure's 'artist plot' onto the career of Joseph Bridau, already launched in *Un grand homme de province à Paris*, *Pierre Grassou* and *Les Deux Frères*.[13] As well as the wealthy marriage that crowns Sérisy's patronage of Joseph, Balzac has added to Laure's text the artist's tall story of a Dalmatian love affair. What is more, in Balzac's text, it is this *mystification* that appears to have forged the bond between Joseph and Sérisy; like the straight man in a double act, Sérisy offers prompts and reactions and moves the story along, almost as if the two men were inventing it together.[14] Transplanted from *Un début dans la vie* into *La Rabouilleuse*, Joseph's marriage of convenience, and its origins in a male comedy of fakes, copies and role playing, foregrounds once more the theme of the artist's relation to the gendering of social realities. Until the last page of *La Rabouilleuse*, marrying or not marrying is never raised as an issue for Joseph. His celibacy is not traced back to the young boy's powerful vocation; it is simply not mentioned. In a single oblique allusion, Joseph repeats to his dying mother what he claims to have told his friend Pierre Grassou: ' "Ce qui me console au milieu de mes luttes, c'est d'avoir une bonne mère; elle est ce que doit être la femme d'un artiste, elle a soin de tout, elle veille à mes besoins matériels sans faire le moindre embarras..." ' (IV, 529). The choice of addressee is interesting in that, genius apart, Joseph's attitude to the relation between art and sexuality appears to have more in common with Pierre Grassou than with Sarrasine or Frenhofer.

(ii) 'Toujours des pastiches'

The eponymous hero of *Pierre Grassou* is celibate not only by force of circumstance ('Ayant vécu dans le travail et dans la misère, il n'avait jamais eu le temps d'aimer') but also by inclination: 'Jusqu'alors garçon et pauvre, il ne se souciait point de compliquer son existence si simple.'[15] When Magus, his picture dealer, turns up at his studio with three would-be portraits and the possibility of a large dowry ('"Ce sera peut-être pour vous des portraits de famille"'), Grassou 'crut entendre Méphistophélès parlant mariage' (VI, 1094): '"Me marier, moi? s'écria Pierre Grassou, moi qui ai l'habitude de me coucher tout seul, de me lever de bon matin, qui ai ma vie arrangée…"' (VI, 1094–95). If the comedy of Grassou's marriage to the bourgeois heiress whose portrait he paints makes this another ironic Pygmalion text, the two threads I have traced through *La Rabouilleuse* — and have found parodically present in *Un début dans la vie* — are here inseparably entwined. In *Pierre Grassou*, the transfer of property and wealth from one man to another is mediated by the woman who is literally — not just metaphorically, as in *La Rabouilleuse* — the artist's model; indeed, the conjugal plot is played out in two settings: the artist's studio, and his future father-in-law's gallery of pastiched masterpieces (the 'fakes' that turn out to have originated in Grassou's own studio). This link between conjugal structures and those of realist art is symbolically illustrated by Grassou's début picture. The 'bad' painting that is refused by the 1819 Salon is the origin of his relationship with Élias Magus, seemingly his exploiter, but in fact the symbolic father — Grassou's equivalent of Sérisy — who will launch his career and broker his marriage. The picture is a laborious pastiche of Greuze's *L'Accordée de village*, the subject of which, appropriately, is the handover of a daughter's dowry from father to son-in-law.[16]

Grassou's pastiche, marginally improved thanks to Schinner's advice, is bought by Magus for fifteen francs and sold on ('"Je suis rentré dans mes fonds avec un petit intérêt"' (VI, 1098)), presumably as a Greuze original.[17] When Magus commissions more paintings (Flemish interiors, an anatomy lesson and so on), Grassou 'aurait serré Magus dans ses bras, il le regardait comme un père' (VI, 1098). He believes his talent has been recognized at last and in a sense he is right, for Magus has astutely spotted the financial potential of this inveterate pasticher. The purchase of the pastiched 'noce de village', and the subsequent, open-ended commission, is the contract that launches the longstanding association of painter and dealer, and Balzac uses a prostitution metaphor — 'il ressemblait à un lycéen qui protège une femme' (VI, 1098) — to convey Grassou's naive pride. That evening, taken to the Opéra by Joseph Bridau, he is impatient to get back to his studio: 'Fougères ne vit pas le ballet, il n'entendit pas la musique, il concevait des tableaux, il peignait. Il quittait Joseph au milieu de la soirée, il courut chez lui faire des esquisses à la lampe, il inventa trente tableaux pleins de réminiscences, il se crut un homme de génie' (VI, 1098–99). If Grassou sounds briefly like Sarrasine here, as he stocks up with food, paints and canvases for 'deux mois de séclusion', the art he cathects is more slavish imitation: 'des paysages hollandais, des intérieurs de Metzu, […] une copie de *La Leçon d'anatomie* de Rembrandt: "Toujours des pastiches, dit Schinner. Ah!

Fougères aura de la peine à être original."' (VI, 1099) After the episode of Grassou's bizarre hallucination in Magus's shop (his crisp, bright paintings seem covered by a dull veil, so much so that they look like old paintings), 'le peintre rentra dans son atelier y faire de nouvelles vieilles toiles' (VI, 1099). It is the beginning of a long apprenticeship in the art of second-rate painting and, by the age of thirty-seven, Grassou has produced around two hundred paintings for Magus, all of which remain 'complètement inconnus' (VI, 1101). Although his full name, Pierre Grassou de Fougères, contains anagrams of *forgerie* and *faussaire*, it is unknowingly that Grassou has been producing fakes; the relentless pastiches are explained, in Balzac's text, by his severe lack of talent.[18]

In *La Rabouilleuse*, Pierre Grassou is the friend who inspires in Joseph the successful joke of swapping round on their easels a Rubens original and his own commissioned copy. As well as illustrating Grassou's naivety (and motivating Philippe's mistaken theft of the copy), the episode reveals that Joseph, in order to earn a living and to pay for his materials, also accepts dubious commissions from Magus ('"il me faut demain pour lui donner tous les tons de l'original et la veillir afin qu'on ne les reconnaisse pas"' (IV, 349)). Earlier in the text Philippe, visiting his brother's studio for the first time, had found him at work on a copy for a dealer: '"Voici donc comment se font les tableaux?" [...] "Non, mais voilà comment ils se copient."' (IV, 317) Like Grassou, Joseph learns from these copies ('"j'étudie la manière des maîtres, j'y gagne de l'instruction, je surprends les secrets du métier"' (IV, 317–18)); however, unlike Grassou, he keeps them in a separate compartment from his real paintings ('"Voilà l'un de mes tableaux"' (IV, 318)). Yet Joseph Bridau's acknowledged masterpieces, such as the painting of the young girl being handed over to a Venetian senator, or the portrait of his mother that will be admired in his studio, are mistaken by connoisseurs for pastiches of Titian and Raphael respectively. As we have seen, the theme of pastiche in *La Rabouilleuse* is marshalled by Barthes in support of his account of realist art: 'car il faut que le peintre lui aussi copie un autre code, un code antérieur' (pp. 61–62). Barthes does not give consideration to the quality and status of the copy, to what theoretical criteria might distinguish Joseph's good copies from Grassou's bad ones, or Joseph's commissioned copies from works of genius by Joseph that are nevertheless viewed as pastiches. 'Code sur code, dit le réalisme', speaking through the voice of Barthes in *S/Z* (p. 61). Balzac, in *Pierre Grassou*, would appear to agree. The slippery issue of the origins of the codes of art is exploited in the mode of parody. Yet these are not empty codes, for it is their relation to the institutional codes of marriage that is comically short-circuited in Balzac's short story.

I have already suggested that Jean-Jacques Rouget's preference for his frames over his pictures, and his commissioning of copies to replace the originals, reads as a parody of sections of *S/Z*. The realist aesthetic that for Barthes is associated with Frenhofer — his obsession with being able to see all sides of a three-dimensional *Catherine Lescault* — is exemplified to humorous effect in two passages of *Pierre Grassou*. The first concerns Grassou's long-awaited success at the 1829 Salon, a first admission to the Louvre engineered by the influence of his now famous friends, Léon de Lora (Mistigris), Schinner and Bridau. The painting, *La Toilette d'un chouan*, *condamné à mort en 1809,* 'qui tenait de Vigneron pour le sentiment et du premier faire de Dubufe pour l'exécution', is not simply an unconscious pastiche: 'Fougères s'était inspiré tout bonnement du chef-d'œuvre de Gérard Dow: il avait retourné le groupe de la Femme hydropique vers la fenêtre, au lieu de le présenter de face.' (VI, 1100) This disguised (and unrecognized) instance of plagiarism depends less on replacing the dying woman by a condemned man ('même paleur, même regard, même appel à Dieu') than on Grassou's ingenious ninety-degree rotation of the whole group.[19] The second passage concerns the first appearance of the three three-dimensional members of the Vervelle family. What enters is a family of fruit and vegetables, led by 'une figure vulgairement appelée *un melon* dans les ateliers. Ce fruit surmontait une citrouille, vêtue de drap bleu, ornée d'un paquet de breloques tintinnabulant. Le melon soufflait comme un marsouin, la citrouille marchait sur des navets, improprement appelés des jambes.' (VI, 1103) Even if, as a note in the Pléiade edition is at pains to point out, *melon* and *citrouille* are both words in French for a stupid person, from a mock sculptural point of view the stress is on an assemblage of shapes, or rather of non-shapely shapes, in that the two rotundities led in by Magus — '"Il n'y a que vous pour pêcher de pareilles boules"' (VI, 1104) — are entirely without contours. These are naked vegetables dressed in clothes, so much so that the grotesque wife bears more than a passing parodic resemblance to the Rabouilleuse, decked out in her finery on the Rouget doorstep in Issoudun, her lace-covered back as mysteriously visible as her lace-covered chest:

> La femme avait sur la figure un acajou répandu, elle ressemblait à une noix de coco surmontée d'une tête et serrée par une ceinture. Elle pivotait sur ses pieds, sa robe était jaune, à raies noires. [...] Des dentelles paraient des épaules aussi bombées par-derrière que par-devant; ainsi la forme sphérique du coco était parfaite. (VI, 1103)

However, in this text, at least, an explanation is provided for the all-round perspective on Grassou's future mother-in-law; Mme Vervelle, we learn, swivels on her podgy feet like one of the rotating statues viewed by Canler in Mlle S★★★'s brothel.

Virginie Vervelle, for better or worse, takes after neither of her parents. Where they form two spheres, she is not even plump; in fact she has 'des bras filamenteux' and no figure at all: 'Suivait une jeune asperge, verte et jaune par sa robe' (VI, 1103). Virginie's features and complexion are the polar opposite of Zéna the Greek's in Joseph's fantasy description. If Zéna's '"teintes bien fondues"' (I, 791) contrast with Virginie's freckles, her '"yeux fendus en amande"', her '"paupières qui se dépliaient comme des jalousies"', and her '"cils comme des pinceaux"' (I, 791) cast a markedly unfavourable light on Virginie's 'grands yeux innocents, à cils blancs' and her 'peu de sourcils' (VI, 1103). Virginie's distinctive attribute is her 'chevelure en bandeau, d'un jaune carotte qu'un Romain eût adoré' (VI, 1103); it is the basis of Magus's attempt to sell her charms to Grassou as aesthetic as well as financial: '"Cent mille francs, [...] et une fille douce, pleine de tons dorés comme un vrai Titien!"' (VI, 1095). However, if Virginie is a true Titian, the one that hangs in the Vervelles' gallery at Ville-d'Avray is decidedly a fake. In one of the dizzying paradoxes that mark the last pages of Balzac's story, we learn, if we have not already guessed, that

Pierre Grassou is its creator. It is a discussion between Grassou and Vervelle on the cost and real value of the pastiched Titian — '"Trois mille francs! dit à voix basse Vervelle [...]; mais je dis quarante mille francs!"' — that produces this comic twist in the story. The discovery that Grassou has painted most of the masterpieces in the gallery, and has sold them to Magus for a fraction of what Vervelle has paid for them, far from denting his reputation, multiplies Grassou's value as an artist. More literally, it doubles his desirability as a son-in-law: '"Prouvez-le-moi, dit le marchand de bouteilles, et je double la dot de ma fille, car alors vous êtes Rubens, Rembrandt, Terburg, Titien!"' (VI, 1110) As for the portrait of Virginie, even at the first sitting '[Fougères] était *in petto* déjà le gendre de la famille Vervelle' (VI, 1106). Now, as Magus had predicted, Pierre Grassou completes the three portraits for nothing, and offers them as gifts 'à son beau-père, à sa belle-mère et à sa femme' (VI, 1110). In an ironic reversal of the norm, Pierre Grassou de Fougères has apparently provided the proof demanded by Vervelle, not that the pictures were authentic originals, but that they were authentic Grassou fakes. If the conjugal plot is framed by the issue of pastiche, it is also predicated upon it.

Not only is this an art gallery of pastiches, it is a pastiche of an art gallery: 'le marchand de bouteilles semblait avoir voulu lutter avec le roi Louis-Philippe et les galeries de Versailles' (VI, 1109).[20] In a scene reminiscent of Flaubert's Bouvard and Pécuchet opening their museum for a public viewing, the Vervelles have staged a *coup de théâtre* with lighting effects and a handpicked audience: not only 'trois voisins, anciens commerçants', but a conjugally contextualized 'oncle à succession' and a 'vieille demoiselle Vervelle' (VI, 1109). The paintings are varnished and magnificently framed, and gold labels display the false titles of the pictures ('REMBRANDT. *Intérieur d'une salle de dissection. Le docteur Tromp faisant sa leçon à ses élèves*' (VI, 1109)). If Pierre Grassou, who had long struggled to enter the Salon du Louvre, is the presiding genius of this museum ('il était à lui seul vingt grands maîtres' (VI, 1110)), marriage into the Vervelle family — 'les Vervelle et les Grassou, qui s'entendent à merveille' (VI, 1111) — will bring him ownership of the art gallery along with everything else.[21] The magnificent frames are a reminder of the picture collection that Joseph Bridau will similarly inherit. But where, in *La Rabouilleuse*, what is thought to be a collection of old *croûtes* is in fact a set of masterpieces, in *Pierre Grassou*, Vervelle's fabulously expensive paintings are worthless fakes. However, in a final Flaubertian gesture that, once again, dissolves the apparent difference between Joseph and Grassou, the latter who, for all his own absence of talent, had always been able to appreciate genius in others, 'achète des tableaux de peintres célèbres quand ils sont gênés, et il remplace les croûtes de la galerie de Ville-d'Avray par de vrais chefs-d'œuvre, qui ne sont pas de lui.' (VI, 1111)[22] Thus, in all probability, some of Joseph Bridau's paintings will end up in the art gallery of Pierre Grassou de Fougères: authentic impostors amongst his friend's fakes.

Given Joseph's admiration for the Titian Venus of Issoudun, it may seem appropriate that his cameo appearance in *Pierre Grassou* should coincide with the Titian Virginie's first sitting for her portrait: 'Vers la fin de la séance, l'escalier fut agité, la porte fut brutalement ouverte, et entra Joseph Bridau' (VI, 1106–07). As Goetz notes, this scene in which Joseph metes out tactless advice on the portrait, and briefly takes Grassou's place at the easel, is certainly an ironic recall of the masterclass in which Frenhofer, in *Le Chef-d'œuvre inconnu*, so energetically reworks the *Marie égyptienne* of his friend Porbus:

> 'Aborde donc la Nature comme elle est! dit le grand peintre en continuant. Mademoiselle est rousse. Eh bien, est-ce un péché mortel? Tout est magnifique en peinture. Mets-moi du cinabre sur ta palette, réchauffe-moi ces joues-là, piques-y leurs petites taches brunes, beurre-moi cela!' (VI, 1107) [23]

In *Pierre Grassou*, both model and audience are unimpressed by the boisterous genius they see as an anti-Grassou, and Joseph himself cuts short the lesson ('"Tiens, suis ces indications"'), hastily returning the palette and leaving without saying goodbye, 'tant il en avait assez d'avoir regardé Virginie' (VI, 1108). What interests me is less the parodic repetition of a key scene from *Le Chef-d'œuvre inconnu*, than the significance of the brief substitution of Joseph Bridau for Pierre Grassou. By letting Joseph take Grassou's place in this comic conflation of conjugal and artistic structures, its significance for Joseph's own case is briefly highlighted. Joseph may be unimpressed by this Titian redhead, but his marriage to a wealthy bourgeois heiress will be a mirror image of that of his friend.[24] It is not because Pierre Grassou is a 'bad' painter that he makes a vulgar bourgeois marriage, nor is it this marriage that confirms his negative qualities as a painter. Joseph Bridau, presented to us by Balzac as a painter of genius, will marry in identical fashion. Virginie, we are told, will adore her husband and 'give him' two children. That two children were similarly planned, on a proof variant of *La Rabouilleuse* (VI, 1325), for Joseph and his unnamed wife, is a further indication that Balzac may have conceived the life-stories of the two artists in relation to each other. That both marriages are 'happy' is incidental to Balzac's representation of a social structure. What is split up in the wide-ranging storyline of *La Rabouilleuse* — on the one hand, celibacy, marriage, prostitution, inheritance; on the other, painting — is ironically conflated in the simple but ingenious plot of *Pierre Grassou*. What in *La Rabouilleuse* is a serious aesthetic strategy for an ambitious realist novel, is comically parodied, in *Pierre Grassou*, in 'the model of painting' that underpins the representation of Grassou's studio, his father-in-law's art gallery, and the runaway theme of pastiche by which Balzac links them. In both cases, the model of painting is contextualized in relation to conjugal structures.

(iii) 'Qu'estimez-vous une copie de Raphaël?'

In *La Cousine Bette*, the fleeting appearances of Joseph Bridau may seem artificial links of the sort discussed by Citron. As a fellow artist and friend of Wenceslas Steinbock, he helps pay the sculptor's debts to get him out of prison and he is mentioned as a guest at his wedding. What is more, a portrait of the singer Josépha Mirah, 'dû au pinceau de Joseph Bridau' (VII, 378), hangs in the exquisite surroundings of the *hôtel* that has been purchased for her and filled with beauti-ful things by the Duc d'Hérouville, Josépha's fabulously rich protector (he is a connoisseur art collector). Pierre Grassou, too, gets a mention in *La Cousine Bette*, for this now consecrated specialist of bourgeois family portraits has been hired to immortalize two generations of Crevels on the walls of Célestin Crevel's house in the rue de Saussayes:

> Les portraits de feu Mme Crevel, de Crevel, de sa fille et de son gendre, dus au pinceau de Pierre Grassou, le peintre de renom dans la bourgeoisie, à qui Crevel devait le ridicule de son attitude byronienne, garnissaient les parois, mis tous les quatre en pendants. Les bordures, payées mille francs pièce, s'harmoniaient bien avec toute cette richesse de café, qui certes eût fait hausser les épaules à un véritable artiste. (VII, 157)

If Grindot 'avait recommencé là pour la millième fois son salon blanc et or, tendu de damas rose' (VII, 156), it is because Crevel's role model is César Birotteau, and the 'ancien adjoint, décoré, garde national, avait [...] reproduit fidèlement toutes les grandeurs, même mobilières, de son infortuné prédécesseur' (VII, 157). When the same forgotten architect is re-employed to do up the *hôtel* purchased by Crevel for Valérie Marneffe, the contrast with Josépha's house is explicitly underlined: 'Grindot avait essayé de lutter avec Cleretti, l'architecte à la mode, à qui le duc d'Hérouville avait confié la maison de Josépha' (VII, 398). The result is a tasteless disaster which is marked, like Crevel who has commissioned it, by the spirit of imitation: 'Ce qu'on admirait chez Josépha ne se voyait nulle part; ce qui reluisait chez Crevel pouvait s'acheter partout. [...] L'hôtel de Crevel était donc un magnifique spécimen du luxe des sots, comme l'hôtel de Josépha le plus beau modèle d'une habitation d'artiste.' (VII, 398) Even Adeline Hulot will supposedly be aware that, *chez* Josépha, 'tout surprenait par la perfection de la chose unique. Les modèles étaient brisés, les formes, les figurines, les sculptures étaient toutes originales.' (VII, 377) Thus, by association with the settings in which they are hung, the portraits by Bridau and Grassou, the two painters I have chosen to read in relation to each other, are again polarized in terms of originality and aesthetic quality. However, in terms of content and context, the pictures are linked by the figure of Crevel. On the one hand, the paired representations of Crevel and his wife, his daughter and son-in-law, incarnate a respectable bourgeois genealogy. On the other, the painting of Josépha Mirah forms the second panel of Balzac's diptych: the beautiful and successful courtesan, now kept by the duc d'Hérouville, was first sold into prostitution to none other than Crevel: ('"j'ai mis, comme on dit, dans ses meubles une petite ouvrière de quinze ans, d'une beauté miraculeuse"' (VII, 63)).

In *La Rabouilleuse*, the metaphorical work of art that is Flore Brazier on two occasions gives way to the literal masterpieces that hang on Rouget's walls. In *La Cousine Bette*, the structure is reversed, and a description of Josépha's magnificent paintings twice precedes her appearance amongst them. In the first episode, Hector Hulot, discovering that he has been thrown over in favour of Hérouville, rushes to Josépha's new establishment in the rue de la Ville-l'Éveque, sends in his card, and is asked to wait in the *grand salon*:

> Il admira [...] ce que des princes seuls ont la faculté de choisir, de trouver, de payer et d'offrir: deux tableaux de Greuze et deux de Watteau, deux têtes de Van Dyck, deux paysages de Ruysdaël, deux de Guaspre, un Rembrandt et un Holbein, un Murillo et un Titien, deux Teniers et deux Metzue, un Van Huysum et un Abraham Mignon, enfin deux cent mille francs de tableaux admirablement encadrés. Les bordures valaient presque les toiles. (VII, 121)

The Josépha who, 'tout en blanc et jaune', silently enters as Hulot is examining the pictures, 'était si bien parée pour cette fête, qu'elle pouvait encore briller au milieu de ce luxe insensé, comme le bijou le plus rare' (VII, 121–22). Five years later, it is Adeline Hulot, hoping for news of her husband, who sends in her card and is shown into Josépha's *grand salon*. The half hour she is kept waiting is spent inspecting the setting already familiar to the reader, admiring its profusion of priceless objects, and imagining the person who lives in their midst: 'Adeline pensa que Josépha Mirah, dont le portrait dû au pinceau de Joseph Bridau brillait dans le boudoir voisin, était une cantatrice de génie, une Malibran, et elle s'attendit à voir une vraie lionne.' (VII, 378) The portrait is not described, nor is it clear from Balzac's wording whether Adeline is supposed to have looked at it. However, the Josépha who eventually appears, her entry heralded by the implicit framing of the doors she has passed through, is a painting come to life. Focalized by Adeline, but described by the narrator as the image of a picture Adeline has certainly never seen, it is as if Joseph Bridau's portrait of Josépha has merged with the famous painting of Judith to which she is compared:

> Après avoir entendu ouvrir et fermer des portes, elle aperçut enfin Josépha. La cantatrice ressemblait à la Judith d'Allori, gravée dans le souvenir de tous ceux qui l'ont vue dans le palais Pitti, auprès de la porte d'un grand salon: même fierté de pose, même visage sublime, des cheveux noirs tordus sans apprêt, et une robe de chambre jaune à mille fleurs brodées, absolument semblable au brocart dont est habillée l'immortelle homicide créée par le neveu du Bronzino. (VII, 378)

Within this general likeness to Allori's portrait, it is Josépha's yellow *robe de chambre* that is picked out for its exact resemblance to Judith's dress. The lavish outfit has been chosen to crush the respectable *baronne* with a courtesan's grandeur — '"Allons, mes plus belles pantoufles, ma robe de chambre brodée en fleurs par Bijou, tout le tremblement des dentelles"' (VII, 377) — a plan abandoned when Josépha-the-artist finds herself moved to admiration in Adeline's presence. However, the initial intention of Josépha-the-courtesan motivates her appearance in the fabulous housecoat that has been embroidered by Bijou, and that is used by Balzac to establish a relation between Josépha and Bijou herself.

Despite its resemblance to the painted brocade that adorns Allori's *Judith*, Josépha's *robe de chambre* has been commissioned as a unique luxury item in keeping with the rest of her surroundings. As she had told Hulot, when he turned up at her *hôtel* three years after his first visit: '"la petite Bijou vient demain m'apporter une robe de chambre brodée, un amour; ils y ont passé six mois, personne n'aura pareille étoffe!"' (VII, 360) The decrepit, ruined and disgraced Hulot has come to Josépha for help, and it is in the 'magnifique salon où il l'avait vue la dernière fois' (VII, 358) that he listens — once more surrounded by Josépha's works of art — to her idea of setting him up as protector of the sixteen-year-old Olympe Bijou:

> 'Veux-tu, lui dirai-je, d'un monsieur de soixante-douze ans, bien propret, qui ne prend pas de tabac, sain comme mon œil, qui vaut un jeune homme? Tu te marieras avec lui au Treizième; il vivra bien gentiment avec vous, il vous donnera sept mille francs pour être à votre compte, il te meublera un appartement tout en acajou; puis, si tu es sage, il te mènera quelquefois au spectacle.'

I leave aside the female alienation that underpins a scheme conceived by Josépha as a good deed to Hulot and Bijou alike, and of which the reality is as follows: '"Ça ferait les *cent* horreurs pour avoir sept ou huit mille francs"' (VII, 360).[25] From Josépha's point of view, what is intriguing is her conscious recreation of the scenario of her own beginnings with Crevel (to which she explicitly refers as she outlines her plan), as if this controlled repetition of her past, in which she acts as the *entremetteuse* and offers her young double to Hulot, were almost a selfish exorcism.[26] Josépha is Bijou's role model ('"Bijou rêve de porter de belles robes comme les miennes"' (VII, 361)), and the child will be encouraged in this aspiration by the gift of Josépha's old dresses. However — as with the structurally reminiscent episode in *La Maison du chat-qui-pelote*, where Guillaume offers his daughter to Joseph Lebas — the significant identification is Josépha's, in that Bijou is clearly perceived as the image of her own former self:

> 'je connais une pauvre famille qui possède un trésor: une petite fille, plus jolie que je ne l'étais à seize ans!... [...] Ah! je sais ce que j'ai souffert quand j'avais faim! [...] Je connais Bijou, c'est moi-même à quatorze ans! J'ai sauté de joie quand cet abominable Crevel m'a fait ces atroces propositions-là!' (VII, 360–61)

All three scenes set in Josépha's *salon* are used by Balzac to trace the reality of the singer's career. However, in this central episode of the three, it is no longer Josépha who enters the room as 'le bijou le plus rare' (VII, 122), but 'la petite Bijou' (VII, 360), substitute version of herself:

> Hulot vit entrer un de ces vivants chefs-d'œuvre que Paris, seul au monde, peut fabriquer à cause de l'incessant concubinage du Luxe et de la Misère, du Vice et de l'Honnêteté, du Désir réprimé et de la Tentation renaissante, qui rend cette ville l'héritière des Ninive, des Babylone et de la Rome impériale. Mlle Olympe Bijou, petite fille de seize ans, montra le visage sublime que Raphaël a trouvé pour ses Vierges. (VII, 362)

From a masterpiece to a Raphael virgin: as in *La Rabouilleuse*, Balzac's description of a beautiful child harnesses the codes of art. However, once again an artist's appraisal is merged with the viewpoint of a lecherous old man. The working-class child is decked out in the cheap finery she deems appropriate for a visit to her patron: 'L'enfant, qui ne connaissait pas sa valeur, avait fait sa plus belle toilette pour venir chez la grande dame.' (VII, 363) As for every artist's model with the potential for prostitution, the clothes are part of the package: 'le tout ficelé d'indienne à soixante-quinze centimes le mètre, orné d'une collerette brodée, monté sur des souliers de peau sans clous, et décoré de gants à vingt-neuf sous' (VII, 363). At the same time, they are simply the outer layer of the finely crafted body so easily uncovered by the discerning observer. In this case, in line with Bijou's name, it is upon an *objet d'art* that Hulot lasciviously gazes: 'mais un teint de porcelaine et presque maladif; mais une bouche comme une grenade entrouverte, un sein tumultueux, des formes pleines, de jolies mains, des dents d'un émail distingué' (VII, 363). To all but the child herself, her worth, enhanced by her 'originality' — she is a literal as well as a metaphorical virgin — is explicitly a value on the sexual market:

— Et, lui dit Josépha dans l'oreille, c'est garanti neuf, c'est honnête! et pas de pain. Voilà Paris! J'ai été ça!

— C'est dit, répliqua le vieillard en se levant et se frottant les mains. (VII, 363)

Contrasting the 'somme fixe' luxury purchased by Crevel (VII, 398) with the 'cachet du vrai luxe' stamped upon Josépha's *hôtel* (VII, 377), the narrator draws on the language of painting to convey the difference between an original *objet d'art* and its mass-produced copy: 'l'un est en Archéologie ce qu'un tableau de Raphaël est en peinture, l'autre en est la copie. Qu'estimez-vous une copie de Raphaël?' (VII, 398). The difference, it seems, is almost tediously quantifiable: 'Un miroir unique vaut six mille francs, le miroir inventé par un fabricant qui l'exploite coûte cinq cents francs. Un lustre authentique de Boulle monte en vente publique à trois mille francs; le même lustre surmoulé pourra être fabriqué pour mille ou douze cent francs.' (VII, 398) 'Le fleuve du million' that separates these two versions of luxury can be crossed by such 'grands seigneurs modernes' as Hérouville who, notwithstanding his aristocratic taste and credentials, has raised the 600,000 francs for Josépha's house — for the purchase of Josépha — from a share flotation. For all that she incarnates a Raphael virgin, the 'trésor' that is Bijou can be bought for a mere 7,000 francs. Is Bijou a Raphael or its copy? In no time at all she will be exploited by a lover, before proceeding to marriage with a wealthy merchant who is, as Josépha exclaims, a clone of Crevel. Josépha herself resembles Allori's painting of Judith not only physically, but down to the yellow embroidered dress that, by recalling the parallel with Bijou, keeps her own past — her purchase by Crevel — in the frame. Joseph Bridau's portrait of Josépha is a sequel to his first acknowledged masterpiece, its subject matter a young girl, modelled from Coralie, and portrayed — like the Rabouilleuse and Bijou by Balzac — at the moment of her delivery into prostitution. Pierre Grassou's artistic career takes him from a pastiche of Greuze's *L'Accordée de village* to a production line of family portraits, of which Crevel *en père de famille* is straight from the mould. Despite their friendship and the similarity of their marriages, Pierre Grassou and Joseph Bridau may appear, superficially, to be worlds apart as artists.[27] Yet viewed in the light of the *Code-Homme*, which is the subject matter of their paintings as well as their own socio-economic context, their two versions of pastiche — 'que vaut une copie de Raphaël?' — emerge from the Bridau cycle as two sides of the same realist coin.

Notes to Chapter 6

1. Agathe's dying words, '"De qui donc Philippe tient-il?..."', suggest that she had perhaps shared the belief of Dr Rouget and Mme Hochon that she was Lousteau's daughter. The heavy underlining in *La Rabouilleuse* of Philippe's resemblance to his grandfather Rouget is a reminder that Agathe is the link between them. Not only does she repeat here her brother's voyeurism, she also re-enacts, here as elsewhere in the novel, the scenario of undisguised parental preference of which she herself had been a victim.
2. See Samuels, 'L'Érotique de l'histoire', for discussion of the military uniform as fetish in paintings of Napoleon as well as in *La Vendetta*.
3. *Illusions perdues*, ed. by Adam (Paris: Garnier, 1961), p. xxvii.
4. *La Rabouilleuse*, ed. by Citron, p. xiii. See too Dorothy Magette, who claims that 'Joseph's unity

of character almost totally disintegrates' in the final part of *La Rabouilleuse* ('Trapping Crayfish: The Artist, Nature, and *Le Calcul* in Balzac's *La Rabouilleuse'*, *Nineteenth-Century French Studies*, 12 (1983–84), 54–67 (pp. 60–61)).

5. *Illusions perdues*, ed. by Roland Chollet, in *La Comédie humaine*, v, 1–732 (p. 473).

6. Camusot's debauchery, unlike Rouget's, is kept separate from his domestic life. Even so, this wonderfully hypocritical figure, unmasked by the hapless Oscar Husson in *Un début dans la vie*, is a fine example of the overlap between 'respectable' bourgeois genealogies and the world of prostitution.

7. The texts in which Joseph Bridau plays a significant part were published close together in time, and seem likely to have been conceived more or less together. At any one time (and 1839 is a good example), Balzac carried an extraordinary number of plots and characters in his head; a character like Joseph might well be waiting in the wings for 'his' novel to be written. According to Guise, Balzac started work on *La Rabouilleuse* 'vers juillet 1839', soon after the publication of *Un grand homme de province à Paris* (the second part of *Illusions perdues*) in which Joseph first appears. The short story *Pierre Grassou* came out in December 1839 (though dated 1840), while the two parts of *La Rabouilleuse*, first published as *feuilletons* in spring 1841 and autumn 1842 respectively, straddle the publication of *Le Danger des mystifications* (*Un début dans la vie*) in the summer of 1842.

8. Joseph's himself points the way here: '"Je connais un officier qui m'a raconté qu'en Dalmatie, il fut arrêté dans des circonstances presque semblables, en arrivant de la promenade un matin, par une populace en émoi..."' (IV, 465) Guise does not seem to find the link odd, stating simply: 'Dans *Un début dans la vie*, Joseph Bridau, qui se fait passer pour Schinner, raconte cet épisode comme s'il lui était arrivé personnellement.' (IV, 1297) Citron rehearses critical attempts to find a real source, before concluding: 'L'allusion ici faite à l'affaire de Dalmatie ne serait qu'un de ces rappels si fréquents par lesquels le romancier soude ensemble les romans de *La Comédie humaine*.' (See *La Rabouilleuse*, ed. by Citron, p. 299.)

9. *Un début dans la vie*, ed. by Pierre Barbéris, in *La Comédie humaine*, I, 715–887 (p. 791). The oval face, long eyelashes and evenly coloured complexion are features of the portrait of Joseph's mother that hangs in his studio in *La Rabouilleuse*, and that Barthes (see the previous chapter), following Balzac's lead, identifies as a shameless pastiche: 'Plus d'un artiste [...] demande aujourd'hui à notre jeune peintre: "Est-ce la copie d'une tête de Raphaël?"' (IV, 277).

10. For the text of *Le Voyage en coucou*, see I, 1447–68.

11. See *Un début dans la vie*, ed. by Nadine Satiat (Paris: Garnier-Flammarion, 1993), p. 14, p. 29.

12. In *Un début dans la vie* the magic word, as in Chaudet's studio in *La Rabouilleuse*, is the name of the father. Bridau, who had died through overwork as a key member of Napoleon's administration, will be repudiated by Philippe, comte de Brambourg, but is willingly and very usefully acknowledged by Joseph.

13. The precise nature of the overlap would be illuminated by more information on the context, chronology and details of what Balzac was given by his sister. However, according to Satiat, 'on ne sait pas exactement quand s'écrivit cette nouvelle' (p. 251).

14. It is a three-way performance in fact, in that Joseph is assisted by the quick thinking and witty Mistigris: '"Ils crient donc en français, ces Dalmates?" demanda le comte à Schinner. [...]. Schinner resta tout interloqué. "L'émeute parle la même langue partout", dit le profond Mistigris.' (I, 793) Though a relatively minor reappearing painter of *La Comédie humaine*, Mistigris (Léon de Lora) is an interesting figure in that he combines verbal and artistic genius.

15. *Pierre Grassou*, ed. by Meininger, in *La Comédie humaine*, VI, 1077–1111 (p. 1102).

16. Greuze's painting (1761) is not named in the text, but was so well known that it would have been immediately identifiable by the description 'une noce de village' (VI, 1096). Diderot provided an enthusiastic account in his 1861 *Salon* (*Œuvres esthétiques*, pp. 519–24) where he used the title *Un Père qui vient de payer la dot de sa fille* (p. 519). According to Brookner (p. 62), the exact title was *Un mariage, et l'instant où le père de l'Accordée délivre la dot à son gendre*. She notes the appearance of more or less explicitly plagiarized versions while Greuze was still in mid-career, such as Perier's *Un contrat de mariage dans un intérieur rustique* and Lépicié's *La Réponse désirée*, both from the mid 1770s.

17. Balzac's correspondence for 1846 contains an entertaining series of letters to Mme Hanska and

Georges Mniszech concerning the acquisition and attempted resale, at a vast profit, of a supposed Greuze original. Balzac believed it to be a study of the artist's wife used for *L'Accordée de village*. See *Lettres à Madame Hanska*, II, 272, 288–89, 291 and 441.

18. The negative qualities of Grassou's art are a major theme of the story. For Goetz, this makes it potentially less interesting than *Le Chef-d'œuvre inconnu*: '*Le Chef-d'œuvre inconnu* était un roman pour les artistes. *Pierre Grassou* n'est peut-être bien qu'un document pour les historiens de l'art.' (*Le Chef-d'œuvre inconnu et autres nouvelles*, ed. by Goetz (Paris: Gallimard, 1994), p. 22.) Many critical accounts link the theme of Grassou's mediocrity to an attack on the bourgeois commercialization of art under the July Monarchy. See, for example, Juliette Frøhlich, 'Devenir des personnages peintres dans *La Comédie humaine*', in *Balzac et la peinture*, ed. by Boyer and Boyer-Peigné, pp. 83–97 (pp. 90–97) and Danielle Oger's catalogue entry for *La Femme hydropique* in the same volume (pp. 230–31).

19. Although Balzac presents this as disguised plagiarism, Norman Bryson discusses the literal 'troping' of another artist's painting as a means of distancing and subverting tradition, at the same time as openly engaging with it. See *Tradition and Desire: From David to Delacroix* (Cambridge: Cambridge University Press, 1984), pp. 32–62.

20. For Goetz's suggestive comments on this 'collection en trompe l'œil', see '"De si vives compensations à la faillite de la gloire": les collectionneurs au centre de *La Comédie humaine*', in *Balzac et la peinture*, ed. by Boyer and Boyer-Peigné, pp. 187–92 (p. 189).

21. The marriage does seem to be with the family, and especially the father, rather than with Virginie herself: 'Il vit avec son beau-père et sa belle-mère. Les Vervelle et les Grassou, qui s'entendent à merveille, ont voiture et sont les plus heureuses gens du monde'. (VI, 1111) Originally it was the family as a whole that had frightened him off ('"Oui, mais quelle famille!"' (VI, 1104)), but when the significance of the dowry finally sinks in ('"Vous serez à l'abri du besoin pour le reste de vos jours"' (VI, 1104)), it is his future father-in-law he first sees in a favourable light: 'En disposant le père de la jeune personne, il lui trouva bonne mine et admira cette face pleine de tons violents' (VI, 1104).

22. With this final gesture, described as an act of revenge 'qui lui dilate le cœur!', Pierre Grassou surpasses Magus's comically contrived 'plot', and complicates perhaps the status of his own naivety. Magus has pulled the creative strings up to this point, marrying his two clients as it were, and knowing that his own exploitative role will be uncovered if Grassou really marries into this family. As a comic genius playing for high stakes, there is a striking parallel between Magus and Mercadet in *Le Faiseur* which, interestingly, was first conceived in 1839, the same year as *Pierre Grassou* (see Hunt, p. 432).

23. See Goetz, *Le Chef-d'œuvre inconnu et autres nouvelles*, p. 326.

24. We are not told what Joseph's wife looks like, so cannot know whether he too has accommodated a split between his aesthetic and financial interests.

25. This reality is spelled out from a child's point of view when Adeline attempts to persuade one of Bijou's successors to marry her elderly protector: '"Je fais tout ce qu'il veut pour un sac de chocolat!"' (VII, 441); '"c'est bien embêtant d'être la femme d'un homme! Allez! Sans les pralines!..."' (VII, 442) It is therefore impossible to accept A. J. L. Busst's claim that, given the age of nubility in this period, these young girls are not perceived by Balzac as children. See 'Baron Hulot: Only a Temperament?', *Quinquereme*, 12.1 (1989), 80–94.

26. Nicole Mozet describes Josépha's 'projet profondément pervers' as an act of revenge for her own 'mise en vente'. See '*La Cousine Bette*, roman du pouvoir féminin', in *Balzac au pluriel* (Paris: Presses Universitaires de France, 1990), pp. 142–58 (p. 156).

27. Frøhlich describes *La Rabouilleuse* and *Pierre Grassou* as 'deux récits construits en jeu de miroir', but only insofar as Balzac has created a contrast of artistic genius and mediocrity. See 'Devenir des personnages peintres', p. 92.

AFTERWORD

❖

In Daumier's 1842 Pygmalion cartoon, the statue takes the sculptor by surprise by bending down to ask for a pinch of his snuff.[1] So much for the unthreatening, non-reciprocal objecthood of Pygmalion's beautifully stony work of art. In *La Cousine Bette*, the prostitute Valérie Marneffe briefly casts herself in the role of the sculptor's model in order to seduce the married sculptor. The subject matter, composition and significance of the Delilah group for which she models are her own invention. By taking control of the sculptor and his art, by stealing him from his wife and transforming him into a malleable gigolo who caters for her pleasure, Valérie overturns the structure that I have tracked through Balzac's small corpus of artist stories.

The symbolic-cum-aesthetic castration discourse of Sarrasine and Frenhofer is demystified once and for all by Valérie's cynical commentary on '"Dalila coupant les cheveux à Samson"' (VII, 260): '"Ce groupe, et celui de la farouche Judith, seraient la femme expliquée. La Vertu coupe la tête, le Vice ne vous coupe que les cheveux. Prenez garde à vos toupets, messieurs!"' (VII, 261) The bathetic punchline reduces her ironically assumed 'castration reading' to the sordidly real context — elderly protectors with false hair pieces — in which she operates. While Hulot ('content de voir là son gendre' VII, 257)) and Crevel ('"je vous paye un exemplaire de ce groupe mille écus!"' (VII, 261)) hover on the fringes, the target audience for Valérie's witty exegesis is a little group of two sculptors and an art critic:

> — Ah! faites nous de la sculpture!... dit Stidmann.
> — Madame est la chose à sculpter! répliqua Claude Vignon en jetant un regard fin à Valérie. [...]
> Et elle laissa les deux artistes confondus, qui firent, avec le critique, un concert de louanges en son honneur. (VII, 260–61)

From the beginning of the scene, when she makes her entry 'suivie de Bette, qui, mise tout en noir et jaune, lui servait de repoussoir, en terme d'atelier' (VII, 253), the main tool of Valérie's skilfully calculated seduction is her manipulation of visual and verbal aesthetic codes. First, she self-consciously assumes elements of an artistic vocabulary ('"Comme cette *réplique*... est-ce comme cela que vous dites?..."' (VII, 260)); second, she weaves in an allusion to Canova's famously erotic statue ('"Dalila est à genoux, à peu près comme la Madeleine de Canova"' (VII, 261)); finally, she rounds off her performance with a carefully placed staging of her trademark pose:

> Mme Marneffe, elle, ne triomphait pas en face comme les autres. Elle se retourna brusquement pour aller à la table de thé retrouver Lisbeth. Ce mouvement de danseuse agitant sa robe, par lequel elle avait conquis Hulot, fascina Steinbock. (VII, 262)

The impact of the shapely rear view of Valérie, as on Hulot and Mlle S★★★'s brothel customer in Canler's memoirs, is purely physical; sculpture becomes, at most, a euphemism and an adulterer's alibi: 'En ce moment Valérie posait en Dalila.' (VII, 267)

As intended by its model, the bronze group is completed at the cost of the sculptor's marriage. Hortense finds an illustration in the *Revue des Beaux-Arts* and shows it to her mother as definitive evidence of her husband's adultery: 'Mme Hulot aperçut une gravure du groupe de Dalila par le comte de Steinbock, dessous laquelle était imprimé: *Appartenant à Mme Marneffe.*' (VII, 317) It is a deliberate echo of the earlier episode where Valérie, as proof of Wenceslas's marriage plans, shows Bette a lithograph in an art magazine: '*groupe appartenant à Mlle Hulot d'Ervy*' (VII, 147). This was the sculptor's first Samson composition, and when Valérie requests from him a bronze group in lieu of interest on a 10,000 franc loan, she proposes an explicit sequel ('"Vous avez commencé l'histoire de Samson, achevez-la..."' (VII, 259)). Thus the history of Wenceslas's passage from marriage to adultery with the prostitute who is kept by, amongst others, his father-in-law, is framed by two pieces of sculpture. In between lies the sorry tale of the decline in the sculptor's talent, for Wenceslas's creative energy is diverted into the physically happy honeymoon period of his marriage ('En fait de statue, il vint un petit Wenceslas ravissant' (VII, 243)), and soon entirely dissipated: 'En deux ans et demi, Steinbock fit une statue et un enfant. L'enfant était sublime de beauté, la statue fut détestable.' (VII, 244) Ironically, the bad statue he is so slow to complete was a commission negotiated and passed on by Hulot as part of his daughter's dowry. Also ironically, its subject is Montcornet, Valérie's natural father. When Valérie finds herself pregnant by one of her four lovers, she easily wields this Pygmalionesque parallel of two sorts of creation to persuade Wenceslas (and Hortense) that he is the father: '"Tu as raté le monument de mon père; mais chez toi l'amant est bien supérieur à l'artiste, tu es plus heureux avec la fille."' (VII, 275).

The story of Wenceslas — an ironic and ultimately failed Pygmalion who is a better lover than sculptor — is constantly mingled with that of his father-in-law. When Hortense enters the art dealer's shop off the Place du Carrousel to spend her savings on Wenceslas's group, the sculptor falls instantly in love with 'le vivant chef-d'œuvre du baron Hulot' (VII, 128). Hulot, meanwhile, who has accompanied his daughter on her mission to purchase a husband ('"Un mari, ma fille, dans cette boutique?"' (VII, 130)), enters into the euphemistic preliminaries of a prostitution contract with 'la jolie petite dame qui, la veille, avait laissé son image au cœur du vieux Beau' (VII, 125). His initial investment in this image, unlike the leap of faith of Schinner, had been neither psychic nor aesthetic, but crudely erotic: 'Le libertin ressentit cette vive impression, passagère chez tous les Parisiens, quand ils rencontrent une jolie femme qui réalise, comme disent les entomologistes, leur *desiderata*' (VII, 101); indeed, Hulot had been overwhelmed with desire for Mme Manneffe, 'dont la robe était agréablement balancée par autre chose que par ces affreuses et frauduleuses sous-jupes en crinoline' (VII, 101). When finally he follows his daughter into the art dealer's shop, it is because he looks up at Valérie's windows that he almost collides on the threshold with his future son-in-law, who emerges in a state of excitement only to rush into 'la maison de Mme Marneffe' (VII, 127).

The fashionable public wedding that is attended, as the newspapers report, by 'quelques-unes de nos célébrités artistiques: Léon de Lora, Joseph Bridau, Stidmann, Bixiou' (VII, 186), is effectively a double one, but not, as in *La Maison du chat-qui-pelote*, of two sisters. As the narrator's ironic discourse constantly underlines, it is father and daughter — or sculptor and father-in-law — whose parallel 'marriages' are first consummated during the interminable wedding ball, the money raised for Hortense's respectably large dowry acting as a cover for the parallel establishment of Mme Marneffe in the rue Vanneau. The public face of the artist's wedding conceals a set of arrangements, financial and sexual, that are every bit as murky as the deliberately discreet marriage of Philippe Bridau to the Rabouilleuse. Prostitution and marriage reflect each other and overlap in both cases. That the sculptor and his father-in-law share an erotic preference, as well as a formal relationship deriving solely from the institution of marriage, cements their suitability as the interlinked mediators of the model's — and the celibate cousin's — revenge. That Valérie, shadowed by Bette, should target that revenge at the female members of the Hulot family (at Adeline and Hortense, two generations of wives), is effectively a mirror image of the female alienation that leads Agathe Bridau and Mme Hochon to hold the Rabouilleuse responsible for her prostitution.

'"Les artistes ne devraient jamais se marier!"' (VII, 259), laments a hypocritical Wenceslas. Yet Balzac finds his fictional artists most useful when they do, not least because it allows him — sometimes literally — to 'tourner le modèle'. As discussed at the outset of this study, according to Barthes, in *S/Z*, this is the obsession not just of the amorous sculptor, but of the realist writer and critic ('tourner le modèle, la statue, la toile ou le texte pour s'assurer de son dessous' (p. 129)). I hope to have shown the analytical advantages, as well as the obvious aesthetic ones, that Balzac gains by exploiting this particular impulse in his artist stories. My claim is not that Balzac's depiction of marriage, adultery and prostitution is ideologically or qualitatively different in the artist stories from elsewhere in *La Comédie humaine*, or that real and metaphorical works of art do not have a function in all manner of Balzacian texts. However, the intersection of representation as aesthetic mode, and of realism as social and psychological content, is highlighted when relations between artists and their models mediate what Barthes so usefully calls *le modèle de la peinture*.

Note to the Afterword

1. *Pygmalion* (see frontispiece) was published in *Le Charivari* (28 December 1842) as part of the series *Histoire ancienne*. It bore the caption: 'O triomphe des arts! quelle fût ta surprise, | Grand Sculpteur, quand tu vis ton marbre s'animer, | et d'un air chaste et doux, lentement se baisser | pour te demander une prise. (Comte Siméon)'.

BIBLIOGRAPHY OF WORKS CITED

❖

Ashton, Dore, *A Fable of Modern Art* (London: Thames & Hudson, 1960)

Assoun, P.-L., 'La Femme et l'œuvre: Le Fétichisme dans *Le Chef-d'œuvre inconnu*', in *Analyses et Réflexions sur Balzac: 'Le Chef-d'œuvre inconnu', 'Gambara', 'Massimila Doni'*, collectif (Paris: Ellipses, 1993), pp. 102–08

Balzac, Honoré de, *L'Œuvre de Balzac*, ed. by Albert Béguin and J.-A. Ducourneau, 16 vols (Paris: Le Club français du livre, 1953–55)

——*La Comédie humaine*, ed. by Pierre-Georges Castex and others, 12 vols (Paris: Gallimard (Bibiothèque de la Pléiade), 1976–81)

——*Illusions perdues*, ed. by Antoine Adam (Paris: Garnier, 1961)

——*La Maison du Chat-qui-pelote, Le Bal de Sceaux, La Vendetta*, ed. by Pierre-Georges Castex (Paris: Garnier, 1963)

——*La Rabouilleuse*, ed. by Pierre Citron (Paris: Garnier, 1966)

——'*La Maison du Chat-qui-pelote', suivi de 'Le Bal de Sceaux', 'La Vendetta', 'La Bourse'*, ed. by Anne-Marie Baron (Paris: Flammarion, 1985)

——*Un début dans la vie*, ed. by Nadine Satiat (Paris: Garnier-Flammarion, 1991)

——*Le Chef-d'œuvre inconnu et autres nouvelles*, ed. by Adrien Goetz (Paris: Gallimard (Folio), 1994)

——*Lettres à Madame Hanska*, ed. by Roger Pierrot, 2 vols (Paris: Robert Laffont, 1990)

Bann, Stephen, *The True Vine: On Visual Representation and the Western Tradition* (Cambridge: Cambridge University Press, 1989)

Baron, Anne-Marie, *Le Fils prodige: L'Inconscient de 'La Comédie humaine'* (Paris: Nathan, 1993)

——*Balzac, ou les hiéroglyphes de l'imaginaire* (Paris: Honoré Champion, 2002)

Barthes, Roland, *S/Z* (Paris: Seuil, 1970)

——*Fragments d'un discours amoureux* (Paris: Seuil, 1977)

——*Œuvres complètes*, ed. by Éric Marty, 5 vols (Paris: Seuil, 2002)

Bonard, Olivier, *La Peinture dans la création balzacienne: Invention et vision picturales de 'La maison du Chat-qui-pelote' au 'Père Goriot'* (Geneva: Droz, 1969)

Borderie, Régine, *Balzac, peintre du corps: 'La Comédie humaine' ou le sens du détail* (Paris: SEDES, 2002)

Boyer, Jean-Pierre, and Élisabeth Boyer-Peigné, eds, *Balzac et la peinture* (Tours: Musée des Beaux-Arts de Tours/Farrago, 1999)

Bremond, Claude, and Thomas Pavel, *De Barthes à Balzac: Fictions d'un critique, critiques d'une fiction* (Paris: Albin Michel, 1998)

Brookner, Anita, *Greuze: The Rise and Fall of an Eighteenth-Century Phenomenon* (London: Elek, 1972)

Bryson, Norman, *Tradition and Desire: From David to Delacroix* (Cambridge: Cambridge University Press, 1984)

Busst, A. J. L., 'Baron Hulot: Only a Temperament?' *Quinquereme*, 12.1 (1989), 80–94

Canler, Louis, *Mémoires de Canler: Ancien Chef du Service de Sûreté 1795–1865*, ed. by Jacques Brenner (Paris: Mercure de France, 1986)

Cellard, Jacques, 'Le *Vicaire* et la *Rabouilleuse*: Autocensure et sexualité dans la *Comédie humaine*, in *Censures: De la Bible aux larmes d'Éros. Le livre et la Censure en France*, ed. by

Martine Poulain and Françoise Serre (Paris: Éditions du Centre Pompidou/BPI, 1987), pp. 140–45

CROW, THOMAS, 'B/G', in *Vision and Textuality*, ed. by Stephen Melville and Bill Readings (London: Macmillan, 1994), pp. 296–314

——*Emulation: Making Artists for Revolutionary France* (New Haven: Yale University Press, 1995)

DAMISCH, HUBERT, *Fenêtre jaune cadmium, ou les dessous de la peinture* (Paris: Seuil, 1984)

DEL LUNGO, ANDREA, 'Fenêtres à l'envers (perversions, effractions, pénétrations)', in *Envers balzaciens*, ed. by Del Lungo and Alexandre Péraud (Poitiers: La Licorne, 2001), pp. 87–102

DICKINSON, LINZY ERIKA, *Theatre in Balzac's 'La Comédie humaine'* (Amsterdam: Rodopi, 2000)

DIDEROT, DENIS, *Œuvres esthétiques*, ed. by Paul Vernière (Paris: Garnier, 1965)

DIDI-HUBERMAN, GEORGES, *La Peinture incarnée* (Paris: Minuit, 1985)

FAILLIE, MARIE-HENRIETTE, *La Femme et le code civil dans 'La Comédie humaine' d'Honoré de Balzac* (Paris: Didier, 1968)

FARRANT, TIM, *Balzac's Shorter Fictions: Genesis and Genre* (Oxford: Oxford University Press, 2002)

FÉDIDA, PIERRE, 'L'Exhibition et le secret de l'enveloppe vide', *Nouvelle revue de la psychanalyse*, 14 (1976), 275–80

FREUD, SIGMUND, *Art and Literature*, Pelican Freud Library, X, trans. by James Strachey, ed. by Albert Dickson (Harmondsworth: Penguin, 1985)

——*On Sexuality*, Pelican Freud Library, VII, trans. by James Strachey, ed. by Angela Richards (Harmondsworth: Penguin, 1977)

FRIED, MICHAEL, *Absorption and Theatricality: Painting and Beholder in the Age of Diderot* (Berkeley and Los Angeles: University of California Press, 1980)

——*Courbet's Realism* (Chicago: University of Chicago Press, 1990)

FRØHLICH, JULIETTE, 'Devenir des personnages peintres dans *La Comédie humaine*', in *Balzac et la peinture*, ed. by Jean-Pierre Boyer and Élisabeth Boyer-Peigné (Tours: Musée des Beaux-Arts de Tours/Farrago, 1999), pp. 83–97

GAUTIER, THÉOPHILE, *Contes fantastiques* (Paris: Corti, 1986)

GIRODET DE ROUCY-TRIOSON, ANNE-LOUIS, *Œuvres posthumes*, ed. by P. A. Coupin, 2 vols (Paris: Renouard, 1829)

GOETZ, ADRIEN, '"De si vives compensations à la faillite de la gloire": Les Collectionneurs au centre de *La Comédie humaine*', in *Balzac et la peinture*, ed. by Jean-Pierre Boyer and Élisabeth Boyer-Peigné (Tours: Musée des Beaux-Arts de Tours/Farrago, 1999), pp. 187–92

GOMBRICH, E. H., *Art and Illusion: A Study in the Psychology of Pictorial Representation* (London and New York: Phaidon/Pantheon, 1960)

HUNT, HERBERT J., *Balzac's Comédie humaine* (London: The Athlone Press, 1964)

KASHIWAGI, TAKAO, *La Trilogie des célibataires* (Paris: Nizet, 1983)

KELLY, DOROTHY, *Fictional Genders: Role and Representation in Nineteenth-Century French Narrative* (Lincoln: University of Nebraska Press, 1989)

KNIGHT, DIANA, 'Skeletons in the Closet: Homosocial Secrets in Balzac's *La Comédie humaine*', *French Studies*, 57 (2003), 167–80

——'Celibacy on Display in Two Texts by Balzac: *Le Cabinet des Antiques* and the Preface to *Pierrette*', *Dix-Neuf*, 2 (April 2004), 1–15

LACAN, JACQUES, *Écrits*, 2 vols (Paris: Seuil (Points), 1966)

LATHERS, MARIE, *Bodies of Art: French Literary Realism and the Artist's Model* (Lincoln: University of Nebraska Press, 2001)

LAUBRIET, PIERRE, *Un catéchisme esthétique: 'Le Chef-d'œuvre inconnu' de Balzac* (Paris: Didier, 1961)

——— *L'Intelligence de l'art chez Balzac: D'une esthétique balzacienne* (Geneva: Slatkine Reprints, 1980) [first published 1961]

MAGETTE, DOROTHY, 'Trapping Crayfish: The Artist, Nature, and *Le Calcul* in Balzac's *La Rabouilleuse*', *Nineteenth-Century French Studies*, 12 (1983/84), 54–67

MARIN, LOUIS, *Lectures traversières* (Paris: Albin Michel, 1992)

MASSOL, CHANTAL, *Une poétique de l'énigme: Le Récit herméneutique balzacien* (Geneva: Droz, 2006)

MASSOL-BÉDOIN, CHANTAL, 'L'Artiste ou l'imposture: Le Secret du *Chef-d'œuvre inconnu* de Balzac', *Romantisme*, 54 (1986), 44–57

——— 'Le Mot de l'énigme', in *Balzac: Une poétique du roman*, ed. by Stéphane Vachon (Paris: Presses universitaires de Vincennes, 1996), pp. 181–93

MAUPASSANT, GUY DE, *Contes et nouvelles*, ed. by Louis Forrestier, 2 vols (Paris: Gallimard (Bibliothèque de la Pléiade), 1974)

MILLER, JANE M., 'Some Versions of Pygmalion', in *Ovid Renewed: Ovidian Influences on Literature and Art from the Middle Ages to the Twentieth Century*, ed. by Charles Martindale (Cambridge: Cambridge University Press, 1988), pp. 205–14

MILNER, MAX, 'Les Dispositifs voyeuristes dans le récit balzacien', in *Balzac: Une poétique du roman*, ed. by Stéphane Vachon (Paris: Presses universitaires de Vincennes, 1996), pp. 157–71

MONNET, PHILIPPE, 'Balzac et les salons', in *Balzac et la peinture*, ed. by Jean-Pierre Boyer and Élisabeth Boyer-Peigné (Tours: Musée des Beaux-Arts de Tours/Farrago, 1999), pp. 41–51

MOZET, NICOLE, *Balzac au pluriel* (Paris: Presses Universitaires de France, 1990)

OVID, *Metamorphoses*, trans. by Mary M. Innes (Harmondsworth: Penguin, 1955)

PAULSON, WILLIAM, 'Pour une analyse de la variation textuelle: *Le Chef-d'œuvre* trop connu', *Nineteenth-Century French Studies*, 19 (1991), 404–16

POE, EDGAR ALLAN, *The Fall of the House of Usher and Other Writings*, ed. by David Galloway (Harmondsworth: Penguin, 1986)

PRENDERGAST, CHRISTOPHER, *Balzac: Fiction and Melodrama* (London: Edward Arnold, 1978)

——— *The Order of Mimesis: Balzac, Stendhal, Nerval, Flaubert* (Cambridge: Cambridge University Press, 1986)

REBOUL, JEAN, 'Sarrasine ou la castration personnifiée', *Cahiers pour l'Analyse* (March/April 1967), 91–96

SAMUELS, MAURICE, 'L'Érotique de l'histoire: *La Vendetta* et l'image de Napoléon au XIXe siècle', in *L'Érotique balzacienne*, ed. by Lucienne Frappier-Mazur and Jean-Marie Roulin (Paris: SEDES, 2001), pp. 105–16

SANDT, UDOLPHO VAN DE, 'Le Salon', in *L'Empire des Muses: Napoléon, les Arts et les Lettres*, ed. by Jean-Claude Bonnet (Paris: Belin, 2004), pp. 59–78

SCHEIE, TIMOTHY, *Performance Degree Zero: Roland Barthes and Theatre* (Toronto: University of Toronto Press, 2006)

SCHOR, NAOMI, *Breaking the Chain: Women, Theory and French Realist Fiction* (New York: Columbia University Press, 1985)

——— *George Sand and Idealism* (New York: Columbia University Press, 1993)

SCHUEREWEGEN, FRANC, 'La Toile déchirée: Texte, tableau et récit dans trois nouvelles de Balzac', *Poétique*, 65 (1986), 19–27

SERRES, MICHEL, *Genèses* (Paris: Grasset, 1982)

SEZNEC, JEAN, 'Diderot et *Sarrasine*', in *Diderot Studies IV* (Geneva: Droz, 1963), pp. 237–38

TODOROV, TZVETAN, *La Poétique de la prose* (Paris: Seuil, 1971)

VACHON, STÉPHANE, ed., *Balzac: Une poétique du roman* (Paris: Presses universitaires de Vincennes, 1996)

WETTLAUFER, ALEXANDRA K., *Pen vs Paintbrush: Girodet, Balzac and the Myth of Pygmalion in Postrevolutionary France* (New York: Palgrave, 2001)
WURMSER, ANDRÉ, *La Comédie inhumaine* (Paris: Gallimard, 1964)

INDEX

❖

SOCIETY FOR FRENCH STUDIES

The Society for French Studies, the oldest and leading learned association for French studies in the UK and Ireland, exists to promote teaching and research in French studies in higher education. The Society's activities include:

• Editing the *French Studies* quarterly journal and its companion *French Studies Bulletin*

• Editing the catalogues of research projects, *Current Research in French Studies* and *Postgraduate Research* — now online at www.sfs.ac.uk

• Hosting an annual conference with distinguished guest speakers and a variety of workshops across the spectrum of French studies

• Maintaining a website with rapidly expanding resources for those working in French Studies (**www.sfs.ac.uk**)

• Supporting research through:

  • Conference and seminar grants for events in the UK and Ireland

  • The R. H. Gapper annual prizes for scholarship at undergraduate, postgraduate, and book-publication levels

  • Subsidising publication of Legenda Research Monographs in French Studies (with 33% discount to SFS members)

  • Grants for postgraduate travel to the SFS annual conference, and reduced postgraduate conference and membership fees

  • Extension of the postgraduate membership rate to new lecturers in their first three years of employment

Membership enquiries:
Dr Chris Tinker, Department of Languages and Intercultural Studies,
School of Management and Languages,
Herriot Watt University, Edinburgh EH14 4AS.
membership@sfs.ac.uk

The Society for French Studies is charity no. 1078038 and is a company, limited by guarantee, registered in England and Wales, no. 3801778, whose registered office is the Taylor Institution, Oxford OX1 3NA.